SAVING AMERICA

SAVING AMERICA

7 PROVEN STEPS TO MAKE GOVERNMENT DELIVER GREAT RESULTS

MARK AESCH

First published by Bibliomotion, Inc.
39 Harvard Street
Brookline, MA 02445
Tel: 617-934-2427
www.bibliomotion.com

Printed in the United States of America

Library of Congress Cataloging-in-Publication Data

Names: Aesch, Mark.
Title: Saving America : 7 proven steps to make government deliver great results / Mark Aesch.
Description: Brookline, MA : Bibliomotion, 2016.
Identifiers: LCCN 2016011825| ISBN 9781629561554 (hardback) | ISBN 9781629561561 (ebook) | ISBN 9781629561578 (enhanced ebook)
Subjects: LCSH: Government accountability—United States. | Public administration—United States—Evaluation. | Administrative agencies—United States—Management. | Government productivity—United States. | Transparency in government—United States. | Organizational effectiveness—United States. | BISAC: POLITICAL SCIENCE / Government / General. | POLITICAL SCIENCE / Public Affairs & Administration. | BUSINESS & ECONOMICS / Government & Business. | BUSINESS & ECONOMICS / Strategic Planning.
Classification: LCC JK421 .A547 2016 | DDC 352.8/80973—dc23
LC record available at https://lccn.loc.gov/2016011825

To Alex and Marie Aesch, my paternal grandparents who emigrated from Switzerland and chose to make America home and raise children.

To Ted and Helen Montgomery, my maternal grandparents who worked every day to give their children an even brighter future than the one they enjoyed.

To Alex and Marie Aesch, my paternal grandparents who emigrated from Switzerland and chose to make America home and raise children.

To Ted and Helen Montgomery, my maternal grandparents who worked every day to give their children an even brighter future than the one they enjoyed.

CONTENTS

INTRODUCTION

My first exposure to American government took place during the blustery winter of 1976 in Mrs. Burton's fourth-grade class. The class was taught in a modular, prefabricated building in our little rural town of Mayfield, New York. I remember I sat in the first seat of the first row because my last name starts with the letters "A" and "e"—Tammy Agnostopolous sat behind me. During the long winter months, bone-chilling winds would blow right through the flimsy building's single-pane windows, and I would bounce my knees up and down below my desk trying unsuccessfully to keep warm. Many of my classmates stayed warm by wearing big wooly sweaters, but I wore only T-shirts. I had one sweater and it was reserved for my work on our family farm. We had a whole herd of cattle to take care of and a sweater worn in a barn smelled like, well, a barn.

Money was tight for our family; my father worked a full-time job in addition to managing the farm, but with four kids to feed and high state and local taxes to pay, we didn't have money for health insurance, much less a fancy "school sweater" for me. To occupy my half-frozen mind in the shoddy schoolroom we were stuffed into, I took to reading. It was the year of America's bicentennial and I enjoyed books about American patriots: Nathan Hale, Paul Revere, Samuel Adams, William Dawes. I would lose myself in writing book reports to Mrs. Burton, sharing the tales of these great American leaders and how they sacrificed and risked all that was dear to them so that they might realize their vision of building a great nation. I wound up writing dozens of book reports that year that weren't even required—my first step down the path of geekdom.

As I grew older, my reading progressed from the Revolutionary War era to the Civil War and eventually to the Second World War. I always perceived America as a "can do" country, a nation of incredible progress, opportunity, ambition, and prosperity. Horace Greeley famously said, "Go West, young man," and we did, exploring the frontiers of our great nation. President John F. Kennedy challenged us to go to the moon, and we did, exploring the "new frontier." America has repeatedly come together militarily to face common enemies; we fought the British in 1776 and 1812, Germany in World War I, and the Axis powers in World War II, emerging victorious each time.

I have always felt that our greatest period as a nation came during World War II. Never before had we been so focused, so aligned; we came together around a clear and compelling definition of success—defeat Hitler, Mussolini, and Tojo. And in achieving that success, we emerged as the world's sole superpower. We could do anything—and we did. We saved the world from fascist tyranny. We led the world in everything that mattered.

Today, we no longer lead. America is in obvious and disturbing decline. We rank seventeenth in education.[1] We rank thirty-fourth in the percentage of children living in poverty.[2] We rank twenty-first in our food quality, abundance, and affordability.[3] We rank twenty-sixth for life expectancy—behind Slovenia.[4] And we rank sixteenth in the quality of our infrastructure, behind powerhouse countries like Iceland and Portugal.[5] We don't face an existential military threat, as we did during World War II; rather, our main battle is against internal financial and social collapse. Our aggressors are distraction, unprioritized spending, and generally poor management. We as a people are striding forward, but we have allowed the government we allegedly command to go backward, creating inefficient government structures—both bureaucracies and buildings—that we cannot sustain. Sadly, national polling shows that for the first time in our history, a majority of Americans believe their children will not enjoy a better standard of living than they do today. Perhaps even more startling: in its 2014 polling of the American people, Gallup found that for the first time ever, Americans identified government itself as the biggest problem facing America today. That's right: Americans believe that the government we have built is a bigger problem than issues like the economy, unemployment, health care, or even terrorism.[6]

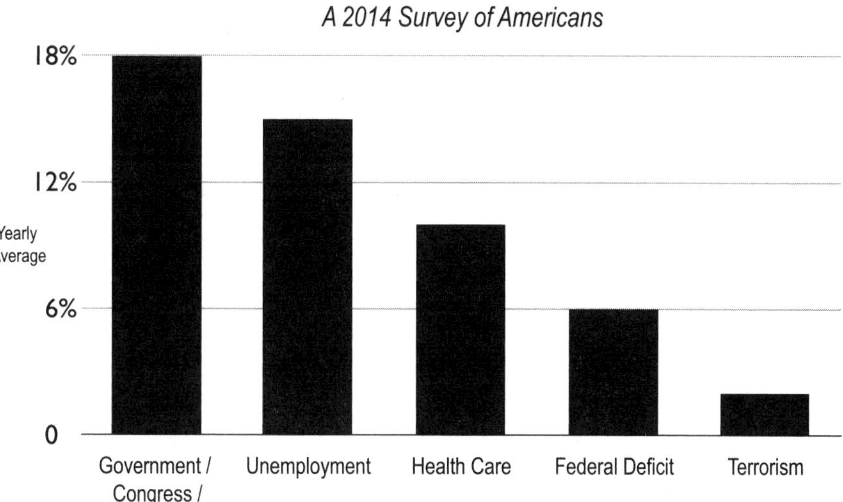

FIGURE I-1

Irresponsible, thoughtless, and unsustainable spending is at the root of the problem. Imagine taking your family out to dinner on a Friday evening. Mom and Dad. Jimmy and Suzie. Heck, bring your in-laws as well. Nothing outrageous or extravagant for dinner: two appetizers for the table, pasta and chicken dishes for everyone, a couple of beers. And your family loves dessert, so you get three for the six of you to share.

The bill comes to $120. But as the waiter places it before you, you do something strange. You hand him two credit cards. As he eyes you quizzically, you stand up at the end of the table and raise your half-finished beer in the air. "So, Ellen and I have some news to share. You might have noticed that Ellen didn't order a glass of wine tonight. That's because we're pregnant. Yes, that's right! We're going to have another baby, and we're so happy you're here to share the joy with all of us." Some people at a nearby table applaud in support.

You continue on with your toast, "With Jimmy and Suzie in so many activities at school, and all the vet bills for Fido, and you know we just had to get a new hot water heater—well, we're going to have to start doing things a little differently around here with another mouth to feed." Your father-in-law starts to reach for his wallet in order to pay for dinner, but you wave him off. You turn to make eye contact with a now totally befuddled waiter, "What we're going to do is only pay $84 toward the dinner bill on my credit card, because that's all we have money for." You point to Ellen's belly. "But I'm going to put the rest—the other $36—on the baby's credit card. We're going to make the baby start paying in six months for what we ate tonight. In fact, who wants coffee?"

Sounds stupid, doesn't it? More than stupid—it's immoral. You're foisting the bill for your own gluttony onto your unborn child. But this is what America does every single day. And let's be clear: this is what we as *Americans* do every day. We eat whatever we want, and we only pay 70 percent of the bill. Health-care insurance for everyone—and pay for 70 percent of it. Prescription drugs for everyone—and pay 70 percent of it. Lavish subsidies for farmers—and pay 70 percent of it. We can certainly decide as a nation whether we actually want health-care coverage, free prescription drugs, farming subsidies, and many other goods and services government provides. Maybe we do want them, maybe not. But we simply cannot continue to eat a full nine-course meal when we're not even paying for our entrée.

Political candidates always try to frame the coming election by telling us that our nation is at a crossroads and voters need to select the kind of America they want. By any reasonable standard, that is a misrepresentation of facts. Our nation is *not* at a crossroads. We *were* at a crossroads decades ago, and we already picked the road. We picked massive deficit spending. We picked government agencies that pay their employees well but deliver mediocre quality. We picked lucrative public employee pensions and generous retiree health-care programs that we don't adequately fund. We chose to define success as throwing more money at a problem rather than ensuring an appropriate result. And as time passed, the path we chose has grown darker and rife with potholes, dimming streetlights, and collapsing bridges. Literally.

Elected officials, candidates, and pundits often point to our decaying public institutions and say that we need to run government "more like a business." They pound podiums and whip crowds into frenzies with calls to make government agencies run like businesses. Really? Does anyone *really* want to dial 9-1-1 when their house is on fire and have the dispatcher ask them for a credit card number? Because that's what running government like a business looks like. On the other hand, when you have a small grease fire in your kitchen, you wouldn't want to see three ladder trucks show up with twenty-two firefighters, all on overtime pay. That is unnecessary and wasteful—and you're paying for it! At least 70 percent of it, anyway.

Most Americans want to eliminate the practice of sticking the unborn children of tomorrow with 30 percent of the cost of today's government. We want to start paying down our trillions in debt, and we believe we should only spend as much money as we take in. At the same time, most Americans want to spend enough money to have our schools reclaim the number-one position in the world for reading and math skills. Most Americans want to spend enough money to ensure that our bridges won't fall down. Most Americans want to ensure that veterans get the medical care they deserve and that middle-class families can afford college for their kids.

We need government that can provide balanced success—that can reduce costs while *improving* quality. Just as most Americans will invest in private companies that have a track record of proven results (Apple, Disney, Google), so too will we invest in government agencies that can deliver results. We want government that is efficient. And productive. And innovative. And responsive. We want government that *works.* In essence, we want public-sector services delivered with a private-sector *mindset*—which is far different from running government like a business. We want to see *value*, with services of a quality commensurate with what we citizens paid for it. When you go to McDonald's, you expect a certain kind of experience, and when you go to Ruth's Chris Steakhouse, you expect a different kind of experience. In each case, your expectations of service match what you pay. What Americans are weary of is paying Ruth's Chris prices for a quarter-pounder.

We want public-sector services delivered with a private-sector *mindset*—which is far different from running government like a business.

It sounds like an impossible task; so many government agencies, from the DMV to the post office, seem like poster children for deficiency and ineptitude. The good news is that it's *not* impossible for public administrators to run efficient, high-performance agencies. My team has built a model for doing exactly that. And we haven't just built it, we've implemented it. And then we've implemented it again. And again. We've rebuilt government agencies that deliver results. We've helped agencies improve quality while reducing reliance on tax dollars.

We created this process during the mid-2000s when we ran a mid-sized public transportation system in the western part of New York State. In 2004, when I became CEO, the Rochester–Genesee Regional Transportation Authority (RGRTA) was on the verge of insolvency. We were staring at deficit spending of more than $27.5 million—about 40 percent of our annual budget. Our buses were on time only 73 percent of the time; the airlines actually beat us in consistency. People thought our buses were filthy, because they were. We drove empty buses around just because we had the bus and could pay public employee drivers and mechanics.

Most public agencies in serious trouble know exactly what to do: they stick their hands out and tell taxpayers they must inject more money in order to keep them going. They tell the people using their service—in our case, the 35,000 people standing at the bus stops every day—that they have to pay a higher fare, most of the time for a product they already think is awful. But we decided to do it differently. We rebuilt the $80 million, 725-employee company from the top down and the bottom up. We rethought the way we provided service, how we spent money and why, and where our money came from.

All said, we created a seven-step plan for transforming the organization from the top down and the bottom up:

- We publicly, and quantifiably, *defined success* so we could hold ourselves accountable for delivering it.
- We built *a plan* to achieve this success, including a corresponding budget to pay for it.
- We built a *performance measurement system* to monitor every single month whether or not our plan was working.
- We created a *culture of ownership*, so employees took responsibility for their results.
- We *managed the results* each month as they came in so we could deliver success on an ongoing basis.

- We encouraged employees to demonstrate *courage in the decision-making* process rather than blindly following restrictive policies.
- And, finally, we *celebrated the results* with employees, our board, the media, taxpayers, and our customers.

The results were astounding. During the Great Recession of 2008, rather than raising fares, we were the only public transportation system in America to *reduce* fares (we cut them by 20 percent). While private companies like General Motors, AIG, Citigroup, and others were sticking out their hand for public dollars, we reduced our reliance on taxpayer dollars by more than 25 percent. We developed a way to measure customer satisfaction, and *increased* it by 26 percent. We increased on-time performance from 73 percent to 91 percent. Even as we reduced fares, we increased revenue by more than 90 percent. And we ran multimillion surpluses for seven straight years.

Taxpayers won—we reduced our reliance on their investment. Our employees won—their wages rose and our workforce grew by 20 percent. Our organization won—we saw unionized bus drivers, mechanics, and bus washers *vote* to tie their paycheck to their results. And our customers won—they were measurably happier with service. And, perhaps most importantly, because she was paying a lower fare, maybe, just maybe, a working mom was able to afford that school sweater for her fourth grader. This is what public service with a private-sector mindset looks like: casting a compassionate eye toward the community while also delivering a measurable way to improve service quality and a reasonable return on investment to taxpayers.

Since 2012, our team at TransPro has helped dozens of public organizations do exactly the same thing we did at the RGRTA. We support transit systems in places like Nevada, Louisiana, and Pennsylvania as they work to deliver measurable value to taxpayers and customers. We support municipalities in places like New York, Michigan, and Florida and school districts in places like Virginia, Delaware, and Florida. And in as about as complicated an environment you can imagine, we helped the City of Detroit save $38 million *and* improve customer satisfaction by more than 40 percent in a single year! Collectively, these organizations have so far saved taxpayers more than $300 million, while also increasing customer satisfaction by double digits. Those are results that should give Americans hope that a brighter future for their children *is* possible.

Anyone can reduce government spending—just cut programs, reduce services, and lay off employees. It really is that simple. Similarly, anyone can easily improve the quality of government programs and satisfaction with service delivery—just spend more money until you've driven success results higher (and, as our federal government does today, whether it's paid for or not). The trick is to achieve *both* of these competing interests, reducing the cost of government while also improving quality. An agency that follows our Seven Steps structure and utilizes the management principles to execute them will deliver excellence both to taxpayers and to those who use their services. And that's what *Saving America* is all about.

Of course, helping public administrators run strong, efficient agencies won't alone erase our massive government debt and fix our decrepit infrastructure. That's because these problems aren't just administrative in nature; they're deeply political as well. Looking at politics, we can, I think, observe three important structural reasons that government today is so bad. First, simply put, we reelect politicians who deliver us crap. More than 90 percent of incumbents win reelection, even though most of us think the government systems they have built and managed are failing. That's like going back to the same restaurant Friday night after Friday night, even though you hate the food, you hate the menu, the prices are high, the service is lousy, the waitress has a bad attitude, and the parking lot is filled with potholes.

Why do we reelect politicians who deliver crap? That brings us to a second problem. We fall prey to deliberate distraction techniques on the part of politicians. As most politicians know, it's easier to blow a "dog whistle" and shake a "shiny thing" in front of voters than to explain why 25 percent of our bridges are rated as deficient[7] and hundreds of thousands of schoolchildren get bused across them every day. Was it really important for fifty United States senators to debate whether the Washington Redskins name is offensive, as they did during the summer of 2014?[8] At roughly the same time, it came out that dozens of war veterans had died because they lacked access to health care *that those same politicians* had promised them. Yes, those elected officials were all too happy to distract us. I've been in the back rooms: they do it on purpose. Making government work efficiently and effectively is hard. Telling us that some team name causes offense is easy.

This begs the question: Why exactly can politicians get away with distracting us? A key answer is that it's too difficult for citizens to evaluate the performance of agencies and politicians. This is the third reason we have become saddled with such poor government services. One candidate tells us during her campaign she cut taxes. Her opponent runs a TV ad informing us that the first candidate actually raised taxes twelve times. Who is right? Good luck figuring that out.

The marketplace makes it easy to evaluate how well publicly traded companies perform; just look at their stock prices. In sports, performance evaluation is easy as well. Imagine going to a football game, not keeping score, not even knowing *how* to keep score or, worse yet, what a score even *was*, and then watching both head coaches hold competing news conferences after the game laying out why their team had a good day. I expect most of us would stop watching football. But that's exactly what we watch in government every day. That's the whole *premise* of politics today: two or more candidates working to try to define the success or failure of the other, the totality of their debate eliciting hopeless confusion in voters. It's no surprise that we all just throw up our hands and reelect incumbents. Because we lack clarity in evaluating the performance of government, voter participation declines, the purveyors of distraction win out, and everyone winds up shaking their heads in disbelief that this is what America has become.

Imagine going to a football game, not keeping score, not even knowing *how* to keep score or, worse yet, what a score even *was*, and then watching both head coaches hold competing news conferences after the game laying out why their team had a good day. I expect most of us would stop watching football.

Our Seven Step program can help ease voter confusion and apathy. In addition to being a proven process for administrators to apply in running agencies, the Seven Steps can serve citizens as a means of grading government agencies. I can't compel Americans to fire failed elected officials any more than I can get owners of a last-place football team to fire the head coach. That's the joy of democracy: we can reelect failed leaders. But I *can* help Americans understand which elected officials delivered success with the same clarity that they might understand the performance of a football team that went 14–2. I can build a system that helps citizens understand which investments of their taxpayer dollars deliver results, and which don't. With that clarity, the American people won't fall prey as easily to the games politicians play. Over time, as the failing incumbents get voted out, more and more of us will be able to engage in political dialogue again with the same passion we talk about sports. If we want to reelect poorly performing politicians, that will be up to us. But at least the choice will be clear, and the debate honest and real.

Saving America thus has a twofold purpose. The book offers a coherent, nonpartisan, practicable plan for administrators to use in rebuilding our nation's public agencies in a sustainable way. And it also provides voters with a tool that lets them know whether those agencies are succeeding and whether they warrant further investment. *Saving America* is not a political broadside or a theoretical academic lecture; rather, it's an accessible path to help local citizens, elected officials, and administrators make American government work again. It is, hopefully, both actionable and inspirational. We can make measurable gains by applying the Seven Steps process to fire districts, school systems, municipal governments, entire states, and to the federal government. When we get public agencies to produce results and when we hold elected officials and administrators accountable for delivering success rather than speeches, we will free up billions that can then be used to rebuild our infrastructure, ensure our food and water safety, take care of our young and vulnerable, and put America on a path of fiscal and structural sustainability, all while keeping taxes stable.

The fourth graders of today, whether they are in Mrs. Burton's class at Mayfield Elementary School or anywhere else in America, deserve to believe that they can build a better life than their parents had. Sadly, when every single fourth grader in America arrives home at the end of the school day, his or her parents hand over a credit card statement with a debt of $57,000 on it. These kids deserve better. This, after all, is the land of the Greatest Generation. Let's demonstrate to our grandfathers and grandmothers, watching down on us, that they were right to fight for America's freedom. Let's focus on issues rather than advertisements, solutions rather than sound bites. Let's rededicate ourselves to rebuilding and renewing the way local, state, and federal agencies do business. Our grandparents had to defeat tyranny. We only have to defeat ourselves.

Let's go save America.

1

America the Broken

In early April 1987, after Sunday morning pancakes at my parents' farm in upstate New York, I made the 225-mile journey west back to college. When I returned to campus after the four-hour drive, I heard the news (this was way before the instant information age, and most people didn't even have the toaster-sized cell phones of that era, including me). A bridge on the New York State Thruway had collapsed, and ten people had died. The bridge was only five miles east of where I had gotten on the Thruway.

Some twenty years later, I turned on the television to learn of another, even deadlier, tragedy playing out across the nation's airwaves. On August 1, 2007, right in the middle of rush hour, the westbound I-35 bridge in Minneapolis collapsed into the Mississippi River. This failure came without warning to the occupants of 111 vehicles idling in jam-packed traffic. Thirteen people were killed and 145 injured.[1] Some of the victims were disfigured for life and remain haunted by the unfathomable events of that day.[2]

One of these victims was Garrett Ebling, who was heading home from a company picnic he had organized. Ebling called his fiancée from the car with an update, then rolled down his windows and cranked up some music for the drive back to his apartment across the Mississippi River. Within moments, Ebling felt a powerful jolt. Brake lights on several cars ahead of him glowed red in unison, then spilled off the road into a gaping hole. A split second later, the ground beneath his own vehicle gave way. Ebling was weightless, and the world cut to slow motion. As his car tipped forward into a downward slide, he braced hard, his feet to the brakes and his back against the seat. He remembers nothing after that.[3]

In the days following the disaster, we all learned, to our even greater horror, that this bridge collapse didn't just "happen." The I-35W bridge had been classified as "structurally deficient" for seventeen years preceding the collapse.[4] Seventeen unbelievable years it had been on a list. But state officials, including Minnesota Governor Tim Pawlenty, asserted that this classification did not indicate an imminent structural failure. Clearly, for sixteen years it wasn't imminent, but on August 1, it became pretty darn imminent. Structurally deficient "doesn't necessarily mean a bridge is unsafe or in need of replacement," Pawlenty said in a press conference two days after the accident, "but I think anybody who looks at the national picture... and says we don't have a problem would be naive."[5] It might have been helpful had the governor held that news conference on July 31.

What happened to Ebling and what could have happened to me should deeply concern *you*. Every day, tens of millions of people drive across bridges that our government has labeled "structurally deficient" and done *nothing* about—other than type it on a list and stuff it in a report to gather dust. In 2007, the Department of Transportation considered roughly 600,000 bridges in the United States to be structurally deficient or functionally obsolete.[6] In 2009, the "Report Card for America's Infrastructure," published every four years by the American Society of Civil Engineers (ASCE), claimed that while $10.5 billion was being spent annually on bridge maintenance and construction, that spending wasn't getting the job done. ASCE recommended that in order to substantially improve bridge conditions, an annual investment of $17 billion was required.[7] In 2012, ASCE president Andrew Herrmann pointed out that America's already thorough bridge inspection program is undermined by the federal government's failure to spend enough on updating and maintaining infrastructure. "Congress basically lacks the courage to do what is needed to raise the funds," Herrmann told ABC News. "Bridges require maintenance, and maintenance requires funding.... Politicians like to show up and cut a ribbon on a brand new bridge, but they don't like to show up and applaud a new paint job that may increase the life of a bridge."[8]

Routine maintenance like paint jobs, foundation repairs, and resurfacing might be unglamorous, but it saves lives. When Garrett Ebling awoke from a coma some two weeks after the bridge collapse, both of his feet and his left arm were broken, as were the bones in his face. His severed colon had required immediate surgery, the first operation in what would become a years-long odyssey. Today, his cheeks, jaw, and forehead are held together by metal—the result of several reconstructive surgeries.[9] Although he eventually married and had a child, Ebling bears emotional wounds that may never heal. "The bridge had done more than crush bone," Ebling wrote in a 2012 book about his ordeal. "It had crushed my spirit."[10]

FROM THE MOUNTAINS TO THE PRAIRIES

Calamities like this are no longer freak occurrences in our country. They are increasing in number and are affecting an ever-widening swath of our population. From the failing state of our infrastructure and institutions of law and order to the safety of our food and water, America is increasingly incapable of keeping its most basic systems working. The most fundamental functions of government are a reliable transportation system; fire, police, and military protection; a safe and reliable energy supply; and uncontaminated water and food. These represent the core of what government is supposed to do—and it's increasingly clear that our government is failing. As former Secretary of Transportation Ray LaHood remarked on the CBS news program *60 Minutes,* "Our infrastructure is on life support right now. That's what we're on."[11]

The engineering lobby would argue that critical infrastructure failures represent an issue of revenue. In the *60 Minutes* interview cited above, Secretary LaHood went on to say, "We haven't made the investments. We haven't got the money." I respectfully disagree; it is actually an abject failure in management. Does any reasonable American think it's more important to "invest" millions of tax dollars in subsidizing artists or weaponry that the Department of Defense doesn't even want than ensuring we inspect and repair our bridges every year? It's unnerving to think that this artist driving to the museum to drop off a taxpayer-funded piece of art has a decent chance of passing over a deficient bridge.

I'm not calling for us to raise taxes so that we can spend more money on infrastructure. I'm calling for us to recognize that we need to spend existing dollars based on measurable return rather than political rhetoric. I'm calling for us to recognize that we as Americans must downsize our government to match what our taxes can afford to sustain. And when we do spend, we must demand excellence: water lines that don't leak, Veterans Affairs hospitals that actually see patients in a timely fashion, and yes, deficient bridges actually repaired, or at a minimum, barricaded. Just imagine if we closed every single structurally deficient bridge. Americans might just demand that we spend money on priorities rather than distractions.

At present, hundreds of public agencies do amazing things and produce fantastic results. Tens of thousands of public employees demonstrate incredible ownership, unselfishly giving of themselves to truly serve. Hundreds of thousands more of their colleagues would do the same, were they not trapped in a failed system that rewards rule-bound behavior over results. At the same time, thousands of public agencies tax too much while delivering too little. And hundreds of thousands of public employees accept or even embrace the notion of "close enough, for government work." We can and must do better.

You might stroll around your town and observe newly paved roads or recently built schools, and think, "Well, *my* neighborhood looks pretty good." It might indeed "look pretty good." The I-35 bridge "looked pretty good," too. Much of America's infrastructural decay occurs sight unseen—until it doesn't. In Harrisburg, the capital of Pennsylvania, the ground has been giving way... literally. In early 2013, a giant sinkhole measuring eight feet by fifty feet opened up in a low-income city neighborhood, swallowing a street and forcing a dozen locals to evacuate the area.[12] "I thought the world was ending," said Sherri Lewis, who saw the road outside her apartment collapse. The sinkhole, which was related to the corrosion of aging water and gas pipes underground, was only one of *forty* such holes that have plagued the city.

In April 2013, a fertilizer plant in West Texas exploded, killing fifteen people and injuring two hundred more.[13] The blast of thirty tons of ammonium nitrate registered as a small earthquake and razed large parts of the town nearby.[14] The plant was not in compliance with OSHA standards and had not been inspected since 1985.[15] And these explosions just keep happening. In the six months after the West tragedy, ten major chemical disasters occurred in the United States according to the States News Service.[16]

Nuclear power plants, long considered to be among the safest forms of power production, are also showing signs of aging. An Associated Press investigation in 2011 found that of America's sixty-five nuclear power plants, 75 percent have leaked a radioactive form of hydrogen.[17] What's most frightening is that plant operators have not been able to figure out how to *quickly* detect leaks in the event that they occur. A follow-up investigation by Congress found that these leaks can go undetected for *years* and show no signs of abating.[18] At least our government *knew* that the I-35 bridge was structurally deficient; heck, they even put it on a list. They just didn't *do* anything about it. When it comes to nuclear power plants, government inspectors haven't even bothered to scrutinize adequately the very plants they are responsible for overseeing.

We'd like to think that our water is safe, but that, too, is wishful thinking. In 2014, a chemical spill near a water treatment facility in Charleston, West Virginia, sickened hundreds of people with rashes, nausea, and vomiting and left three hundred thousand more without clean tap water for drinking, bathing, or washing. Roughly five thousand gallons of an industrial chemical used in coal mining gave tap water in the region a "sweet, licorice-like smell," prompting public officials to declare an emergency and sending "near-panicked residents in search of fresh water."[19]

Sixty-year-old Curtis Walls was in the tub when his wife frantically told him to get out.[20] Jason Eldridge, thirty-five, skipped work and drove for hours in surrounding towns to find water to take home, where his two-year-old daughter suffered flu-like symptoms. He never found the water he sought.[21] The governor implored people not to panic,[22] but few listened. On the streets, conditions deteriorated with each passing hour.[23] Some citizens posted on Internet discussion boards that neighbors were becoming violent in their quest for water. "It's survival of the fittest," one woman wrote in her description of the general hysteria she witnessed.[24]

In the end, some five hundred people in the area were admitted to hospitals, including a legislator in the West Virginia House of Representatives, who almost lost her eyesight.[25] Delegate Tiffany Lawrence woke in a Charleston hotel room to find one of her eyes swollen shut. It took an emergency room visit, fifteen rounds of antibiotics, and five days in the hospital to clear up the aggressive staph infection that could have taken her sight and, worse, spread to her brain. "We must... do all we can to ensure this never happens again," Lawrence later told fellow delegates in a speech on the House floor.[26]

I hate to say it, but this sounds an awful lot like Governor Pawlenty's news conference held next to the I-35 bridge two days *after* the fact. It might not surprise you to learn that state inspectors hadn't visited the offending plant for thirteen years. Whether the House of Delegates failed to vote to provide adequate budgetary resources to the department charged with chemical plant inspections, or whether they had simply failed to hold employees there accountable for performing their responsibilities, Ms. Lawrence and her peers had the ability to safeguard the water well *before* the incident. Rather than give speeches on the House floor, Ms. Lawrence would have been well served to look in the mirror and roll up her sleeves to become proactive rather than reactive in identifying and solving problems across the entire portfolio of services managed by her state's government.

I've focused on the Charleston chemical spill, but a 2009 *New York Times* analysis showed that over the last decade some sixty-two million Americans drank water that violated federal health guidelines.[27] A related report exposed the fact that more than 20 percent of water treatment systems in the United States violated the Safe Drinking Water Act in the same five-year period. "Since 2004, the water provided to more than 49 million people has contained illegal concentrations of chemicals like arsenic or radioactive substances like uranium, as well as dangerous bacteria often found in sewage," according to the *Times* report.[28] Incredibly, state and federal authorities penalized fewer than 6 percent of violators. The report cited waning government oversight as a key reason that water pollution was on the rise. Most ominously, it appears that "violations have occurred in parts of every single state."[29] This is not a worry just for the good citizens of West Virginia. Uninspected, unsafe water is a problem that affects all of us. Most of us would rate it as a top priority of government. We'd put it right up there with safe bridges. Simply put, our government is not getting it done.

HELLO...911?

Let's say that because of old, leaking municipal water pipes underground, a sinkhole suddenly appeared in your backyard. Or let's say there was an accident at a nearby industrial facility that hadn't been inspected in ten years. Or let's say your kitchen stove just happened to catch on fire. Would help arrive in time? In Westfield, New Jersey, in 2012 a retired widower named Roy Rentrop was knocked unconscious by a blast in his second-floor apartment and suffered severe injuries from smoke inhalation in the ensuing blaze. Firefighters from twelve nearby towns fought the fire all night, but a lack of personnel in the Westfield department meant that a crucial piece of equipment had to be left at the fire station. Rentrop almost died and spent the next six weeks in the hospital recovering. Westfield had seen a 25 percent reduction in its firefighting force over the previous two years.[30]

A month later, while Rentrop was still in the hospital recovering, a beloved Westfield restaurant called Ferraro's caught fire. This time, six fire departments from the surrounding area and more than one hundred firefighters struggled all night to extinguish the blaze. But the first ladder truck on the scene did not come from Westfield; it came from the town of Cranford—after an agonizing twelve minutes. Westfield's ladder truck, a hundred yards away, never left the station.[31] Because of budget cuts and a hiring freeze, Westfield's fire department didn't have enough personnel on duty at the time to man the ladder truck.[32]

The same year, Westfield resident Ellen Dilorio lost her house in a fire. She and her husband survived; they were rescued from the bedroom on the second floor. But the hardest thing to accept was this: Westfield's firefighters waited fifteen minutes for Plainfield's fire department to arrive before they began their work. Again, manpower was the issue: according to state law, when two firefighters enter a building, two more must remain outside for safety reasons. Westfield only had six firefighters on duty at the time, and three had responded to another call. The three who did respond were left to watch from the outside until sufficient backup arrived. "If we had had children across the hall or an elderly parent who was bedridden, we would not have been able to rescue them, and they could have possibly lost their lives," Dilorio impressed upon Westfield's town council.[33]

A 2005 *Boston Globe* investigation found that in 2002, the last year for which data were available, only about 54 percent of local fire departments in Massachusetts, "met the fire industry goal of arriving within 6 minutes of the first alarm at 90 percent of building fires."[34] Departments nationwide did worse; just 35 percent met the same standard.[35]

Just like a bridge that is found to be structurally deficient with nothing done for seventeen years, these numbers are the difference between life and death. The *Globe* investigation revealed that in the sixteen years between 1986 and 2002, more than four thousand people perished in fires where responders failed to meet the six-minute standard.[36]

THE BIGGEST PONZI SCHEME EVER

I've just cited a few examples of dangerous lapses in service; I could tell you about slower police response times, an increase in dangerous oil spills on our nation's railroads, underperforming schools, poorly inspected food supplies—the list goes on and on. However you slice it, Americans simply aren't receiving the high-quality performance we need from government. As a result, our country is far more dangerous and less livable than it was just thirty years ago. What makes our relentless fall into mediocrity puzzling—and indeed, maddening—is that we're actually spending more money on government than we've ever spent before, certainly enough to fund the core functions of a first-world nation.

Remember all those lists of economic and health criteria that show America lagging behind other developed countries? Well, there's something we do rank highly on. We rank second in debt relative to the size of our economy.[37] In fiscal year 2013, the U.S. government took in \$2.7 trillion in revenue, the most it ever has in a single year.[38] But it spent about $3.5 trillion.[39] In total, the United States ended 2013 on the hook for $680 billion, and that was just for one year![40] We spent 28 percent more than we took in. As of this writing, the total U.S. debt is closing in on $19 trillion and rising every single year.

So let's get this straight: we're spending $3.5 trillion, approximately 30 percent more than we take in every year, and we *still* get low-quality government—we can't get our bridges fixed, our children educated to lead the world, or our nuclear plants inspected on schedule. It might be one thing if we balanced our books every year, and were even paying down some debt. We might accept fewer police officers, long fire response times, and schools that didn't perform as well. But that's not the case. We actually *print* money to pay for the Ritz-Carlton of government, and instead we get the Bates Motel.

We're spending $3.5 trillion, approximately 30 percent more than we take in every year, and we *still* get low-quality government—we can't get our bridges fixed, our children educated to lead the world, or our nuclear plants inspected on schedule.

Because our government agencies have become so distracted, so unfocused on delivering the most fundamental of services, good Americans have had to step in. Have you seen those "Adopt-a-Highway" signs? That's the program through which kindhearted individuals, civic groups, and companies look after a stretch of road because government has given up. You may have seen groups like Wounded Warriors, which raises millions to support our returning war heroes. Groups like this shouldn't need to exist, because those selfless Americans already paid taxes to government agencies like the Department of Transportation and the Department of Veterans Affairs to deliver those services. A proud nation shouldn't be having bake sales to cover the costs of track chairs for our veterans.

A proud nation shouldn't be having bake sales to cover the costs of track chairs for our veterans.

Today, we pay for elected officials to proudly stamp their names on roadside signs for new buildings, delivering an unspoken message about what a good job they are doing for us. Instead, what if on either side of a deficient bridge we required a large sign that said, "This bridge

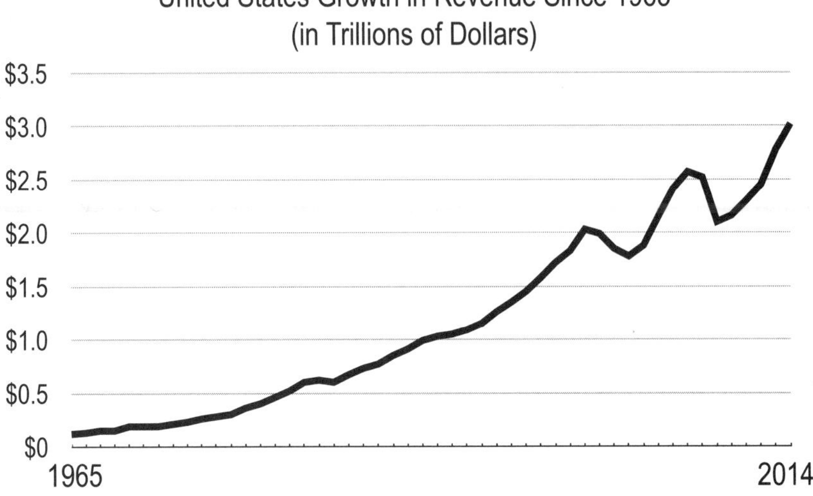

FIGURE 1-1

is rated as structurally deficient because I spent your money on other things. Cross at your own risk. Have a nice day!" And then we proudly listed the elected officials for that district and their phone numbers. What if we did the same thing next to every water fountain that fails to meet clean water standards? And every nuclear power plant that wasn't inspected on schedule?

If our infrastructure of roads, bridges, and water supply is broken, that's because *the government* that runs it is also structurally unsound; core deficiencies in the one ultimately produce sinkholes in the other. There are many talented people working at all levels of public-sector management, and you'll have a chance to meet some of them in the chapters that follow. Thousands more come to government service, whether elected or appointed to office, determined to build high-performance departments, agencies, and state governments. Far too often, they wind up frustrated, confused, and even astonished at the level of inefficiency, finger-pointing, and dysfunction they encounter.

The great tragedy—and it is exactly that—is that well-meaning, competent individuals become trapped in a flawed system that rewards status quo behavior rather than risk taking and actual results. We'll have occasion to explore some of the structural causes of dysfunction, but

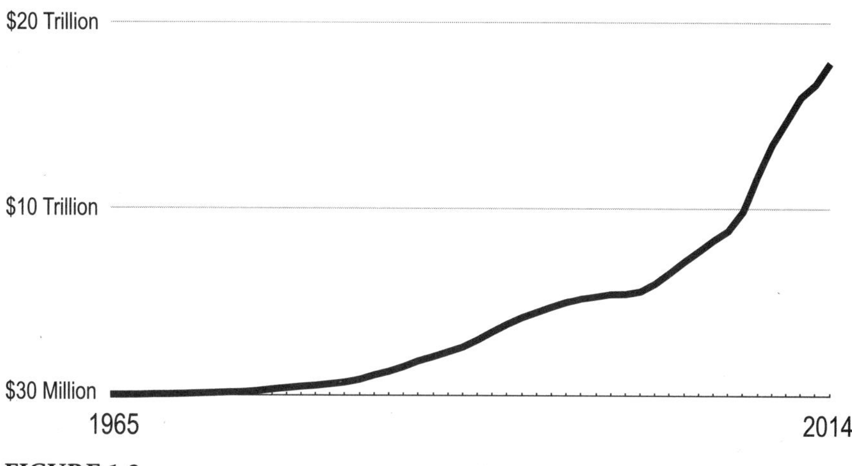

FIGURE 1-2

they include a failure to specify clear organizational goals, inadequate performance measurement, and a culture that values box-checking accountability rather than ownership of results. If we want to repair the infrastructure of America, we must rebuild the infrastructure of American *government*. This book intends to provide precisely that structure.

CHASING SQUIRRELS

We citizens bear ultimate responsibility for our decaying country, and that's because we're ultimately in charge. Many credit nineteenth-century thinker Alexis de Tocqueville with having said, "In democracy, people get the government they deserve." In election after election, we routinely reseat incumbents who continue to contribute to the country's problems, whether through inaction, incompetence, or arrogance. Congressional approval ratings dropped in 2012 to an all-time low of 21 percent, but voters still returned 90 percent of their sitting representatives that year to the U.S. House and 91 percent to the Senate.[41] In both 2006 and 2008, 94 percent returned![42] As citizen conductors we have fallen asleep at the switch and are letting others drive our national train off the tracks. We simply cannot say in polling that the greatest problem facing America is government itself and then rehire more than 90 percent of the management team. We are neglecting our constitutional duty to hold public officials accountable for their failure to deliver what we hired them to do.

> We simply cannot say in polling that the greatest problem facing America is government itself and then rehire more than 90 percent of the management team.

When I was in fifth grade, I would come home with a ninety-five on a school test, and my Mom would proudly display it on the refrigerator and make my favorite dinner as a reward. When we reelect officials more than 90 percent of the time, we are giving them a gold star for their F performance. They would be fools to do anything different in their next term than what clearly worked the last time around. Elected officials perform the way they do because we reward them for building us a low-quality government that costs more than we can afford. And they have intentionally designed the system so it is difficult to understand whether they succeeded or failed. This lets them campaign on distraction issues rather than on actually delivering results. It is in their interest to make government more complicated than necessary, so that voting Americans are unable to determine with clarity whether they merit more time on the job.

So why don't we clamp down on our politicians? One reason is that we allow ourselves to become distracted by issues that should not really be issues at all. How many bullets a gun will hold, legalizing marijuana, whether there's global warming—they're all deck chairs, figuratively, and we spend most of our time rearranging them as our *Titanic* sinks deeper and deeper into an ocean of debt. Debating such issues is the privilege of citizens of a rich nation. These questions would have been great topics for the 1950s, before we chose the road that headed us toward the cliff. Of what consequence are any of these things if the whole enterprise burns down and turns us into a subsistence-level society? Debating global warming today is akin to a scenario in which parents who can't afford to feed their children dinner tonight argue about how much they should be saving each month for their children's college education. The question isn't whether there is or isn't global warming, it's the fact that people driving to the conference to debate it likely

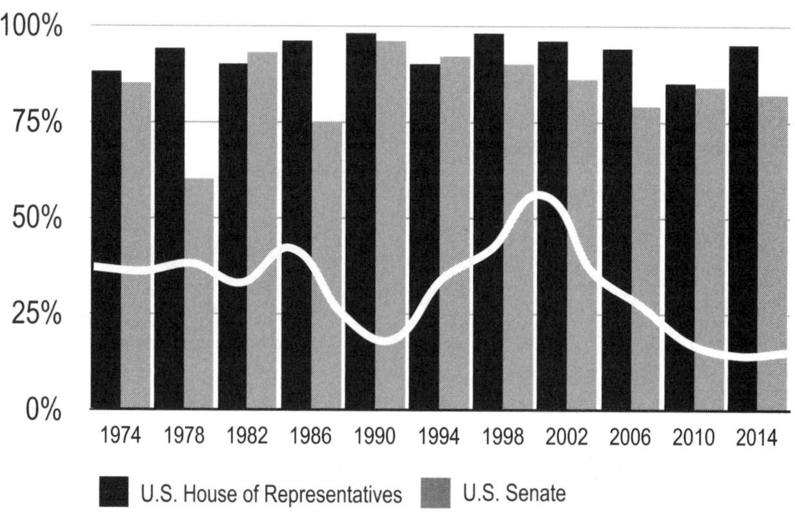

FIGURE 1-3

drove over multiple structurally deficient bridges to get there. Do you think Garrett Ebling in Minneapolis wished his member of Congress or state legislator spent more time debating prayer in schools or ensuring that substandard bridges were repaired? Do you think Sherri Lewis in Harrisburg wished her mayor or city council member spent more time on how much ammunition a gun could hold, instead of preventing the street in front of her house from collapsing? Before any of these attention-grabbing "problems" can be solved, we need to focus on the multitrillion-dollar gorilla in the room.

In the same week in the summer of 2014 that the national embarrassment of our incompetence to provide contractually agreed-upon health care to our veterans was making news, *fifty* United States senators were signing letters to Daniel Snyder, the owner of the Washington Redskins, objecting to the offensive name of the team's mascot.[43] Now, some might say that it's possible to "walk and chew gum" at the same time—i.e., to focus on both issues. Ask the veterans who stood in lines for months waiting for life-saving health procedures if the United States Senate is capable of walking and chewing gum. Better yet, ask the widows of the several dozen veterans who passed away waiting for the health care they were promised. I look forward to the day when an issue that commands the attention of any United States senator, let alone fifty of them, deserves to be *anything* related to a game that grown men play.

In a scene from the popular animated Disney move *Up*, the star dog has his two front paws up on the shoulders of the curmudgeonly Carl and is totally focused on explaining his ability to speak: "My master made me this collar. He is a good and smart master and he made me this collar so that I may talk. Squirrel!" Suddenly the dog's head swivels and his attention shifts to the nearest distraction—a squirrel! Elected officials count on us to chase squirrels. They throw them into the national discourse, and we keep chasing them, one after the other. And then we reward those officials with more votes.

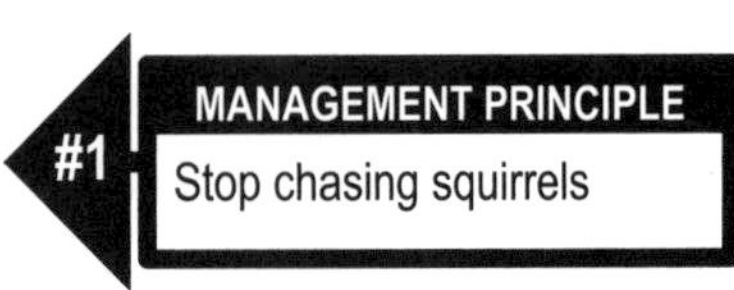

What's wrong with us? While Congress was putting the final touches on the National Defense Authorization Act of 2014 (the legislation that funds our $700 billion-a-year military), America became obsessed with homophobic comments made by Phil Robertson, the patriarch of the hit TV show *Duck Dynasty*.[44] While the Obama administration was trying to figure out how to deal with Syria after revelations the Assad regime had gassed its own people with chemical weapons, Americans were captivated by Miley Cyrus twerking with a foam finger at the MTV Video Music Awards.[45] Soon after that, an anchor on MSNBC interrupted her guest, a former congresswoman invited to speak about NSA spying, to deliver breaking news about Justin Bieber.[46] If Paul Revere were to ride through Massachusetts today to alert residents of a mortal national threat, we wouldn't even hear him . . . we'd be watching *Dancing with the Stars*.

Our disinterest in the activities of government has gotten so bad that many of us can no longer even engage in civic discussions in a responsible way. Jimmy Kimmel, who routinely combs the streets of Los Angeles to prank pedestrians for his "Lie Witness News" segment, asked passersby to reflect on the recent death of Franklin Delano Roosevelt, and they fell for it.[47] Jay Leno for years tripped up citizens on the streets with similar antics in a popular segment called "Jaywalking." A 2013 study by the Center for the American Dream at Xavier University found that one in three American adults would fail the civics section of the citizenship exams taken by immigrants.[48] According to that survey, only a third of people questioned knew the name of one of their senators, only 29 percent could say how long a senator's term of office is, 9 percent knew how old the Constitution was, and only 7 percent could say how many amendments had been made to that document since 1789.[49]

It seems that most of us plain don't care. Only about 18 percent of people followed the Bridgegate controversy that consumed New Jersey governor Chris Christie's administration for multiple news cycles, according to a Pew poll.[50] That's a stark departure from the 44 percent of people who reported following the extremely cold weather of the same period with fervent interest.[51] About one-third of respondents to a summer 2013 Pew poll gave a collective shrug in the wake of revelations by NSA contractor Edward Snowden that the government was overstepping its bounds by spying on U.S. citizens.[52] In his show on Fox News, host Bill O'Reilly gave his own interpretation: "The Internet has created a generation of self-absorbed, addicted, distracted, and ignorant people.... The result is that a very few shrewd people are now wielding enormous power and many Americans are now voting for what they can get, not for what is best for this country." O'Reilly goes on to suggest that we are a "nation in decline" because the populace fails to take an interest in the country's workings and welfare.[53]

I would argue that it goes deeper than that. Our government leaders have intentionally designed a system that makes it difficult for Americans to monitor their performance. *That's* how we wind up rehiring the same elected officials that delivered a failing government for us. Rather than simply lamenting the distraction of Americans and allowing elected officials to take advantage of that, we need a system of government management that makes it easier for a distracted electorate to compare performance with promises. We know *what* to look for; we have just given up demanding that government can and should deliver the same clear service and results that we expect when we spend money in other areas of our lives.

A March 2014 Gallup poll showed that the Americans who *are* paying attention are deeply concerned about five issues in particular: the economy, federal spending and the budget deficit, "the availability and

Americans Are Losing Sleep Over These Issues
1. The economy
2. Federal spending and budget deficit
3. The availability and affordability of health care
4. Unemployment
5. The size and power of the federal government

Source: Rebecca Riffkin, "Climate Change Not a Top Worry in U.S.," Gallup, March 2014

FIGURE 1-4

affordability of healthcare," "unemployment," and "the size and power of the federal government."[54] A full 85 percent of Americans think that government should only spend as much money as it takes in. More than half of Americans think that taxes are too high. Americans also think that fifty cents of every dollar of government spending goes to waste, inefficiency, and bureaucracy.[55] Yet, our politicians fail to address these issues, and because we are so easily distracted by them, we essentially say, "Thank you, do it to me again, please."

Reporters, too, are quick to distract us by citing a politician's favorability rankings in opinion polls. That's about as important as the sixth-grade class presidential election at Mayfield Elementary School, in which the most popular kid would win. Since when is leadership about doing what is popular? My mom used to make us eat her disgusting "end-of-garden pickles," an amalgamation of all the gross things that couldn't stand on their own as vegetables. Her end-of-garden pickles were hardly popular with us kids, but she didn't care. "I'm in charge of this family," she would implicitly (and sometimes explicitly) say, "sometimes my decisions will be popular, and sometimes they will not, but I will work to convince you that my unpopular decisions are in this family's best interests."

True elected leaders are more like my mom: they don't parrot back to people what they want to hear but instead take people to a place that is best for most of them. President Lyndon Johnson is purported to have said, "You need to do what's popular in order to be around long enough to do what's right." Maybe, but America today needs elected leaders, not elected followers who simply conduct polls and feed people cheeseburgers and pizza, which they know are bad for us. America needs some end-of-garden pickles on its plate, elected officials with the courage to put them there, and reporters with the intelligence and integrity to keep us focused on what's *really* important to us.

The bottom line is that we Americans have built ourselves a government that is dangerously unaffordable, unsustainable, and unsuccessful. Our federal debt will be more than $20 trillion when President Barack Obama leaves office.[56] That's already more than we can hope to rein in—let alone pay off—before several generations have passed.

The first thing you do when you're in a hole is stop digging, yet through our political choices we have opted to get more shovels and dig even deeper. We realize on some level that we're in trouble, but we don't know what exactly the problem is, or what to do about it. Polls in the last few years have revealed that Americans harbor deeply negative feelings toward their government over the debt and other economic factors, feelings that undermine the optimism and vitality for which Americans are famous. In 2014, the Associated Press–NORC Center for Public Affairs Research found that only one in twenty Americans thinks that the country works well and requires no adjustments.[57] And, as I said in the introduction, Americans today believe that the number-one problem facing America today is government itself—greater than terrorism, job creation, or health care.

If we could change one metric in our nation—just one—it should be the incumbency reelection rate. Rather than giving this industry an A+ year after year with a reelection rate of over 96 percent, can you imagine the tsunami of performance improvement if we could just get the incumbency reelection rate to the mid 70 percent range, which would be like giving government a "C"? And if we actually gave our politicians failing grades, by only reelecting 50 percent of our incumbents? We are the supervisors in this employer–employee relationship, and our failure to terminate politicians who don't produce the results they were hired to deliver has brought us to the edge. We need to get our *own* houses in order if

Can you imagine the tsunami of performance improvement if we could just get the incumbency reelection rate to the mid 70 percent range, which would be like giving government a "C"?

we are to have any hope of saving America. We need a system that will clearly, quickly, and accurately inform a distracted electorate whether politicians have delivered success or simply empty speeches.

SEVEN STEPS TO SAVING AMERICA

Plenty of public figures from both the left and the right have lamented America's decline. "The persistent blues, the lack of faith, the bet that things won't get better—it just doesn't sound like America," wrote Peggy Noonan, a conservative columnist. She was opining on a 2014 poll that two-thirds of Americans think the United States is on the wrong track.[58] George Packer, a writer for the *New Yorker*, starts his 2013 book on America's gloomy state this way: "No one can say when the unwinding began—when the coil that held America together in its secure and sometimes stifling grip first gave way." Other writers have depicted America as a decaying world power, a behemoth unable to sustain its present course. Many of them are articulate, to be sure, but beyond poignant assertions by intellectuals and blustery bumper-sticker speeches by politicians, solutions to our problems have not materialized. Meanwhile, Republicans and Democrats have both effectively demonstrated over the past decades that neither party has developed the model to deliver anything other than low-quality, high-cost government services.

There is a clear solution, and it's not just to pump more money into the system. American government does not need more money. Instead, it needs to do two things: spend the money it takes in on core functional responsibilities, and spend it in such a way that provides both a financial and quality-of-life return on investment. When we get those core functions of government right, then by all means, let's open the floor for debate on other programs we should consider.

In the private sector, Apple has chosen to be great at innovation—and it is. Ritz-Carlton has chosen to be great at quality—and it is. Walmart has chosen to be great at low prices—and it is. In the public sector, our federal, state, and local officials have chosen to be everything to everybody, and as a result they are great at building wasteful and unsustainable governments. Trying to be good at everything is a commitment to be mediocre at all of them. Therein lies the challenge, but also our greatest hope. Government *can* work better, every bit as well as well as our for-profit companies do. What American policymakers and elected officials need is a systematic approach for rooting out dysfunction and designing, managing, and overseeing government agencies so that they work efficiently and well. Policy makers need a process that allows them to establish what is important and that focuses them on delivering it. And the tens of thousands of idealistic public employees who are trapped in a flawed structure need a new one that rewards them for results rather than for punching a clock.

Our federal, state, and local officials have chosen to be everything to everybody, and as a result they are great at building wasteful and unsustainable governments. Trying to be good at everything is a commitment to be mediocre at all of them.

In the chapters that follow, I will lay out our proven seven-step method to turning unfocused public organizations around and demonstrate the tremendous opportunities available for measurable performance. From defining a success moment to creating a plan to achieve it to measuring the impact of new efforts at efficiency, the rest of this book will show how together we can save America. It comes down to demanding that we have a government judged on its efficiency and results rather than on who gives the best speeches and evokes the warmest emotions.

We judge the greatness of football teams not on the basis of whose coach gives the best pep talk in the locker room, but on the basis of which team puts the most points up on the scoreboard. With this book, American taxpayers will finally have the tools required to hold their government executives every bit as accountable as we hold our football coaches. Public employees will have a clear, practicable process for making their organizations every bit as effective and helpful as they always

We judge the greatness of football teams not on the basis of whose coach gives the best pep talk in the locker room, but on the basis of which team puts the most points up on the scoreboard.

2

Define the Success Moment

In the fall of 1963, a group of businessmen climbed aboard a twin-engine Beachwood Queen Air turboprop and took off over a sultry Florida swamp just south of Orlando. They had been on a lengthy trip with stops earlier in St. Louis, Niagara Falls, and the Baltimore–Washington, D.C., region. Their days on the road were coming to a close, and after this last flight they would be heading home to California.

The men flew over the coast and then headed inland, looking down at the unspoiled vastness of the region. From the air, the landscape did not appear welcoming; it was an almost endless expanse of swampland and citrus groves punctuated by lakes.[1] On a hazy day, you couldn't even see the horizon; the trees just faded into steamy oblivion. It seemed an unusual choice for a construction site, but where other people only saw the mosquitos and alligators that inhabited the place at the time, Walt Disney, the rich and powerful entertainment magnate from California, saw opportunity and the successful realization of his dream.

Disney envisioned building a theme park that would far surpass his original Disneyland in California. It would be a fantastical land of castles, amusement park rides, and Disney characters come to life, as well as a futuristic city known as the Experimental Prototype Community of Tomorrow, or EPCOT. Disney had spent years researching sites that might fit his vision; he wanted a large tract of land so he could control the businesses that would spring up around his new park.[2] Niagara Falls in New York was beautiful, but it was hard to get to, and the winters were harsh.[3] Southern Louisiana offered an alluring subtropical climate, but the Big Easy's politicians demanded too much in their negotiations.[4]

Disney liked St. Louis, Missouri, but there he clashed with beer mogul August Busch, Jr., who publicly criticized Disney's position of prohibiting alcohol sales in the park.[5] Now Disney gazed into the sun glare of central Florida's lakes and ponds and said to the men on board with him, "That's it."[6]

The site was perfect. The region was sparsely populated and cheap, and the nearby construction of Interstate 4 would one day cross over the Florida Turnpike—almost literally saying X marks the spot. The confluence of two major highways and an airport in Orlando would make the trek to the park accessible for millions.[7] With the location set, Disney could now define a series of specific success moments for himself and his team to accomplish. There were tens of thousands of acres to be acquired (and in secrecy, no less, so as to prevent land speculation). He wanted construction to be complete by 1971. And he expected six million visitors in the first year.

Disney died in 1966, but the vision he laid out as well as the specific success moments that led to it were so clear and unwavering that his brother and business partner, Roy O. Disney, was still able to drive progress. The Magic Kingdom opened in October 1971 and welcomed ten million visitors in its first year, far exceeding the goal.[8] The hordes who showed up were greeted by a spectacle that really did seem like magic: a pearly white castle that dominated the city's pristine pedestrian avenues, manicured gardens, and throngs of beloved Disney characters—all where a swamp had once been. Asked what Walt Disney might have thought of the new park, his widow was quoted as saying, "I think Walt would have approved."[9] Today Disney World attracts more than fifty million visitors annually, making it the world's most frequented resort. Indeed, Disney had defined success.

TEN MILLION iPHONES

The establishment of a success moment—a clear definition of what must happen *in the short term* to accomplish a broader vision—is the first step in our Seven Step process. Business schools and consultancies offer a range of definitions for a company's vision, but they usually agree that a vision statement should spell out where a company is broadly headed, or, as the Boston Consulting Group, rated as the best change management provider by Kennedy Information, puts it, "an ambitious image of the future that is radically preferable to the current state."[10]

A success moment, on the other hand, is a tangible, quantifiable, trackable *event* that holds the same meaning for all members of the organization. While a vision describes an organization's *destination,* often years down the road, a success moment represents its *temporary resting point* after a finite period of time.

Well-defined success moments share three basic characteristics. First, they express a single, *quantifiable* goal—i.e., how much money to shave from a budget, how many PCs to roll off a factory assembly line, or how many motorists check the "satisfied" box in a customer survey at the DMV. Second, strong success moments specify a time frame within which the quantifiable goal should be achieved. President Kennedy said in 1961 that he wanted a man on the moon and safely back to earth before the decade was out. That was a perfectly clear objective—it stated what we are going to do, and by when. Third, strong success moments focus on the big issues. The new principal of a failing school should not waste time thinking about how quickly she can get the gym walls painted. She should be thinking about how to raise test scores 10 percent past her state's minimum standards before the school year is out.

Success moments, as I'm defining them, are not by any means new; in fact, what sets all great organizations apart is an inspirational vision *coupled with* focused execution around clear, well-communicated, shorter-term goals. A great example is Apple. When Steve Jobs came back to run the company in 1997, Apple was "producing a random array of computers and peripherals, including a dozen different versions of the Macintosh."[11] Finally, in a now infamous meeting, Jobs had enough.

> "Stop!" he shouted. "This is crazy." He grabbed a Magic Marker, padded in his bare feet to a whiteboard, and drew a two-by-two grid. "Here's what we need," he declared. Atop the two columns, he wrote "Consumer" and "Pro." He labeled the two rows "Desktop" and "Portable." Their job, he told his team members, was to

> focus on four great products, one for each quadrant. All other products should be canceled. There was a stunned silence.[12]

Jobs imposed a focused discipline on the company's management, designers, and engineers, deciding that Apple was going to produce a very limited line of high-quality computers and be "best in class." He defined what the company was going to be great at. It was going to stop being mediocre at *everything*, and be amazing at *one* thing. Jobs would continue to do something similar several more times over the ensuing years. Whenever the company moved into a new product space (like music players) or invented one from thin air (like tablets), Apple chose to make a limited number of models—and in some cases just one—to keep the quality high and the focus sharp. With his broader vision clear, Jobs established clear success moments for the delivery of Apple's products.

In the summer of 2007, for instance, Apple unveiled the iPhone, giving birth to a new global smartphone market.[13] Jobs gave the company a sales target in a specified time frame. He wanted to sell ten million iPhones by the end of 2008.[14] The message was simple, it was clear, and it was easy to track. Employees throughout the organization could understand how their role in sales, shipping, marketing, and so on would contribute to realizing it. Apple achieved that success moment at the end of October 2008—two months early—and only a few weeks after the debut of the second-generation iPhone.[15] By 2012, the iPhone was estimated to be responsible for more than half of Apple's profits, thanks to both a vision and the focused discipline afforded by success moments.[16]

The world of sports offers many strong examples of success moments defined and achieved. In major league baseball, general managers of the top teams usually (but not always) have broad, multiyear visions. During the 2000s, when Theo Epstein, the young general manager of my beloved Boston Red Sox began to rebuild his team utilizing Moneyball principles (see chapter 4), the Red Sox won three out of ten World Series titles. Each title represented an individual success moment on the way to attaining the larger vision of building a dynasty. Juxtapose that with the Florida Marlins, which in 1993 were the worst in their division, and which in the following off-season acquired an entirely new team of free-agent superstars. In 1997, the Marlins won the World Series—and then promptly got rid of all of their new superstars. Predictably, they finished last the subsequent year. The vision of their general manager, Jim Leyland, was simply to win the World Series once, and it became his success moment as well. The Marlins succeeded in achieving this very narrow vision/success moment.

Both teams achieved success by clearly defining the success moment in spring training, *before* the team began to play games. They then aligned every single person in their organizations—from the first baseman to the trainer to the batboy—around what a good year looked like. For both the Red Sox and the Marlins, success was quantifiable and a time frame was specified. Most importantly, everyone on these teams understood viscerally what success would *feel* like (that glorious moment when the ball settled into the left fielder's mitt and they could rush the pitcher's mound, piling on top of one another beneath a pile of confetti, with tens of thousands of cameras flashing).

If you start looking for success moments, you can find them everywhere. Marathon runners have a vision of finishing the race and embracing loved ones. The success moment? The first time they run sixty miles in a single week training for the race. A dieter might take as his goal dropping his forty-inch waist down to a thirty-four by next Christmas. The success moment? Losing twenty pounds during the first ninety days of that journey. A recent college graduate plans to pay off her hefty student loan in ten years. The success moment? Paying off the first $6,000 of that loan at the end of year one.

TWO SCOOPS OF GOVERNMENT MINUS THE SUCCESS

If success moments—to track the journey to the ultimate destination—are so common, not to mention commonsensical, it's surprising to find that so few of our public officials make use of them. Most elected leaders, regardless of party affiliation, can articulate a strong vision. Republicans often campaign on balancing the nation's budget, Democrats on taking care of those in need. Hopefully all elected officials believe we should work to prevent acts of terrorism against Americans and America's interests both at home and abroad. Yet politicians typically fail to define shorter-term markers of success. You don't ordinarily hear politicians getting specific, stating that it will be a successful year if we reduce our deficit by 5 percent, or put one million police officers on the street, or provide eight million Americans with health insurance. You also rarely, if ever, see public administrators building success moments into their organizations' overall management infrastructure as the starting point for excellence. As a result, our city, state, and federal governments stay stagnant, failing to achieve the larger vision. And, of course, by design, it's harder for voters to hold them accountable for performance, because success isn't clearly defined.

Consider what happened with the Troubled Asset Relief Program, or TARP. In the fall of 2008, during the near collapse of the American financial system, Congress provided nearly three-quarters of a billion dollars to banks across the country, ostensibly to catalyze capital available for borrowing. The banks were supposed to take the newfound, unanticipated revenue from the federal government and loan it out as mortgages to families. There was not, as we shall see, a success moment. Simply a vision and then debate about the tactics.

In early 2009, Congress held hearings to get answers about the previous fall's allocation of $700 billion from the Troubled Asset Relief Program. On February 11, 2009, the representatives on the House Financial Services Committee hauled America's top Wall Street bankers in to find out how the "bailout" funds they received were being spent.[17] Under the glare of television lights, the hearing devolved into a fracas, with sarcastic members of Congress hurling insults at the eight men. They might as well have sold popcorn in the hallway.

At issue were two basic questions: Why were the banks still refusing to free up capital for lending despite the hundreds of billions of taxpayer dollars given to prop them up? And why were the banks still doling out enormous bonuses and retirement packages to executives whose imprudence and reckless risk taking had helped create the financial crisis in the first place? The representatives seemed delighted to devote the most dramatic act in that year's political theater to shaming these scions of American finance. The lectures, finger-pointing, and recriminations dragged on for hours.[18] But no one in the chamber asked the one question that should have been asked that day. Someone should have inquired of the irate congressmen, all puffed up for television cameras, why *they* gave away an amount of money equal to the Pentagon's annual budget to countless private companies without knowing precisely how that money was going to be used. The problem in this case was not so much corporate greed as government incompetence.

One of TARP's most important goals was the preservation of home ownership after the housing market collapsed.[19] In the run-up to the bill's passage, the U.S. Treasury told Congress that the $700 billion in bailout funds would be used in large part to purchase risky mortgages from the banks. Once the government owned those loans, Treasury would then modify their terms to help distressed borrowers keep their houses. But that promise was not kept. In 2011, TARP's outgoing special inspector general wrote in the *New York Times*:

> Almost immediately, as permitted by the broad language of the act, Treasury's plan for TARP shifted from the purchase of mortgages to the infusion of hundreds of billions of dollars into the nation's largest financial institutions, a shift that came with the express promise that it would restore lending. Treasury, however, provided the money to banks with no effective policy or effort to compel the extension of credit. There were no strings attached: no requirement or even incentive to increase lending to home buyers, and against our strong recommendation, not even a request that banks report how they used TARP funds.[20]

Addressing banking executives during the infamous February 2009 hearing, Representative Gary Ackerman from New York remarked, "When the press makes inquiries as to what you did with the first tranche of money that we gave you, many billions of dollars, your answer is it's none of your business."[21] Seriously, the congressman was suggesting that the *press* was the investigative wing of the federal government because that very congressman hadn't put proper controls in place before handing out $700 billion dollars of tax money. The congressman went further, asking, "What did you do with the new money?"[22] The mere fact he had to ask should make every taxpayer shudder with indignation.

It was sadly apparent; no success moment had been defined. And without a success moment, Congress had no way to firmly hold parties accountable, much less frame and execute a plan to achieve success. Congressman Ackerman's constituents could determine with great clarity whether the then New York Jets head coach, Rex Ryan, had a successful year—that was evident in his win–loss record. But they had no clarity as to whether their congressman had a successful year, which is exactly how members of Congress from both parties design it. And, in this case, Congressman Ackerman had no way of knowing whether his vote to spend $700 billion of our money had been successful.

The TARP legislation is hardly the only instance in which political leaders failed to define a success moment. In presidential politics, it's a rarity. In December 2014, a friend of mine shared a post on Facebook that described what a successful presidency looked like: Dow Jones

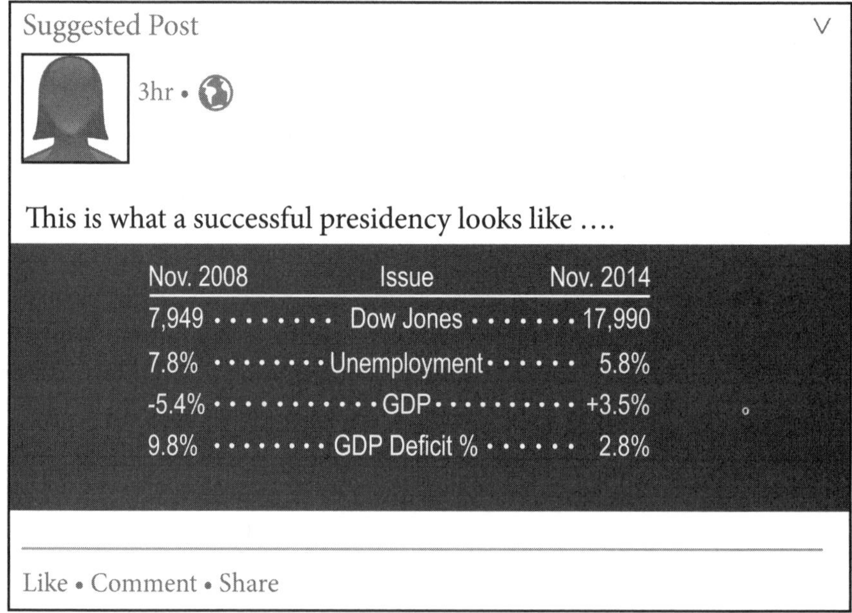

FIGURE 2-1

Industrial Average of almost 18,000; unemployment rate under 6 percent; gross domestic product growth of 3.5 percent; and so on. These were all metrics achieved under the Obama administration by the fall of 2014, and the point of this post was that Obama's had been a "successful" presidency. There's no question about it: those are impressive results. But hold on. While we can all have a rational debate about causation and correlation (whether these things just happened, or whether the president's policies caused them to happen), we should ask: Who decides whether these metrics, as opposed to others, define success? When President Obama leaves office, our national debt will exceed $20 trillion, more than half of which was amassed during his presidency.[23] More than half of Americans think that race relations are worse today than in 2008.[24] Real household income is flat,[25] and food stamps eligibility and utilization are through the roof.[26] You get the idea; there are any number of metrics that *didn't improve* or even got worse during the Obama years.

Now, I'm not suggesting that one set of metrics is more or less important than any other. I'm just asking: Who gets to decide? Maybe the Dow Jones should be at 22,000 instead of 18,000. Maybe unemployment should be even lower—4 percent, not 5.5 percent. Maybe it's race relations or the size of the national debt that counts, not the economy. The problem is that *nobody* defined success—not the president, not the electorate, not even the media. If the president had selected the metrics listed in that Facebook post in his campaign as criteria for judging, if he had set goals for them, and if he had then delivered them on the schedule promised, then we could say that he had clearly delivered success. Instead, partisans and talking heads cherry-pick the metric that works best for their argument and try to trumpet that as success. As a result, success is literally defined by whomever talks the loudest.

Partisans and talking heads cherry-pick the metric that works best for their argument and try to trumpet that as success. As a result, success is literally defined by whomever talks the loudest.

What's frustrating is that politicians are actually quite adept at defining success moments for themselves *as candidates*. During election campaigns, they identify internal monthly, quarterly, and annual fund-raising goals for their campaigns. Externally, they design detailed platforms and legislative agendas that they promise to enact in a given term of office. They make bold claims to constituents about the dollars they will bring to their districts, or the exact number of jobs their policies will help create, or the precise number of families that will be benefited by a certain tax-reduction proposal. So they clearly know *how* to do it. But once election day passes, that focus typically gives way to vague descriptions of success and progress. Distraction, cynical political maneuvering, and double-talk win the day. Imagine how much more dynamic and productive public organizations would be if employees could cross the finish line and celebrate success, and then try to run the race faster the next year.

LET THE GERBIL WHEEL SPIN

In the absence of success moments, both elected officials and administrators often perform what I call "gerbil wheel management." Others who report to them—teachers, bus drivers, analysts at a state pension fund—come to work day after day, month after month, year after year, performing the same job over and over. The gerbil never gets anywhere. There's never a victory. No one ever rushes the pitchers mound. Round and round the wheel goes. Employees "succeed" by making it to retirement, when they can finally get off the gerbil wheel, to be replaced by someone else who immediately begins the ride. Pretty depressing, isn't it? Sadly, that's the way the structure is built.

It gets worse. By failing to step up and define success moments, public officials actually make it *harder* to achieve their longer-term visions. When an organization doesn't explain what success looks like, others get to do it for them. Sometimes they are hostile outsiders. Other times they are uninformed critics, or perhaps an auditor. And quite often, they may just be inquisitive journalists.

Consider the case of health-care enrollment figures for the Affordable Care Act, President Obama's signature legislative achievement. In September 2013, just before the HealthCare.gov website was scheduled to go live, NBC reporter Nancy Snyderman asked Obama's health and human services secretary Kathleen Sebelius what success looked like to her. Sebelius attempted to navigate away from the question. In the end, after more needling from the reporter, she murmured, "I think success looks like at least seven million people having signed up by the end of March 2014."[27] Earlier in June she had told reporters, "We're hopeful that seven million is a realistic target."[28] Sebelius's comments comprised a clear definition of success, one that supported President Obama's larger vision of making health care more affordable and accessible for all Americans. There was only one problem: the success moment had been established in a television interview. Because the administration hadn't defined success itself, a reporter was able to drive the debate, and now the administration owned it, like it or not.

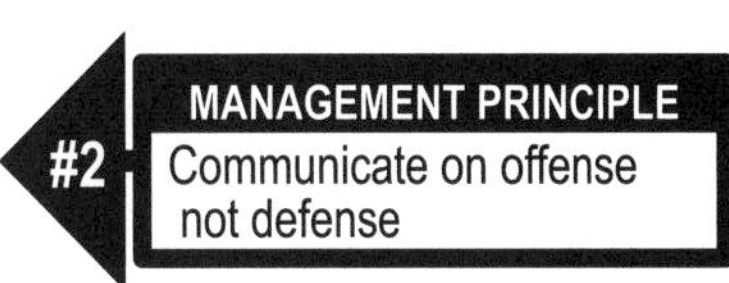

During the months that followed, as difficulties with HealthCare.gov emerged, the American public began to lose confidence in the administration's plan. Toward the end of March 2014, less than a week before the deadline to enroll those seven million people, the administration extended the deadline by two weeks in order to give people who had had trouble with the website more time to sign up.[29] Did the administration realize that it was not going to meet its target of seven million enrollees on time? The administration's extension was not accompanied by a release of the actual number of people who had already signed up, so it didn't take too great a leap to figure out what was happening: they hadn't made it.

Only a month earlier, Secretary Sebelius reported in testimony to Congress that about 4.2 million Americans had enrolled in a healthcare plan so far, well below the desired 7 million.[30] Worse, Sebelius tried to claim that the seven million figure had been contrived by the Congressional Budget Office, a contention immediately debunked by the press.[31] The president and congressional leaders who had so vigorously promoted the new law also refused to "own" the low enrollment numbers. In fact, in testimony before the House Ways and Means Committee, Secretary Sebelius was repeatedly grilled as to what success *now* looked like for Obamacare. Now, the secretary steadfastly declined to be specific, repeatedly saying that "success looks like access to affordable health care for millions of Americans," with no mention as to *how* many millions or by *when*.

Jay Carney, the president's spokesperson, spent months trying to move the White House away from Secretary Sebelius's clear definition of success. Only in April 2014, *after* the deadline had passed, did the president finally embrace his secretary's definition of success. Speaking in a Rose Garden pep rally–style event, he proclaimed, "Last night, the first open-enrollment period under this law came to an end. And despite several lost weeks out of the gate because of problems with the website, 7.1 million Americans have now signed up for private insurance plans through these marketplaces—7.1." Again, picking the metric to be judged by after the game had been played.

Let me be clear: I'm not taking a stance on whether the Affordable Care Act is good or bad legislation; I'll leave that to health-care experts. Second, I applaud the Obama administration for having a vision as to what the president wanted to achieve and I applaud his designee, Secretary Sebelius, for clearly defining success. However, the Obamacare case illustrates two important points. First, when an organization fails to define a success moment at the outset of a major change or new initiative, other people get to. That NBC reporter had no idea what success was supposed to look like when she talked to Sebelius that day, but just by posing the question and pushing the secretary to respond, she forced the Obama administration to define it in the least desirable way possible—publicly and under duress.

Second, the administration then made matters much worse by failing to own its failures. The goals an organization sets, no matter how realistic they may seem at first, are not always achievable. When we realize we may fall short, it's better to miss the target and own the shortfall on our own terms. That way, we can adjust quickly and focus on the next success moment in order to deliver the grand vision. Vice President Biden, for his part, seemed to understand this. "We may not get to seven million," he told reporters, "we may get to five or six, but that's a hell of a start."[32]

Organizations large and small embrace this principle of ownership all the time when they hold fund-raising campaigns. They paint a huge thermometer on plywood and position it at the end of Main Street, right by the old courthouse, leaning it up against the big oak tree. At the top of the thermometer they paint a line indicating what the success moment is for the fund-raising campaign. And as the community makes progress toward that goal, the group paints the thermometer in red—raising the level ever upward—until one of two things happens: success is realized and a celebration ensues, or everyone can understand that the organization came up 6 percent short this year. Public officials *owe* it to citizens to project a similar transparency. If they do, they'll find it much easier to overcome opposition and move forcefully toward fulfilling their larger, more ambitious promises. And voters will have a much clearer sense of which agencies are succeeding and which are struggling.

WHY DO WE EXIST?

The process of defining a success moment is quite easy. First, leaders should grasp and articulate their organization's mission. This comes down to a few simple questions: Why do we exist? What do we do? For whom? It's easy to get distracted and start talking about why you *wish* you existed. A school superintendent might give a speech saying that "the public education system must be protected." Really? I don't think so. The *true* purpose of education is to prepare children for success as adults, not to protect the education system. Why would we protect *any* structure that is failing to deliver desired results?

So often the management teams we work with want to blow right past this conversation. They treat it as a bunch of gobbledygook. I have had senior executives responsible for budgets of hundreds of millions of dollars tell me that "they're too busy doing work to make time to figure out what work they ought to be doing." I've watched smart, experienced executives rush into decisions about *what* they're going to do, *what* they're going to spend money on, and *what* projects they want to advance, rather than answer the difficult question of why. Why spend money on a high-speed rail network if success is defined as preventing terrorist attacks? Conversely, if success is defined as reducing automobile travel by 30 percent by 2020, then why are you spending so much on preventing terrorist attacks? Why not spend *more* money on high-speed rail?

Understanding and articulating *why* the organization exists in the first place is critical; you're talking about the purpose of the entire organization, the reason everyone bothers to get up in the morning to come to work. If anything deserves to be clear and precise, this is it. It is the foundation on which the entire organization sits. Take your time, and deliberate over the nuances. We have spent hours working with teams to narrow their mission statements to exactly the right vocabulary and phrasing. In the case of the Pasco County (Florida) School District, that work yielded a very tight mission statement: "To provide a world-class education for all students." That's it. That is the reason there is a school district in Pasco County. The district, like nearly all public organizations, doesn't exist to deliver projects, but rather to drive performance in what it does every single day. In this case, educate children, not build schools.

WHAT DO WE SEEK TO BECOME?

The next step is to develop a *vision* that detaches the organization from the status quo and opens up alternate possibilities. Leaders must develop a picture of the future that everyone can understand and rally around. Simplicity is key. Bill Gates and Steve Jobs were able to describe simple and elegant visions of where they wanted their companies to go; government can and must do the same. Make sure to involve *everyone* in the process. When working with a school district, we work with the superintendent *and* the bus drivers. At a toll road or turnpike, we work with the chief financial officer as well as the toll takers. At a library, it's the board and the custodial staff. Consumers of public services must also be heard as well. How? By gleaning their desires from quarterly customer satisfaction tracking systems. Consider, too, what taxpayers who *don't* use your public service have to say by engaging them at public meetings. They are, after all, investors—whether by choice or not.

When framing a vision, an organization simply must choose where it wants to be best in class, and where it's willing to be second or third best. No organization can be good at everything, although a lot of them try, especially in government. America is full of well-intentioned agencies and institutions whose thinly stretched efforts result in diminished quality—and indeed, mediocrity—across the board.

When framing a vision, an organization simply must choose where it wants to be best in class, and where it's willing to be second or third best. No organization can be good at everything.

When I was CEO of the RGRTA, my team knew that there were many things we were just *not* going to be great at, such as project management, employee training, and security. The key is we selected proactively those areas that we were willing to be less good at than others. What we *were* going to be great at was delivering low fares to customers. We had selected this area to excel in because low fares were something we could control, and they were a key component of our vision of becoming "economically sustainable." When framing a vision for your organization, spend some time specifying what you're willing to forgo or back away from. Steve Jobs has famously said that a major reason Apple was so successful was that leaders decided what initiatives they would *not* advance every bit as much as those products they developed. Commit to trading lower performance in some areas for stellar performance in others. The more sharply your team can understand organizational priorities, the more energized and directed it can become.

#3 MANAGEMENT PRINCIPLE
Select one thing to be best in class

Now, you might say, "That's great for Apple. They can just decide not to build a computer. But in my county government we must have parks, provide a police force, fight fires, license businesses, and so on." Yes, that is absolutely true. Government is indeed different from Apple. But you still can and must decide what to be great at. If your county government is committed to low taxes, then you're not going to mow the park lawns every week; it might be twice a month, and you and your constituents should be willing to tolerate longer wait times at DMV. Conversely, if high-quality customer satisfaction is your government's core focus, then you had better be prepared to tax people in a manner consistent with that and point complainants toward the value they are receiving—i.e., wait times of less than sixty seconds at the DMV.

Now, those aren't always crystal-clear choices. Perhaps if you want to be best in class at lowering taxes, and you also want to mow the lawns in the park, clean the bathrooms, and offer after-school education programs, you can achieve all these things. But you're going to have to be willing to eliminate concerts in the park on Sunday afternoons. You can't have it all; you just can't. You can't eat ice cream sundaes every night and think *Sports Illustrated* is going to call to put you on the cover. Excellence comes with choices—and that's true in life as well as in government. To deliver excellence, you simply have to choose what is the most important, and stick to it.

WHAT WILL WE NEED TO GET THERE?

Before any organization can crystallize vision into meaningful success moments for everyone, a team must take time to determine what tools the organization will call upon to achieve its vision, and what obstacles will crop up during their journey. Perform a classic SWOT analysis (identifying the organization's strengths, weaknesses, opportunities, and threats), again bringing all relevant voices to the table. Once leaders collect and synthesize what the rank and file considers the coming year's key issues, leaders are in a far better position to analyze what the organization must do to realize success as they have defined it.

> Make sure what you say about the organization in the room matches what you say about it to your loved ones when you get home.

When we work with organizations through this part of the process, we break it down into three steps. First, we go department by department and unit by unit through the organization, meeting with mid-level and entry-level employees in small groups to perform the SWOT analysis. We do this without senior leaders, department heads, or bosses in the room. We establish one rule from the outset: honesty. Make sure that what you say about the organization in the room matches what you say about it to your loved ones when you get home. And we focus discussion around the goal of achieving the vision. We're not interested in identifying strengths or opportunities that won't help us achieve our vision. We're also not interested in having employees simply bitch about those things they don't like. Rather, we want them to talk about weaknesses that we *must* fix in order to realize success.

Step two is to do the SWOT process with senior management, without sharing with them what their employees have identified; that way, they can perform the exercise more objectively. In step three, we identify gaps between what employee groups and what senior leaders have identified as the strengths, weaknesses, opportunities, and threats bearing on execution of the vision.

With everything on the board, we take the senior team through a process of prioritizing their SWOT—selecting key issues that they must take advantage of, repair, and guard against—in order to realize their chosen vision. This process always separates the wheat from the chaff, making it very clear where the organization must focus in planning for the coming year (I'll discuss the process of actually building the plan in chapter 3).

HOW WILL WE BEHAVE?

After figuring out what resources an organization can muster to pursue its vision and what obstacles it must overcome, leaders should achieve consensus around the foundational values that will govern how team members behave during the journey. One of my team's values has long been the principle of saying in a meeting what you're going to say at home that night. In so many organizations, people's heads nod in passionate agreement during a meeting, and then when they are at the water cooler talking to colleagues or having dinner with their family, they gripe about what a foolish idea the boss had that day. Such double-talk benefits nobody. The employee becomes disengaged, and the boss and organization fail to benefit from the employee's thinking. For us, honesty is so important that we want to see it in action at all times as we strive to achieve a success moment.

For some institutions, personal integrity is a highly treasured character attribute among team members. For others, it's blind devotion to the bottom line. Some organizations preach timeliness, scrupulousness, and attention to detail; others spurn caution, insisting instead on risk taking, creativity, and ultracompetitiveness. Because government organizations serve the public (under the direction of representatives elected or appointed in their name), a more service-oriented approach to values development is generally appropriate. The National Park Service lists as guiding principles adherence to productive partnerships, citizen involvement, heritage education, and employee development, among others.[33] Customs and Border Protection emphasizes vigilance, courage, valor, service to country, and integrity as its core values.[34] The Food and Drug Administration's Office of Regulatory Affairs is frank about its desire to develop better values for the future, among them team and partnership building, investment in FDA's people, and continuous improvement.[35]

It largely doesn't matter what your organization's values are. What does matter is that you identify these values in a collaborative and engaging way and then hold every team member responsible for realizing them.

WHAT DOES SUCCESS LOOK LIKE?

Only now, once you've established a mission, vision, SWOT analysis, and values, are you ready to frame that simple, precise statement of what success will look like. Again, keep it simple, clear, quantitative, and realistic, and be sure to share the success moment with employees, board members, taxpayers, and customers. *Everyone* must know the organization's short-term performance goal, as well as what they must to do help deliver on it.

When I was a kid, my dad would deliver his version of a success moment over pancakes during our family's Sunday morning breakfast. He would explain that three wagonloads of hay needed to be baled up and stored in the barn, and he specified what each of us would have to do to complete the task. After dealing with the hay, he said, we would need to repair the wire fencing around two fields; my role was to put all the tools in the back of the trailer by 2:30, while my brother was responsible for loading the trailer full of fence posts. At 5:00, we would all meet up on the hill to cut the brush back from around a field Dad wanted to plow in the fall. Finally, at 7:00 we would meet up with my mom and sisters at our pond for a swim, a picnic, and some celebration of our day's work. It was a clear vision for the day as well as specification of what needed to be achieved and by when. With everything set out so clearly, we all had the direction we needed to get the job done. If a small family farm could achieve so much during a single day, then surely we can get our public agencies to operate in a similar way for taxpayers.

A COSMIC SUCCESS MOMENT

On November 22, 1963, the very same day that Walt Disney selected a central Florida backwater as the site of his masterpiece, President Kennedy was assassinated in Dallas, Texas. Like Disney, this young and inspiring leader was attuned to seeing the future and then defining meaningful success markers along the way to that destination. Indeed, one of Kennedy's most fantastical dreams would outlive him. Just over a year before his death, Kennedy spoke to a crowd at Rice University about a vision he had for putting an American on the moon. For several years, the Soviet Union had beat America in the space race. In 1957, the Russians launched Sputnik, the world's first satellite.[36] The Russians' second satellite launch that year took a dog up, too.[37] Then in 1961, Soviet cosmonaut Yuri Gagarin became the first human being in space.[38] By September of 1962, President Kennedy had had enough. "Those who came before us made certain that this country rode the first waves of the industrial revolutions, the first waves of modern invention, and the first wave of nuclear power," Kennedy announced, "and this generation does not intend to founder in the backwash of the coming age of space. We mean to be a part of it—we mean to lead it. For the eyes of the world now look into space, to the moon and to the planets beyond, and we have vowed that we shall not see it governed by a hostile flag of conquest, but by a banner of freedom and peace..."[39]

Now *that* is the end zone! A clearly articulated vision for the president's team, the government, and indeed the nation to rally around: leading humanity in the exploration of space. But Kennedy broke this vision down and focused on the first step along the journey. Before the country would explore more distant planets, it would have a man walk safely on the moon. It would accomplish this feat within a specific length of time: as Kennedy went on to say, "We choose to go to the moon in this decade." Kennedy also specified the values that the country would adhere to in pursuing this success moment, those of "freedom and peace" rather than hostility and conquest.

Fifteen months earlier, in May of 1961, the president had appeared before a joint session of Congress to flesh out his success moment. Reviewing his remarks, we recognize key elements I've set forward in this chapter:

> Since early in my term, our efforts in space have been under review. With the advice of the Vice President, who is Chairman of the National Space Council, we have examined where we are strong and where we are not, where we may succeed and where we may not [**SWOT analysis**]. . . . But the facts of the matter are that we have never made the national decisions or marshaled the national resources required for such leadership. [**Prioritization**] We have never specified long-range goals on an urgent time schedule, or managed our resources and our time so as to insure their fulfillment. [**Success moment**] Recognizing the head start obtained by the Soviets with their large rocket engines, which gives them many months of lead-time, and recognizing the likelihood that they will exploit this lead for some time to come in still more impressive successes, we nevertheless are required to make new efforts on our own. For while we cannot guarantee that we shall one day be first, we can guarantee that any failure to make this effort will make us last. We take an additional risk by making it in full view of the world, [**Transparency**] but as shown by the feat of astronaut Shepard, this very risk enhances our stature when we are successful.[40]

We all know what happened. The country rallied, and in 1969 Kennedy's success moment was achieved and summarized in Neil Armstrong immortal words, "That's one small step for man, one giant leap for mankind." If our government could put a man on the moon in 1969 using a metal craft with less computing power than an iPhone, then it can do anything. What we need is true leadership, a disciplined structure, and competent management rewarded for results. And it all starts with spelling out what people can, should, and will achieve by a certain date on the way toward realizing a greater goal.

People in any organization will struggle through new initiatives and projects, but if they have a clear vision of what success looks like step by step, the struggle will be meaningfully focused on performance rather than a form of drudgery. Opening a new school is not success. Opening a new school on time, on budget, with a certain percentage of taxpayer support and a defined number of students signed up to attend—now *that* is success. Mission and vision aren't enough; a clear definition of success is the bedrock on which we can rebuild our broken government and its infrastructure. Define it, describe it, prioritize the big issues, and lay out the values with which the organization will operate. Then rush the mound as a team. It worked for Walt Disney. It worked for Steve Jobs. It worked for President Kennedy. And it can work for all public agencies at all levels of government, too. With success clearly defined, it's time to construct an actionable plan to deliver it. A Success Plan.

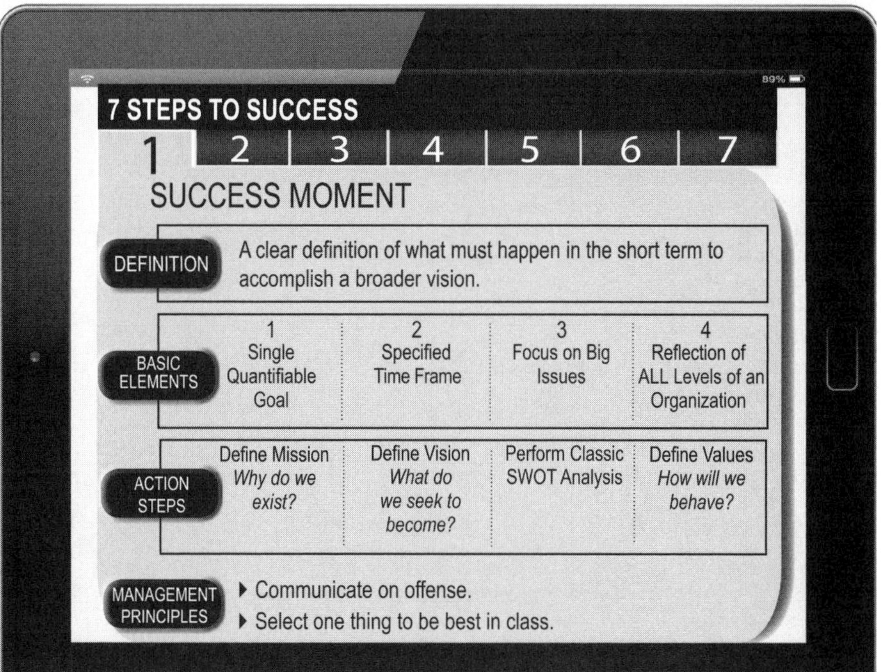

FIGURE 2-2

3

Plan Your Miracle

When I was a kid and my mom made a decision I didn't like, she used to counter my objections by saying to me: "Let it go, Mark. In ten years, it won't matter." By and large, she was right—I've forgotten most of the things she either didn't let me do or made me do. With one exception. On February 22, 1980, during the winter Olympics held in Lake Placid, New York, only a three-hour drive from our family farm, the American men's ice hockey team took to the ice in the semifinal medal round against the Soviet Union team. I was in eighth grade, and I desperately wanted to see the game. It aired at 9 p.m., and my parents had a strict rule that we kids had to be in bed by nine, no exceptions. I begged and begged, but the answer was still no.

Decades later, I joke with my mom and tell her that her refusal to budge on my bedtime that night *still* did matter. Because of her, I missed one of the most thrilling and emotional sports competitions of all time. American goalie Jim Craig played the game of his life, stopping thirty-six shots after having been knocked violently to the ice halfway through by a Soviet skater during a heated exchange in front of the net. As the game wound down with America ahead 4–3, people all over the country wept and broke into stirring spontaneous renditions of "God Bless America" and "The Star Spangled Banner." Afterward I heard and read stories of people listening to the game on the radio as they drove down major interstates, pulling over to the side for the last few minutes, and total strangers hugging one another as eighteen-wheelers sped by spraying rain and slush.

"Do you believe in miracles?" sportscaster Al Michaels asked during the game's final seconds.[1] To many Americans, "miracle" seemed a good word for it. Not six years earlier, Americans had seen the first-ever resignation of a president as well as a quiet exit from the brutal war in Vietnam. Our Cold War adversary, the Soviet Union, had just invaded Afghanistan, which would lead to our boycott of the Moscow summer Olympic games that same year. American consumers had suffered double-digit inflation and fuel rationing thanks to the 1973 Arab oil embargo. And in Iran, college-aged terrorists had overrun the American embassy. After a failed rescue attempt and the killing of some of our special-forces troops, dozens of Americans were still being held captive. We needed a boost, something to cheer us and affirm that we "still had it" as a superpower on the world stage. A stunning upset victory over the Russians' powerhouse hockey team, followed by victory over Finland in the gold medal match, gave us exactly that.

Victory over the Russians was frankly the more meaningful accomplishment. The United States had been seeded seventh out of the eight teams in their bracket, the Soviet Union first. The Soviets had won four straight Olympic gold medals and six of the last seven. In fact, just two weeks earlier, they had trounced the American team in New York City, and they had also won the 1979 Challenge Cup against all-star players from the National Hockey League. Most experts believed that not a single member of the American Olympic hockey team was good enough to have made the Soviet team, let alone skated their way off the bench into an actual game. By comparison, Soviet goalie Vladislav Tretiak was (and still is) considered by many to be the greatest goalie to ever play the game.

How had the Americans done it? Coach Herb Brooks, the highly successful head coach from the University of Minnesota, had built a team of amateur college kids, and out of the gate he knew he had problems. His top players came from two schools, the University of Minnesota and Boston University, that were fierce rivals in hockey. Some of these players had known one another since high school and maintained personal rivalries, seeing one another as "the enemy." Brooks had a clear vision (to win the gold medal) as well as at least one key success moment along the way (defeating the Russians). But merely having the destination and the journey in mind wasn't enough; Brooks needed a plan to execute it. Somehow, he had to get his players to put aside their rivalries and come together as a team aligned around a common goal.

The initial part of Brooks's strategy was to get his players to hate *him* more than they hated one another. He already had a reputation for being mean, but now he dialed that up—big time. Brooks screamed at his players, telling them that they weren't talented enough to win on talent alone, and that they were playing worse and worse every day. In one game, forward Rob McClanahan wanted to come out of a game after suffering a severe charley horse. In the locker room between periods, Brooks got into a nose-to-nose screaming match with McClanahan, cursing him out in front of the entire team as a "cake-eater" (among some other not so polite phrases). McClanahan went back out onto the ice despite his injury, while his teammates sympathized with him.

On another now infamous occasion, during an exhibition game with Norway, the Americans put in a lackluster performance, skating to a 3–3 tie. As fans exited the rink, Brooks told his players to stay on the ice. He ordered them to all line up on the goal line and then skate as fast as they could to the nearest blue line and back; then to the next line on the ice and back; then to next; then to the far line and back—all without stopping. It's an exhausting exercise that is sometimes done once after a practice but never after a game. On this night, however, Coach Brooks had the team perform rotation after rotation. When each player reassembled on the goal line, heaving and gasping for air, Brooks shouted, "Again!" and blew his whistle to signal the start. The maintenance workers turned the lights out in the arena—and still the players skated. One player broke his stick over the boards in anger, but Brooks wouldn't relent. Finally, after nearly an hour, the team doctor stepped in. "Herbie, Herbie, stop, please stop. They've had enough."

With his players now totally aligned against him, he was ready to move to his plan's second phase, in which he directed the passion and unity he had aroused toward beating the Russians. On the one hand, Brooks tried to get his team to see the Russians as beatable. He ridiculed individual Russian players, telling his team that the great Soviet right-winger Boris Mikhailov looked comical, as funny and ridiculous as Stan Laurel of the classic comedy duo "Laurel and Hardy." "You can beat Stan Laurel, for crying out loud, can't you?" On the other hand, Brooks depicted victory over the Russians as a great and inspiring challenge for players to embrace. "Risk something, or you will forever sit with just your dreams," Brooks told them. "What is courage? Let me tell you. An indefinable quality that makes a man put out that extra something when it seems there is nothing else to give. I dare you to be better than you are. I dare you to be a thoroughbred."[2]

By the semifinals game against the Russians, Brooks's group of amateur college players was a unified team working toward a clear objective. It had gone 4–0–1 in the preliminary round, beating teams like Czechoslovakia, Germany, and Sweden that were far superior on paper. And it had shown its mettle on several occasions by coming back to win in the final period of games. In the quiet of the locker room, Brooks gave one final, rousing speech that galvanized players against the Russians. "Great moments are born from great opportunity," he told his team, "and that's what you have here tonight, boys. That's what you've earned here tonight. One game; if we played them ten times, they might win nine. But not this game, not tonight. Tonight, we skate with them. Tonight we stay with them, and we shut them down because we can. Tonight, we are the greatest hockey team in the world. You were born to be hockey players—every one of you, and you were meant to be here tonight. This is your time. Their time is done. It's over. I'm sick and tired of hearing about what a great hockey team the Soviets have. Screw 'em. This is your time. Now go out there and take it!"[3]

And that's exactly what the Americans did. When U.S. captain Mike Eruzione smacked home the winning slap shot with ten minutes to play in the third period, he and his teammates inspired a nation. Two days later when all the players, in an unprecedented fashion, climbed atop the medal podium, all of America stood right there with them, our hearts swelled with pride (my parents actually let me watch this match!). The victory may well have been the "miracle on ice," as it became known, but behind the miracle was the wisdom of a plan designed by a master coach. In hiring Brooks, the U.S. Olympic Committee had wanted a "respectable showing." Brooks had a more precise vision, and he had put in the careful thought required to achieve his objective. In this respect, he stands as example not only to others in sports, but to any leader seeking to guide an organization to greatness—even and especially leaders of public-sector organizations. To rebuild America, leaders at government bodies and agencies at every level must get far more serious not merely about defining success, but about figuring out exactly how to achieve it.

TRAIN TO NOWHERE

Often, elected officials and public-sector leaders will give media interviews and speeches and talk about "how we're working to get everyone on the same page." A critical part of getting everyone on the same page is actually having, well, a page: a precise game plan, just like NFL coaches have in their hands on the sidelines on Sunday afternoon, that lays out clearly what will be done, by whom, and in what order. Everyone knows his part, so that when the quarterback barks the signals, each player can execute his part of the plan to precision, knowing exactly what is expected of him. Coaches spend hours working to get the plan just right—and this is the key word—*before* they start to play the game. Coming up with a plan to deliver success may seem obvious, and it is—in the private sector. Public-sector managers, by contrast, often seem to think that adopting an annual budget is the same thing as creating a plan. They want to skip conversations about planning, perceiving them as airy-fairy, just as disconnected from the organization's everyday business as conversations about vision. These managers might say they do strategic planning because they make time for a one-day off-site with senior managers. But they often put little thought into the off-site, and as a result, the event changes very little in the organization. Successful organizations recognize that planning is not an event, it is an environment. And it requires high-performing leaders to create that ongoing environment to deliver success.

Successful organizations recognize that planning is not an event, it is an environment.

Could you imagine a tractor-trailer driver who was "too busy" doing his "real work" pulling away from the dock fully loaded and driving eighty-five miles per hour down the interstate without having taken the time to chart the most efficient way to make his stops and deliver his packages? Could you imagine the dock workers burying the materials for the driver's first delivery at the front end of the trailer because they were "too busy" with their "real work" to load the trucks strategically? Of course not.

Lack of planning goes hand in hand with the "gerbil wheel management" discussed in the last chapter. Without a plan, employees and managers at all levels of public agencies lack the ability to perform intentional, directed work. They go through the same motions day after day, year after year—not because what they do makes sense or will contribute toward a strategic goal, but simply because that's the way they've always done it. The organizational stasis that results yields poor service, deficits, layoffs, bankruptcies, and any number of other toxins that destroy government's ability to deliver effectiveness.

Amtrak is a case in point. Formed in 1971 as the National Railroad Passenger Corporation, Amtrak was initially intended to become a for-profit corporation. The railroad came into operation with a $40 million federal grant and a $100 million loan guarantee, not to mention equipment given to it by railroads as well as $197 million in cash.[4] Working with these start-up resources, Amtrak was supposed to slowly wean itself off public funding. President's Nixon's transportation secretary, John Volpe, was quoted in the *New York Times* in 1970 as saying that Amtrak "could be profitable within perhaps three years."[5] That statement was as close as anything to a success moment in the passenger rail industry, which had seen massive declines in ridership since peaking in the 1940s.[6] (During World War II, Americans traveled by intercity rail an average of 67 billion miles. By 1971, that number had cratered to about 4.4 billion.[7])

That statement was also wishful thinking. Amtrak has never made a cent of profit.[8] Anthony Haswell, the founder of the National Association of Railroad Passengers and perhaps the closest thing to Amtrak's founding father, has called it a "massive failure."[9] But should we be surprised? With its CEO appointed by the president and its budget allocated by Congress, Amtrak is effectively a ward of the state. In fact, one lawsuit working its way through the courts is trying to establish whether

Amtrak is a corporation or a public agency. Because of this ambiguity, Amtrak has enjoyed virtually endless streams of public revenue, and therefore has lacked incentives to plan or innovate.

In 2011, in response to criticism of its consistent financial losses, Amtrak's new CEO, Joe Boardman, developed a five-year strategic plan.[10] The plan was intended to find efficiencies in the railroad's services by reorganizing the company into six separate business lines that would each be held accountable for performance and revenues.[11] Boardman told Congress that, "When we're done, Amtrak will look more like a business and less like a government agency. Customers will find that our system is easier to use, more convenient, timelier, and more comfortable."[12] Missing from that statement was any mention of profit, the founding aim of the company.

Amtrak updated its strategic plan again in 2014. This time it embraced a template resembling our pillared approach, which we'll discuss later. The railroad listed as its three strategic "themes and goals" safety and security, customer focus, and financial excellence.[13] The document does not prioritize those strategies, but it does emphasize financial excellence as its chief focus, revealing for the first time in generations that it sought to generate an operating profit from all its services.[14] The company even lists performance measures alongside all of its strategic aims (a subject covered in chapter 4). Amtrak has posted impressive results since Boardman introduced this process of intentional planning, rather than simply adopting a budget. Annual operating subsidies provided by the government have declined by 20 percent, debt has fallen by $1.4 billion, and ridership has jumped more than 12 percent.[15] This is a good start for Amtrak. However the pending litigation is decided, Boardman has the agency/corporation on the path toward delivering a public-sector service with a private-sector mindset.

Stockton, California, is a much different case. Stockton filed for bankruptcy in 2013, partly due to an ill-conceived series of revitalization projects in the city's downtown. Stockton officials had been encouraged in the late 1990s by a home-building boom by Bay Area residents looking for more affordable housing alternatives.[16] As the population grew by 20 percent in a decade, tax revenues soared.[17] Bewitched by the sudden growth, planners announced a $114 million development of the waterfront, including a ten-thousand-seat arena, a smaller minor-league baseball park, a huge parking deck, a marina, and a new government headquarters, all of it paid for by the city.[18] In addition, the city granted employee retirement health benefits *for life* to workers employed for as little as a month, and their spouses, too.[19] After the housing collapse of 2008 and a commensurate spike in unemployment, Stockton saw an exodus of city employees, especially public safety officials.[20] The failure to spend and build with a well-reasoned plan put Stockton almost a billion dollars in debt by 2012.[21]

Stories like Stockton's are all too common. Eight cities and towns in the United States filed for bankruptcy in the five years following the 2008 financial crisis, with almost thirty more utilities, water boards, and hospital systems meeting the same fate.[22] Government organizations are seduced by temporary revenue streams or assume that the economic exuberance of the moment will continue to bring dividends. They adopt budgets first and then develop a work plan to spend that money. They have it all backward. In the private sector, building a strategic plan is considered "real work," and in fact, is the single most important thing leaders do. Leaders are expected to see into the future and prepare for it. In his textbook *Principles of Management*, Tony Morden writes that strategic planning "is typically concerned with management planning into the medium to long-term future"[23] and also requires that a leader "visualize and anticipate the kind of future environments in which the organization is likely to have to operate," not just its current environment.[24] In the public sector, leaders have traditionally forgotten about the future, assuming that the structures, policies, and practices of the past will never die. Sadly, the primary thing leaders managing in the "adopt a budget for next year" mindset pass on to the future is debt and decay.

COLLABORATION VERSUS CONSENSUS

Building a plan is one of the hardest things a leader does. The key in this process is to appreciate the distinction between two words that many often confuse: collaboration and consensus. Years ago I had a college president tell me proudly that his style was to manage his team to consensus.

A collaborative leader creates an environment for robust dialogue, debate, and disagreement.

Even then it struck me as odd. Today, it strikes me as unworthy of the title of president. You could smack a Mike Eruzione slap shot between the definitions for a *collaborative leader* and a *consensus manager*. In a 1981 speech, British Prime Minister Margaret Thatcher said she viewed consensus as merely "the process of abandoning all beliefs, principles, values, and policies in search of something in which no one believes, but to which no one objects—the process of avoiding the very issues that have to be solved, merely because you cannot get agreement on the way ahead."[25] By contrast, a *collaborative* leader creates an environment safe for robust dialogue, debate, and disagreement. Team members feel as comfortable speaking their minds in the boardroom as they do at the water cooler. They know their ideas will be heard and considered, if not ultimately implemented.

#4 MANAGEMENT PRINCIPLE
A collaborative leader or a consensus manager

At the public works department of a major city, the process of designing a new city redevelopment plan involves more than the director of public works and his primary staff. It also includes the heads of the organization's subordinate divisions (e.g., engineering and construction, utilities, traffic operations, and streets and sewers) as well as those of human resources and finance. Each of these departments employs scores of workers who have a stake in the planning process and who can bring valuable insight to bear. The public works leadership would be remiss to forget about its engineers, road crews, contract specialists, and even the administrative staff. Finally, external stakeholders to consider might include union reps, small business owners, elected officials, and, of course, residents.

At the transit system in Rochester, our input process was extensive, and we went through it *every year*. We gathered data and suggestions from our major financial partners, forming revenue projections over the next several years. We had a scientific customer input component, which gathered insight on what our consumers wanted to see us focus on. We did employee engagement surveys to incorporate the knowledge, experience, and talent of our workforce. And we also solicited input from elected officials and community groups.

That's not to say we made decisions by consensus. We didn't. In the summer of 2010 our team gathered at our annual two-day off-site at a cabin deep in the woods of Letchworth State Park in upstate New York. We revisited our mission and vision statement. Check and check. We worked our way through establishing our success statement for the coming year. Check. And then we began to lay out our broad strategic pillars: maintaining financial stability, building a strong customer focus, engaging better with employees, and delivering quality. With everyone agreeing to these strategies, we turned our attention to safety and security. Our director of operations made, as he had in years past, an impassioned plea as to why safety deserved to become a strategic pillar. Around and around the table the conversation went for all of an hour.

Finally, our brand-new head of operations, Randy Weaver, asked if I'd be willing to put it to a vote. The question was a simple one: Who believed we should add safety and security as a strategy? I agreed to lock down what people's positions were. We started to my left and worked my way from person to person. Eleven affirmative head nods later, only two people were not in agreement: our head of Information Technology and me. In my judgment, safety didn't conform well with the low fares that we had already agreed we'd prioritize under the "customer focus" pillar. And so we didn't add safety as a strategic pillar.

We'd collaborated in making the decision; members of our team fought for their position. Yet the *final* decision was not based on consensus. It was made by the CEO. Both our chief financial officer and general counsel were in the majority—and that's a key point. So often we watch public entities let their financial executive and legal counsel drive every decision. "Our lawyer just told us we should do thus and such. It seems to me we ought to do what they tell us." Subject matter experts like those in finance, legal, risk management, and a dozen others have a responsibility to provide the best advice through their prism, but they provide counsel rather than conclusions. If their advice deserved to be the controlling one, then we should put *them* in the corner office. In truth, their input is but one of many factors to be considered.

Because of the collaborative nature of the conversation at Letchworth, participants knew they had been heard, had argued passionately for their beliefs, and now, while not pleased that their argument hadn't carried the day, they could still be invested in our plan of action. It's important to note that in this situation and others like it, safety and security didn't just fall off the radar screen because it wasn't selected as a strategic pillar. Many metrics related to those issues emerged as inputs into our performance scorecard (see chapter 4) and remained frequent topics of daily conversation. The issue just didn't receive the strategic focus of a pillar in delivering success.

Collaboration certainly doesn't end once a plan is constructed. Once a plan is drafted, but before it is complete, share it in draft form with all stakeholders to get feedback. Everyone involved in the plan's development internally should see the draft; even if they disagree with a goal or a milestone, they'll at least be able to register their opinions and offer recommendations. Sharing draft plans with an organization's external stakeholders is critical, too, as it increases the chances of their ultimate acceptance. Union leaders are more apt to go along with a planned redevelopment if they feel satisfied that the appropriate safety precautions have been built into the plan. Small business owners are more likely to support a proposal if they know that street closures are not going to wildly reduce access to their storefronts, or even better, if they realize that the construction strategy will boost traffic flow on their street over the long term. If community residents feel peace of mind that their health will not be compromised by particulate dust or that their home values will not decline as a result of a poorly positioned access road, then they are less likely to end up in an antigovernment picket line. If these groups do not support the plan, organizational leadership will at least know this at the outset and have a chance to make adjustments. Sharing the draft plan also helps executives correct for blind spots, bad information, or erroneous assumptions.

CRAFT YOUR PILLARS

With the core principle of collaboration in mind, let's explore the planning process in more detail. In an organizational context, building a plan means forging three separate courses of action: a multiyear strategic plan to focus on delivering the vision, an annual operational plan to deliver on the strategies, and an annual financial plan to pay for the operating tactics. A strategic plan offers an overarching approach toward achieving the final results as envisioned in the vision statement. The operational plan is a detailed list of the purposeful work tasks that must be performed *this year* by departments and individuals to bring the strategic plan alive and to deliver upon the success moment. The financial plan pays for the tactics to ensure that what is in the plan is fiscally realistic. Put all three ingredients together, and you have the recipe for a gold medal performance, or as we call it, a comprehensive "Success Plan."

The first step is to create the strategic plan, which in turn is composed of "strategic pillars." In architecture, pillars are used to bear the greatest loads in a structure. They are often the most visible and prominent components of a design, and they tend to stick around long after the rest of structure has been devoured by time. You design the pillars first and then the other elements of a building. It's the same with organizational planning.

To develop pillars, the management team identifies the big areas where the organization must focus. Almost every organization has at least three natural pillars: finance, customers, and employees. For some government institutions, these pillars might also be described as budget, citizens, and workforce, but I would argue that if we're going to get government to perform with a private-sector mindset, the original language is probably best. Other pillars might be quality, safety, productivity, and so on. A local fire department's strategic pillars would likely include a budget to keep fire engines maintained and firefighters paid at a level that matches their risks, a focus on the needs and expectations of the citizens they are sworn to protect, and finally, a commitment to recruiting and training the absolute best candidates for the dangerous job at hand. Most organizations have three to five key strategic pillars.

Keep in mind, pillars are focus areas to deliver success, not protect bureaucracy. Too often, as we do work around the country, we make great initial progress with a public-sector team, helping them define success and lay out the key strategic pillars to deliver on it. Just when the team is starting to feel good about itself, team members realize that they have eight departments that don't fit underneath their pillars. Their response? "Let's develop more strategic pillars so we can defend why the departments exist!" Buzzer sound. If a department isn't functioning to help the agency deliver success, the last thing we should do is adjust our strategies. Rather, we need to take a hard look at the department to determine why it exists in the first place, and whether it still deserves to exist.

The specific language that a team selects in describing strategic pillars is critical. When I became CEO of RGRTA, the organization was hemorrhaging money, so our first financial strategy was to "Achieve Financial Stability." Once we had stopped the bleeding over two years, this transitioned to "Maintain Financial Stability." Eventually, as we began running multimillion dollar surpluses, we plotted a strategic course to "Long-Term Financial Success." The title of the strategy sent a clear message about where the organization was going, helping us align appropriate operating tactics underneath the pillar. In America, our strategic pillars to national success might be "job creation," "economic growth," "debt reduction," and "national security." If *those* were the pillars our leaders arranged national efforts around, then other distraction issues like medical marijuana would (correctly) be ignored. We might just let the Washington Redskins go play football games, rather than worry about what they were called.

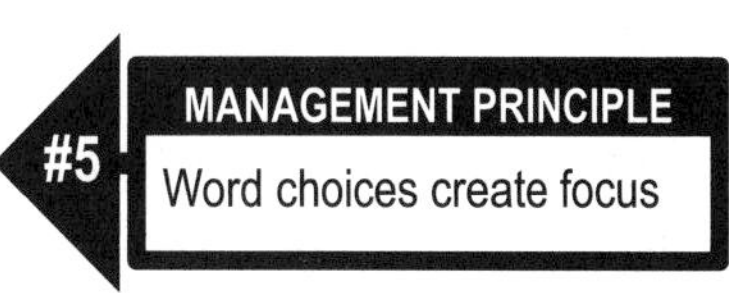

PRIORITIZE YOUR PILLARS

Once the strategic pillars have been erected, it's time to weight them by assigning each one a numerical value reflecting its importance in the overall success plan. All pillars are important—that's why we selected them—but some are going to be more vital than others. We distribute one hundred points among the various pillars as an easy and effective way to convey their relative importance. The chief of the local fire department may lead his team to collaboratively decide that balancing the budget for the next year is the absolute most important strategic area. After all, nothing happens in the department if it can't even afford to pay its firefighters and if it can't purchase new equipment to replace aging inventory. Plus, with the economy in recession and tax revenues down, the fire chief knows that the department must find ways to save money. The financial pillar will therefore be weighted at fifty.

The chief and his leadership team might select the workforce as the second "heaviest" pillar, assigning it a thirty; in order for the department to be effective at its mission of fighting fires and protecting the public, its firefighters need to be trained, professional, confident, and alert. The chief has found that the public's attitudes toward the department remain generally favorable as long response times stay high and damage from fires is minimized. In other words, their satisfaction need not be as high a strategic priority as long as the first two pillars receive the proper attention. The public, then, gets twenty points. And there it is, one hundred points total.

This notion of weighting pillars sounds simple, but because it involves making choices, it runs counter to the way most elected officials think. Officials have to acknowledge that it is more important to focus on public safety than it is to buy new books for the library; as a result, the "Moms for Books" constituency will be mad at them. What elected official sets out to anger a core group of voters? In truth, prioritization is absolutely critical, and our failure to prioritize is one of the key reasons our public institutions are in such poor condition (you will recall Steve Jobs being hyperfocused on prioritization and focus from chapter 2). Why choose fixing bridges, terrorism, or balancing a budget over legalizing marijuana if you get reelected 90 percent of the time? Just don't prioritize. You can see where that approach has gotten us. In the private sector, Walmart has selected price over quality, Ritz-Carlton has selected quality over price, and Apple has selected innovation over price. At RGRTA, we selected low fares over security. Choices must be made; we simply cannot be all things to all people.

> Prioritization is absolutely critical, and our failure to prioritize is one of the key reasons our public institutions are in such poor condition.

Most organizations would select "balancing the budget" as their heaviest pillar, even though workforce engagement also ranks highly. Some, however, would opt for the latter and select their employees. There is no right answer, but there must be *an* answer. And it is almost always better for the organization, its leaders, and those whom they serve to have come up with the answer proactively. Knowing at the beginning of the year that fiscal concerns are paramount provides a prism through which to make any decisions that come up. It also provides the basis for defending those decisions when outside actors attack.

When I led RGRTA, auditors were frequently sent into a local agency like ours. Time and time again, it appeared to us the assignment was to find anything they could write a negative report about. In one instance a draft report criticized us for spending $150,000 more than the audit team felt proper on overtime in our maintenance department. The auditor ignored the context of his so-called "findings" in his draft report to us, so I wrote him a letter. I explained that RGRTA was an $80 million organization and that in just the last year we had posted an $11.3 million surplus (finance pillar), while reducing fares (customer pillar), increasing on-time performance (employee pillar) and improving rider satisfaction (customer pillar). We had weighted our financial strategy most heavily and added more than $10 million to the balance sheet as a result. If we were a publicly traded company, our stock price would have led the NASDAQ.

Even if the auditor was right in his conclusion, which we disputed, we had still run a massive multimillion surplus. He was trying to identify what was important for RGRTA, because that's what he had been able to do at other public agencies. But since my team already had identified and prioritized our pillars, we controlled the dialogue and avoided reputational damage.

CONNECT STRATEGY TO OPERATIONS

After the strategic pillars have been propped up and properly weighted, it's time to focus on everyday, nitty-gritty tactics. The organization's management must construct a work plan that conforms to the strategy so that the work performed by all employees is purposeful. Here is where we pivot away most directly from the gerbil wheel of everyday deskwork—paperwork, meetings, administrative tasks—and lay down specific tasks designed to deliver the success moment. It's also about giving ordinary workers the knowledge and confidence that their everyday tasks matter. Traffic engineers should be able to see that the controversial blockage of a major artery for construction is only temporary and done with the noble intent of completing the overall development project on time. The secretary in finance has to know that the overtime hours she works this year will mean the difference between scorn and praise from her family and friends affected by the city's project. Real success is forged through the matching of the grand plan with the daily one.

Think of it this way: Olympians don't reach the medal stand if they get bogged down in constantly shifting priorities meted out by coaches and trainers. They build tactical plans—for exercise, nutrition, sleep, even alignment—and they execute, all with the strategic goal in mind of reaching that podium. In the case of that fire department we've been talking about, let's say the chief wants to reduce the practice of replacing equipment that may be old but not outdated. Perhaps the department in previous years has been too eager to purchase newer, shinier ladders when all that's wrong with the old ones is they begin to squeak. Sure, the department can recoup some of the value of these ladders through resale, but ladders get more sophisticated and more expensive every year. So to address this problem and satisfy the chief's budget priorities, the firehouse makes a tactical decision to construct a monthly process that commits more time to oiling the ladders and tightening the bolts rather than tossing them out.

#6 MANAGEMENT PRINCIPLE
Rushing the mound or riding the gerbil wheel

In a similar way, the firehouse designs tactics that support every other pillar of its strategy. This is the exact opposite of so many public-sector management teams that gather on Monday morning and have a totally new set of priorities based on the front-page, above-the-fold news article that ran over the weekend. Of course, the newspaper is now setting the agenda rather than the management team, and, of course, the newspaper will have a brand-new screaming headline the following Sunday, and the management team a new set of priorities based upon that. You can almost hear the gerbil wheel spinning as you pick up the newspaper.

While leadership should define success, ground-level employees provide essential input as to what the team should be working on to deliver that success. In small work sessions, teams develop a proposed work plan for their department or team for the coming year. Because we empower employees in this way, they're able to fully embrace the final plan. Rather than impose directives on them, we inspire them to excel by defining success with them (the "what") and then allowing them to lay out the specific activities necessary to achieve it (the "how"). This way, the employees (the "who") actually own their work, because they were involved in designing the path to the destination. And *that* is how you get everyone on the same page, literally, because it all goes into the plan.

Once the organization has drafted its operating tactics, the list goes back to all employees for further review. Groups of employees arrange action items in order based on their impressions of how well each one will advance the organization's strategy. Using a numbering method similar to that used for prioritizing pillars, these groups determine how much each tactic should be valued for a given pillar. The organization winds up with a single list of operating tactics strategically aligned beneath each pillar to deliver the success moment. It really is crystal clear as to what the organization must focus on to deliver success as the team has defined it.

Once the organization settles on its tactics, each one is assigned a team of employees as well as an owner. That team does three things: it identifies quarterly milestones; establishes a budget proposal that outlines the financial resources needed in the coming year; and estimates the number of hours the department will need to perform the work effectively. This whole process balances the work agenda with the eventual budget and staffing levels. It ends with the team agreeing to perform all necessary work within an allocated time estimate. Finally, it gives employees of an organization exactly what you'd want from a leadership standpoint: ownership, clarity, deadlines, and accountability—all aligned to deliver success.

HOW WILL YOU PAY FOR IT?

Now that the organization has fully mapped out its route to success, it has to work out a budget to pay for the journey. Whatever the nature of their organization, leaders should create two separate budgets. The first is the operating budget, which will pay for ongoing expenses incurred throughout the year. A school's operating budget would include things like insurance, the electric bill, and cleaning. The second, a capital budget, accounts for long-term expenses. The construction of a new wing of that school, for instance, might cost hundreds of thousands of dollars and would have to be budgeted over a long period.

Public organizations are *great* at creating budgets. Unfortunately, they rarely tie budgeting processes to strategies and tactics. Elected officials debate tactics rather than hammer out a detailed plan for achieving a goal, and as a result the bureaucracy is left to simply increase spending on what exists today. It is gerbil wheel management at its worst, and one of the great failures in American government today. Programs grow and expand year after year, transitioning away from their original purpose as their tentacles strengthen, never to be cut or even shrunk. When you see this happen as often as I have, you realize that as a nation we have more than enough money to achieve top national priorities. With federal revenues at their highest level in American history, we simply need to spend those dollars with purpose rather than indulging our knee-jerk reflex to protect historical programs.

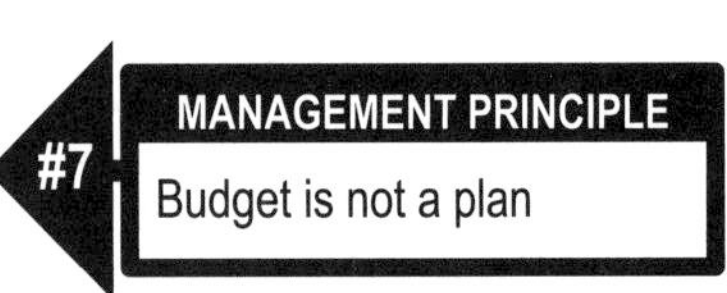

For inspiration, I often reflect on President Kennedy's statement before a joint session of Congress on March 25, 1961, in which he described his proposal for space exploration. On this occasion, he delivered both a speech and a budget that matched his rhetoric. I quote it at length, inserting in boldface my analysis:

> I therefore ask the Congress, above and beyond the increases I have earlier requested for space activities, to provide the funds which are needed to meet the following national goals: First, I believe that this nation should commit itself to achieving the goal, before this decade is out, of landing a man on the moon and returning him safely to the earth [**success moment**]. No single space project in this period will be more impressive to mankind, or more important for the long-range exploration of space; and none will be so difficult or expensive to accomplish.

We propose to accelerate the development of the appropriate lunar space craft [**strategy to deliver success**]. We propose to develop alternate liquid and solid fuel boosters, much larger than any now being developed, until certain which is superior [**strategy to deliver success**]. We propose additional funds for other engine development and for unmanned explorations—explorations [**strategy to deliver success**] which are particularly important for one purpose which this nation will never overlook: the survival of the man who first makes this daring flight. But in a very real sense, it will not be one man going to the moon—if we make this judgment affirmatively, it will be an entire nation. For all of us must work to put him there. Secondly, an additional 23 million dollars, together with 7 million dollars already available, will accelerate development of the Rover nuclear rocket [**budget tied to tactic to deliver success**]. This gives promise of some day providing a means for even more exciting and ambitious exploration of space, perhaps beyond the moon, perhaps to the very end of the solar system itself. Third, an additional 50 million dollars will make the most of our present leadership, by accelerating the use of space satellites for world-wide communications [**budget tied to tactic to deliver success**]. Fourth, an additional 75 million dollars—of which 53 million dollars is for the Weather Bureau—will help give us at the earliest possible time a satellite system for world-wide weather observation [**budget tied to tactic to deliver success**]. Let it be clear—and this is a judgment which the Members of the Congress must finally make—let it be clear that I am asking the Congress and the country to accept a firm commitment to a new course of action, a course which will last for many years and carry very heavy costs: 531 million dollars in fiscal '62—an estimated seven to nine billion dollars additional over the next five years. If we are to go only half way, or reduce our sights in the face of difficulty, in my judgment it would be better not to go at all. Now this is a choice which this country must make, and I am confident that under the leadership of the Space Committees of the Congress, and the Appropriating Committees, that you will consider the

> matter carefully. It is a most important decision that we make as a nation. But all of you have lived through the last four years and have seen the significance of space and the adventures in space, and no one can predict with certainty what the ultimate meaning will be of mastery of space.

Pay attention to the way Kennedy explicitly connects his financial plan to strategies that will deliver on his definition of success, mobilizing precise words and numbers. The president defines success, specifies a strategy to obtain it, and discusses annual work tactics to advance the strategy. He also includes a budget that funds those annual activities. He even talks about it being "a choice which this country must make." This is intentional management at its best, and it reaped incredible rewards. Rather than spending billions, running up deficits, and delivering mediocre quality, President Kennedy's management approach helped create one of the greatest triumphs of American patriotism: Neil Armstrong's glorious walk on the moon and his planting of the American flag, followed by his mission's safe return to earth four days later. More than simply demonstrating American innovation, commitment, and resolve, President Kennedy and his team showed future generations how to tie success, strategy, and money. They say history has a way of repeating itself. For our nation's sake, let's hope so.

MAKE FINAL ADJUSTMENTS

At the end of the planning process, be prepared to make adjustments. In some cases, leaders will have to revise all three plans wholesale. No matter how scrupulously a plan has been developed, realistic budgets may not support the most well-intentioned tactics. The organization faces difficult choices: identify more sources of revenue or eliminate certain tactics, and with them, certain staff positions. Here the success moment created earlier provides valuable guidance, as does the prioritization of tactics in the operational plan. Although leaders might find the decision wrenching, they can take comfort in knowing that in the end the organization will benefit. And because they and the organization have made the effort to collectively prioritize tactics, leaders have a strong and defensible basis for making decisions that are usually made on gut instinct alone.

A draft Success Plan should feature a detailed and purposeful work plan that connects the organization's strategic pillars with the resources to fund them. Now everyone from management on down is aware of the work he will be expected to perform in the next year. Each employee knows who is responsible for what and how much everything will cost. Most importantly, everyone is equipped to know when he has finally arrived at the success moment.

WHAT HAPPENED IN VEGAS *SHOULDN'T* STAY IN VEGAS

Las Vegas evokes images of chaotic excess and after-hours debauchery, but the municipal government there offers a great example of a public organization that used the principles discussed in this chapter to turn itself around. In 2006 and 2007, Las Vegas was a boomtown, with numerous developments blooming out of the desert and people standing in lines to buy houses.[26] For almost a decade, the city was building a school a month.[27] But then the crash came in 2008, and activity halted. When Elizabeth Fretwell took over as Las Vegas's city manager in 2009, Las Vegas had America's highest foreclosure rate and an unemployment rate higher than Detroit's.[28] The city had lost 20 percent of its sales tax revenue, and the economy was still spiraling down.[29] "We went to the bottom of every list you want to be at the top of," Fretwell said, recalling her first weeks in office.[30]

Within a couple of years, Fretwell had put Las Vegas back on a path to recovery. She oversaw a large reorganization of the city and reduced the budget by 20 percent in an effort to align costs with revenues.[31] By 2012, she had reduced the structural deficit of the city by 80 percent and returned Las Vegas to an "AA" bond rating,[32] with revenues eventually beating expenditures by more than a 2 percent margin.[33] How did she do it? By dedicating the city to defining success and then building a plan to achieve it.

For Fretwell, who regards planning as "in my blood,"[34] the process begins and ends with collaboration. Various city councils, the community, and other stakeholders must come to an agreement on what should be prioritized in the coming administrative cycle. Every couple of years, Las Vegas surveys its citizens to gather their assessment of the city's current priorities, services, and performance. Then the city's various councils come together in retreats with other local, regional, and state stakeholders to formulate updated strategic priorities (pillars). The retreats—so successful that city councils actually ask for them now—begin with presentations during which "thought leaders" put forth what they think the priorities should be. Three weeks later, the stakeholders head into workshops to hone the broad categories they identified. The retreats end with a formal short list of priorities rank-ordered by committee (in 2014, for instance, the city's priorities were economic development and diversification, transportation, public safety, and education). The new and approved priority list is then shared with Las Vegas's workforce and the community. As Fretwell says, the city is not afraid of transparency in the least: "What we want is to be found guilty of implementing our strategic plan."[35]

As for operational (tactical) planning within the organization, Fretwell admits that this is hard, mostly because of all the pressures and distractions from the city's noncitizen stakeholders. Again, transparency and collaboration are key. Once Fretwell has identified how to frame the city's goals based on the new strategic priorities, managers present those goals to Las Vegas's three thousand employees. They do so by taking a "cascading approach," passing the goals to mid-level managers and in turn all the way down to entry-level employees. At each step, leaders determine how best to execute the intent of the stated goals with the resources at their disposal. The whole process takes a tremendous amount of communication, communication, and more communication, Fretwell reports.

Throughout the process, participants take great care to match financial initiatives with the latest strategic priorities. Las Vegas's fire department, for instance, is one of the best resourced in the country, its firefighters receiving generous compensation and the best equipment. Citizens have noticed: in a recent survey, 96 percent of respondents voiced approval for the fire department. Given this level of success, increasing the department's budget incrementally each year will yield diminishing returns.[36] So budget discussions in the public safety arena have recently shifted to the city's police force, which has been struggling in recent years.

Because the city's number-one strategic priority is frequently economic development and diversification, Las Vegas has boosted financing in that area. "When we began this, downtown redevelopment was a black eye for us, but now it is a shining star," Fretwell said.[37] The city spent more than $500 million to reinvest in infrastructure, helping Internet retailer Zappos relocate its headquarters downtown next to a brand-new city hall, and also building a museum and performing arts center (formerly Las Vegas had been the only major city in the country without a performing arts center). All of this happened because Fretwell matched funding to the most important strategic priority her team identified, and her elected officials endorsed it. It's a far cry from the way administrators did things back in the "bad old days" in Stockton.

Although Las Vegas's turnaround has been impressive, the planning behind it hasn't been easy. As Fretwell will tell you, it wasn't just about holding a press conference or issuing a memo. It was about following through on each part of the process month by month and quarter by quarter. It was about thoughtfully allocating scarce resources, saying "no" to attractive initiatives when other priorities ranked higher. It was about handling finances responsibly and funding tactics and strategies that the city could actually afford. Finally, it was about staying focused on the city's mission and vision, making sure that the concerns of state and regional authorities took a backseat to the city's core priorities. "One thing I am keenly aware of is that we can only *really* impact our 130 square miles," Fretwell said. "Many times people go too big."[38]

Elected officials and administrators like to give speeches and cut ribbons. But as the City of Las Vegas and the other success stories in this chapter demonstrate, real leadership requires a lot more than that. President Kennedy could have delivered great speeches about all the wonderful things his administration would achieve and left it at that. Instead, he chose to build a plan around his speeches that defined success. He and his team constructed strategies, work activities, and budget priorities. Likewise, Coach Herb Brooks could have simply delivered the "respectable showing" that the United States Olympic Committee desired. Instead, he chose to beat the Russians, and he built a plan to achieve it, pulling off a Miracle on Ice.

If you manage an agency or a department, I urge you to not just dream big; do the hard work required to make the dream actionable and to align everyone behind it. If you're a concerned citizen, demand that leaders at every agency make planning their primary responsibility. Working together, we can build a plan to deliver a successful America. After all, whether it's beating an unbeatable team or walking on the moon, "miracles," as we think of them, do happen. But we have to get off the gerbil wheel, define success, and plot out our future moves to deliver it. And then we get to step on the gas pedal! Once we have a plan, we need to execute it, and, just as importantly, determine whether it is actually *working*.

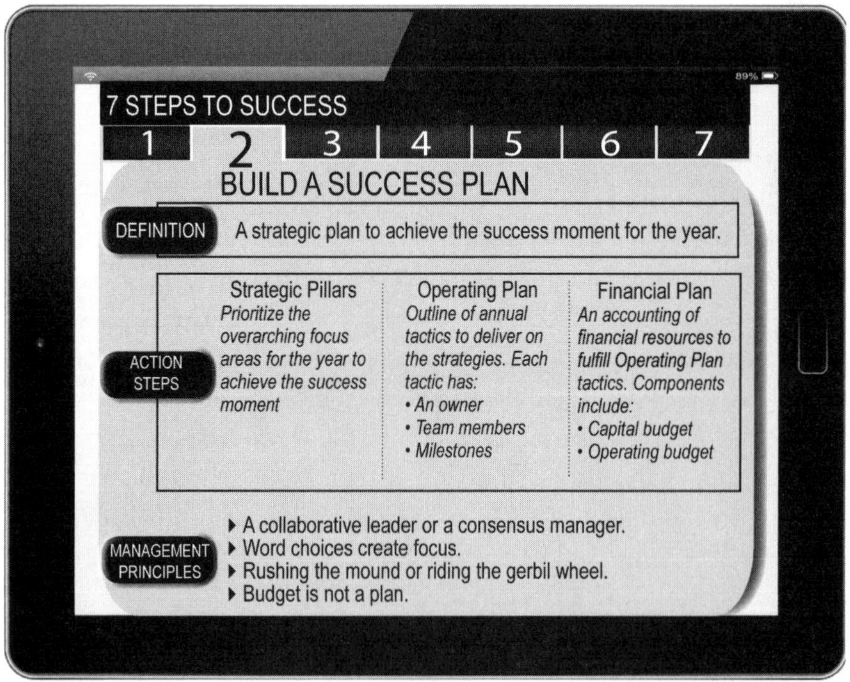

FIGURE 3-1

4

The Performance Scorecard

It was a cool summer evening at Network Associates Coliseum in Oakland, California. Hot dogs were sizzling on the grill. Vendors were strolling through the stands selling popcorn and Cracker Jack. And a sellout crowd of more than fifty-five thousand was cheering on the home team. Some of these fans had arrived hours earlier to get a seat, an unusual amount of support for the Oakland A's, who had one of the league's lowest attendance records.

The fans had turned out for a simple reason: to potentially see history being made. For nearly a century, the American League record for most consecutive games won by a team was stuck at nineteen. The Chicago White Sox had won nineteen in a row in 1906, and the New York Yankees had done it again in 1947. But no other team had done it since—until 2002. For nearly a month, beginning on August 13, the Oakland A's were unstoppable. Nobody had defeated them. And on this night, September 4, 2002, they would get their shot at that record, facing a fourth-place team with a losing record, the Kansas City Royals.

At first, it seemed as though the A's would make easy work of the Royals and break the nearly hundred-year-old record. By the third inning, they had jumped to an 11–0 lead. Excited fans waved homemade signs that read, "There's an 'A' in Domination" and "It's 'A' Beautiful Thing" and "Can You Say 20?" Then Kansas City battled back, scoring five runs in the fourth inning and five more in the eighth. By the bottom of the ninth inning, the game was tied at eleven. With one out, Oakland sent up first baseman Scott Hatteberg to pinch-hit. What followed was what every little leaguer has replayed in his dreams a thousand times. Hatteberg patiently took the first pitch for a ball. He got into position again, checked his bat a few times, and waited for the second pitch. It came in, hanging just a little too high. Hatteberg swung and there was a mighty crack of the bat. The ball soared into deep right field. It was going... going... it was gone! A game-winning and record-setting home run!

The fans went wild. Those close enough to the A's dugout extended their hands to high-five the players. The A's players swarmed the mound, hugging one another and jumping for joy. A giant sign reading "20" was unfurled high in the stands. Watching the celebration, a television announcer remarked, "This is a game nobody here will ever forget." Hatteberg summed it up in his own way, telling a reporter: "It's some kind of magic right now."[1]

The A's would lose their next game to the Minnesota Twins, so as of this writing, the American League record for most consecutive wins by a team stands at twenty. It's an incredible feat, and one that no one would have predicted given the A's recent history. For most of the previous decade (from 1993 to 1998), the A's were one of the most hapless teams in professional baseball, posting six consecutive losing seasons. They were also one of the poorest, with the sixth-lowest total team salary in 1998.[2] Lacking the payrolls of the top teams, the A's simply couldn't compete to sign and retain the very best talent, let alone set off on a record-setting tear.

In 1999, the A's still had one of the lowest payrolls in the league, but their fortunes had appreciably changed. For four years in a row under general manager Billy Beane, the team logged winning seasons, going to the playoffs every single year. In 2002, their twenty-game winning streak set them on the path to win 103 games, finishing the season tied for the best record in baseball.[3] They didn't make it past the first round of the playoffs—much less win the World Series—but they won as many games as the Yankees, a team whose $126 million payroll that year dwarfed the A's paltry $40 million.[4] And they ended the season with a place in baseball history.

How did the A's reverse their fortunes without appreciably increasing the size of their payroll? As financial author Michael Lewis related in his best-selling book *Moneyball*, it came down to one word, and a particularly unsexy word at that: metrics. Like organizations in other industries, baseball clubs had long collected data, lots of it: earned run average, batting average, number of walks, runs batted in, number of stolen bases, and so on. Baseball's scouting Brahmins also valued subjective measures of performance—the power in a player's throw, how swift he was on his feet, how quick his bat speed was.[5] Beane, however, took a much different approach to data. With the help of an innovative statistician on his staff, he began to focus on overlooked objective metrics like a player's on-base percentage (including walks) and total bases.[6] On this basis, Beane began drafting and trading for new and cheaper players who exhibited undervalued traits, and he began spurning pricier players whose performance he came to view as overvalued.[7]

Beane's core insight was that an organization could win by aligning data with its most important goals and managing accordingly. The goal of any major league team is to win, and the ultimate goal is to win the World Series. Through painstaking analysis, Beane determined that most traditional metrics didn't influence whether a team won or lost games. Many of these metrics were "input" metrics; they measured the performance of team members, but they didn't directly bear on a team's overall *output*. One metric did, however, relate to team output: how many runs the team scored. By comparison, how well a team did defensively—how many runs it gave up—didn't matter so much. So Beane stopped focusing on defense and set an offensive performance target, a success moment, for the team: score eight hundred runs. He stopped focusing on data and started focusing on meaningful *information*.

The team's plan entailed doing specific things required to score lots of runs. Going back to the data, Beane discovered (not surprisingly) that the team scored more runs when players got on base. A player's on-base percentage (including walks) and total bases mattered much more than the team had realized. And players who waited until the third pitch to swing also got on base more. So the team started to obtain players who were patient batters, paying less attention to players who might hit more home runs or drive in more runs. The A's also started to make other managerial decisions that seemed counterintuitive or even crazy. In one instance, the A's moved a player who had spent his entire career as a catcher to first base (that player was none other than Scott Hatteberg!). Beane didn't need Hatteberg as a catcher, but he knew from metric analysis that Hatteberg was a patient batter who got on base often. He wanted Hatteberg in the lineup, even if he would make more errors than a traditional first baseman. The number of errors wouldn't matter; it was scoring runs that would help the A's win—and on the night of September 4, 2002, Beane's approach brought Scott Hatteberg to bat in the bottom of the ninth inning, so that he could deliver his game-winning and record-setting home run.

Beane's finely tuned, information-driven approach to decision making transformed baseball. Previously marginalized players were promoted, players like Scott Hatteberg were given new life, and teams that had been written off for decades began to win. Beane's "Moneyball" approach is widely viewed as the reason the Boston Red Sox won the World Series in 2004, 2007, and 2013.[8] Unlike the A's, the Red Sox possessed a hefty checkbook (not just performance metric analysis) to put behind the management philosophy of Moneyball. The result was nothing less than historic, with my beloved Red Sox winning their first World Series since 1918.

I HAVE A PLAN—IS IT WORKING?

> If a CEO's most important responsibility is to define success for the year and develop a plan to achieve it, her second most important is to construct a performance measurement system that will apprise her of whether the plan she built is actually *working*

No organization can operate to its full potential unless it uses metrics that matter. We want to measure those elements that will enable us to deliver success. If a CEO's most important responsibility is to define success for the year and develop a plan to achieve it, her second most important is to construct a performance measurement system that will apprise her of whether the plan she built is actually *working* (Figure 4-1). Constructing such a system—step three of our seven-step process—entails two fundamentally important tasks: figuring out which data is information, as opposed to mere

FIGURE 4-1

noise, and developing a structure that generates *accurate* information for those relevant metrics. I can't promise you that a public agency that tracks performance more strategically will suddenly go on a twenty-game winning steak, but I can promise this: the thousands of underperforming public organizations out there that require a makeover can only succeed when they learn to turn data into information.

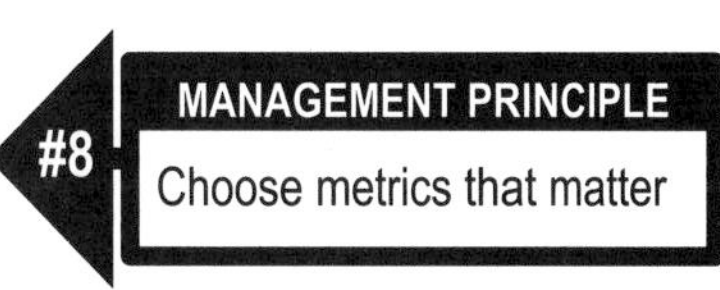

TOO MUCH DATA, NOT ENOUGH INFORMATION

The Moneyball story may sound a bit nerdy, but in truth taking a more sophisticated approach to data is just plain common sense. Individuals and teams use data strategically all the time to track progress against many kinds of strategic plans. The U.S. Olympic hockey team had a clear goal: to win its game against the Russians. In the game itself, it had a meaningful "output" metric of which everyone on the team was constantly aware: the score that appeared in lights on the scoreboard. Students have test results, semester-by-semester course grades, and grade point averages that allow them to grasp how they're doing in real time. Individuals with medical issues keep track of input data such as blood sugar levels, "good" and "bad" cholesterol, and blood pressure as they take steps to improve the desired output—their health. People saving for a new car look to their savings account balances to see how much progress they're making. A person trying to lose weight steps on a scale. All of this data is meaningful, as it connects with outputs and is tied closely to the intended result or strategic goal. All of this data also issues from sources known to be reliable, objective, and even authoritative. All of this data is now *information.*

Dr. Peter Drucker is credited with popularizing the phrase "What gets measured, gets done." I respectfully disagree. Lots of things get measured. Who doesn't religiously step onto a scale week after week and watch the same number staring back? In fact, I would argue that in government agencies, far *too* much gets measured. As a result, no one knows which metric to focus on, and almost nothing gets done. Agencies wind up with a library full of data that no one focuses on until a reporter, auditor, or investigative panel of some sort pulls it out to use as a two-by-four over the agency's head. Simply measuring something doesn't mean that it gets done; it doesn't mean that anyone focuses on it or fixes it. (You might recall that the government does a pretty effective job of measuring the number of deficient bridges it has.) It simply means they measure it. What government is lousy at is turning raw data into usable *information,* and then making decisions based on what the information says.

Agencies wind up with a library full of data that no one focuses on until a reporter, auditor, or investigative panel of some sort pulls it out to use as a two-by-four over the agency's head.

Government has to get much better at connecting metrics with success, rather than simply measuring the inputs.

Government has to get much better at connecting metrics with success.

SPINNING DATA INTO INFORMATION

In the children's fairy tale "Rumpelstiltskin," the main character was able to spin straw into gold. Likewise, my good friend and deep thinker Ray Melleady, managing director at the USSC Group, speaks of "spinning" data into information. Our maintenance team at RGRTA once saw a dramatic uptick in the number of buses that were breaking down in service. Analysis revealed that we spent $400 each time we had to send mechanical staff out with a new bus, shift customers from the broken-down bus to the new bus, and bring the original bus back to the garage. Worse, nearly 40 percent of bus "breakdowns" were simply due to the farebox not working properly. In the transportation business, the farebox is the equivalent of the cash register at a retail store. Any retail organization that has its cash register break down regularly must correct that stat. Right?

> **#9 MANAGEMENT PRINCIPLE**
> Spinning data into information

Maybe not. Our head of operations got the team to dig a little deeper rather than simply reacting based on what their instincts told them. They learned that more than 60 percent of our customers paid for their rides with either a monthly or weekly pass. In other words, we already had their money. Another 25 percent were purchasing a day pass with their first ride of the day. We had their money too. So we were down to less than 15 percent of our customers who lacked the ability to pay cash when they boarded because the farebox failed. What did the team conclude? That we should do nothing to fix this problem of broken fareboxes. If a bus got called in by a driver for a breakdown related to the farebox after 10 a.m., the dispatcher told the driver to keep going; the team would fix the farebox that night when the bus came in to the garage. By strategically doing *nothing*, the team saved us more than $200,000 a year by eliminating the expensive $400 apiece bus change-off process. They focused on sound information, and not their instincts.

> **#10 MANAGEMENT PRINCIPLE**
> Information not instincts

All the metrics cited above were *input* metrics: change-offs, fare payment, overtime costs, and so on. The desired *outputs* or results were customer satisfaction and financial performance. Do you think customers felt more satisfied now that they weren't shuffled from a "broken-down" bus to a different one in the frigid February snow? They could just remain on the bus they boarded. Do you think our financial performance improved because we were now saving more than $200,000 by not fixing an input metric? Had we adhered to Drucker's argument that "What gets measured, gets done," our maintenance team would have negatively affected two key output metrics. By spinning data into information, team members were able to move away from their instincts and make a fantastic, information-driven decision not to fix the wrong problem.

MEASURE RESULTS, NOT HOW MUCH YOU TRIED

A glaring weakness of so many government metrics is a neglect of precisely what we described above as "outputs." Much of the time, the reams of data agencies compile relate to what they do, not the *results* of what they do (i.e., the extent to which a government agency's activities actually deliver against the agency's stated strategic goals). It is this "time clock–punching mindset," whereby agencies care more about the *effort* that an individual, unit, or organization puts forth than about the *results* they produce, that causes public institutions to fall behind.

Agencies care more about the *effort* that an individual, unit, or organization puts forth than about the *results* they produce.

A Young Presidents' Organization (YPO) friend of mine describes this type of effort as eating tomato soup with a fork. There is a flurry of activity—clearly someone is very busy trying to achieve her objective—but at the end of each day, very little soup has been eaten. It's one of the fundamental reasons public agencies struggle to perform: they reward the effort of eating tomato soup rather than actually eating it.

I first became attuned to the difference between results and effort one Sunday morning while working on my parents' farm. We were sitting around the kitchen table having pancakes before beginning the day's work, and my dad made an announcement. A roofing crew had finished replacing the barn roof earlier in the week, and, as they are apt to do, had strewn hundreds of stray nails all over the place. Stray nails on a farm are analogous to land mines in a military context. They puncture tractor and wagon tires. The cows step on them and injure their hooves. My dad said that he would pay each of us a penny for every nail we picked up off the ground. He could have paid us by the hour; that would have been an effort-based (eating tomato soup with a fork) metric. Instead, he paid us for our actual results.

In government, a great example of an agency that lacks results-based metrics is the Federal Emergency Management Agency (FEMA), the agency charged with responding to natural disasters and other emergencies. Before 2009, FEMA's performance measurements did not provide information on the effectiveness of its programs. Interested parties could not, for instance, understand how efficient the agency was in closing down temporary aid sites and finding permanent housing for people affected by disasters. As the General Accounting Office noted, "Having results-oriented measures, such as the amount of time that households live in group sites before returning to permanent housing, and developing numerical targets can help identify potential problems in meeting program goals and could be used to make decisions about resources needed and actions to be taken. Without measures that reflect program results and clearly link to the agency's goals, FEMA will not be able to demonstrate program results and progress in achieving its intended objectives."[9]

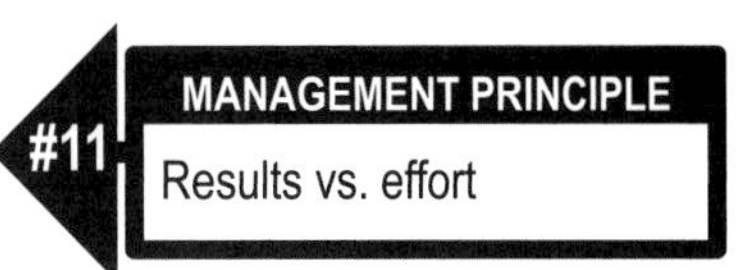

Government agencies at all levels often fail to specify at the outset what they're trying to achieve and then let measurement flow from there. Time and time again I watch government leaders stand up and puff out their chests, or create shiny reports describing all the good things they did in the previous year. Far too often, those are reports of what happened rather than whether it happened on schedule or on budget. They are a reflection of what the elected official or agency could scrounge up that was positive, rather than a balanced reporting of true performance, good and bad. But, again, this is simply cherry-picking metrics after the game has been played, rather than accounting for an established goal. And, pay close attention here, these reports are often reports on projects, rather than on actual organizational performance. Installing new license plate–reading technology is a project—it is effort. Reducing queuing times by 17 percent and raising customer satisfaction levels by 6 percent are performance—they are results. For example, many transit systems measure traditional inputs like how long it takes staff to inspect a bus before it goes on the road, or how often drivers report on time for departure. The output—what *should* be measured—is how often buses actually arrive on time. But there's something else that should also be measured: the customer's *impression* of how often the buses arrive on time. We've worked with organizations whose actual on-time performance is 92 percent, and whose customer impressions of on-time performance is only 76 percent. Numbers like these tell us that we don't need to fix on-time performance; rather, we need communications that advertise the *true* on-time performance so that customers know how good we are. The larger lesson is that agencies shouldn't just measure "customer service" (i.e., the actions they take to serve customers) but customer *satisfaction,* which also encompasses how customers feel about what agencies do. Customer service metrics are the input, whereas the desired *output* is higher customer satisfaction levels.

Have you ever eaten at a restaurant where you received quick service but suffered through a lousy experience overall? The hostess may have greeted you within one minute of your arrival and seated you within two minutes. The waiter may have brought your drinks within four minutes of your order and your food within ten minutes. Yet the food may have been overpriced, and your steak may have arrived terribly overcooked. As you departed the restaurant, the owner might have given you a big smile and asked how everything was and if you enjoyed yourself. You may have nodded, smiled politely, and when you got to the car, announced to your spouse, "We're never going back

#12 MANAGEMENT PRINCIPLE
Customer satisfaction is the goal – *not* customer service.

there again." Looking only at its customer *service* metrics, the restaurant might congratulate itself on hitting every single one. But on the equally important measure of customer *satisfaction*, employees still failed miserably. A restaurant that only looks inwardly and evaluates customer service will quickly close its doors. Satisfaction matters. That's why agencies that provide public services must measure both the quality of their service delivery and their consumers' satisfaction with that service.

When we work with teams like the Capital Area Transportation System (CATS) in Baton Rouge, we go even further, building out a Customer Satisfaction Index (CSI). Their CSI includes information that captures actual performance (metrics like on-time performance or the number of bus breakdowns) as well as the grading of performance by customers (metrics like bus cleanliness, driver attitude, and *perceived* on-time performance). Again, the voices of customers are heard, as the metrics are actually weighted relative to one another (e.g., on-time performance might be given more weight than bus cleanliness). For each metric, we calculate point values that reflect how far actual performance deviated from our performance goal. We award a point value for meeting the goal, and then add or subtract points for every 5 percent that actual performance exceeded or missed the goal. This allows us to recognize overachievement and underachievement compared to the plan. Because he had the right structure in place, the CEO of CATS was able to hold a news conference in the fall of 2014 announcing that the system's customer satisfaction rating had shot up from a relatively low score of three to nineteen, nearly double the industry standard. It was a stunning improvement in a short period of time.

Working with the leadership for the call center at the transit system in Las Vegas, we've watched that team achieve similarly positive results. By focusing on three overarching strategies—excellence in customer satisfaction, call productivity, and employee engagement—the team identified eleven metrics to drive performance, and we set goals around each. In 2014 alone, the department saw overall performance shoot up 34 percent! Average hold times dropped by more than 60 percent, and unforeseen employee absences plummeted by 62 percent. By measuring what *mattered*, Las Vegas got it done.

EPISODIC OR AN EPIDEMIC?

Why is it so important to have a CSI to begin with? Imagine two different board meetings. The first measures customer service based on complaints. The second has built a customer satisfaction index.

Board meeting #1: a dozen people show up for the meeting. They make an impassioned plea about the poor quality of the local parks department. The bathrooms are always filthy, they say. The lawns are never mowed. The lights are always out. All their neighbors are embarrassed to take friends from out of town to the parks. The board simply must do something about it. Board members turn to the city administrator and begin to ask about how many complaints the city has been receiving about the parks. The city administrator turns to the director of the parks department. The parks director shuffles through papers and says he hasn't really heard anything about that. The board apologizes to the people and promises that they'll look into it. The local newspaper reporter corners people after the meeting and asks questions. The headline the next day screams: "Residents Up in Arms Over Bad Condition of Parks." The resolution the board passed at the meeting to cut taxes is ignored. The twelve residents have hijacked the agenda. The next day, the city administrator calls for an emergency meeting to look into the quality of the parks. The city is on defense.

Board meeting #2: a dozen people show up at the board meeting. They make an impassioned plea about the poor quality of the local parks department. The bathrooms are always filthy, they say. The lawns are never mowed. The lights are always out. All their neighbors are embarrassed to take friends from out of town to the parks. The board simply must do something about it. The chair of the board responds to all twelve people collectively. He apologizes that they have had a bad experience, and he tells them that the director of parks is here tonight and would be happy to meet with them to get more details of their experience. At the same time, the chair says, the city receives feedback from five hundred users of the parks every single quarter and (he puts on his glasses for dramatic effect and looks down at the report in the package in front of him to cite from it) their last customer satisfaction rating was

92 percent. There is always room for improvement, of course. The headline in the local newspaper the next day is "Board Votes to Cut Taxes for Third Straight Year." The next day the city administrator and the rest of the team are having their regularly scheduled meetings to drive performance throughout city hall. The city is on offense.

So often we hear from people that perception becomes reality. I've had board members tell me exactly that. Perception *only* becomes reality if an organization and its leadership allows it to. An organization that stays on defense and that has the logging of complaints as its only means of tracking customer sentiment will likely see perception becoming reality. However, a more aggressive organization that possesses a customer satisfaction index with metrics selected and prioritized by real customers can determine whether complaints it receives are *episodic* or an *epidemic*. Are the complaints the result of an individual citizen's personal experience, or is there truly a widespread problem that requires attention and an adjustment in approach or policy? The agency will know it has an epidemic on its hands even before the boisterous crowd reaches the doorway, and can have a plan in place to fix the problem. A customer satisfaction measurement device provides precisely that long-distance clarity. Administrators can respond proportionally, appropriately, and confidently.

> Perception only becomes reality if any organization and its leadership allows it.

THE TRANSITION TO PERFORMANCE

Such relative sophistication has begun to seep into public-sector management, albeit slowly. Efforts to track government performance emerged in earnest in the 1990s during the Clinton administration. The Government Performance and Results Act of 1993 aimed to "provide for the establishment of strategic planning and performance measurement in the Federal government," but financing did not fit into the equation.[10] Then in 2002, the Bush administration's Office of Management and Budget launched the Program Assessment Rating Tool (PART) to identify federal programs that were not meeting performance expectations.[11]

The idea was to make these programs improve or lose funding. But PART never really took hold in Washington.[12] The Obama administration has reignited the torch, this time requiring that federal agencies adopt more analytical capabilities, especially in designing and submitting their budgets. The 2014 budget focused heavily on evidence and results.[13]

Some in the public sector are now seizing on that momentum, as well as the popularity of the *Moneyball* book and film, to urge public organizations to adopt Beane's information-driven approach to policy making.[14] A nascent movement called "Moneyball for Government" is being touted by the nonprofit organization America Achieves through its Results for America initiative.[15] Results for America is a bipartisan campaign that advocates for the building of awareness around "evidence-based" policy making so that public money is invested in "what works."[16] It asks that organizations measure their performance in an attempt to separate what works from what doesn't and craft their future budgets accordingly. America Achieves has even developed its own scorecard to track how well certain federal agencies, such as the Departments of Education, Labor, and Health and Human Services, track their own performance.[17] This is all good news, but it still falls way short of what is needed: a broader transition in public management away from instinct-based to information-driven decision making.

MONEYBALL FOR YOUR TEAM

One day, when I was still CEO at the RGRTA in Rochester the phone rang in my office. It was fellow Red Sox fan and local television reporter Pat McGonigle. "Hey, I was wondering if you've ever heard of the book *Moneyball*?" Pat asked.

"Are you kidding me? I'm looking at it on my desk right now. We use a lot of the concepts in the book in how we run this place."

"I *knew* it!" Pat yelled into the phone. "We were all sitting around in the newsroom talking about all the things you say in news conferences, and we had a bet that you were a *Moneyball* devotee—and I just won! I want to do a story on how you're running a public agency with baseball management principles. People are going to love it."

TOPS RGR SCORECARD

TRANSIT ORGANIZATIONAL PERFORMANCE SCORECARD

STRATEGIC PILLAR	METRIC	PLAN GOAL	Actual 1st Quarter	Actual 2nd Quarter	Actual 3rd Quarter	Actual 4th Quarter	% Variance from Plan	Earned Points	Goal Points
FPI Long-Term Financial Success	EOY Net Income (Deficit) (000's)	$(717)							19.00
	Pension Liability Coverage	100.0%							2.00
	Cost Recovery Ratio	38.1%							5.00
	Available Unrestricted Net Assets (000's)	$17,258							5.00
	Multi-year Budget Projection (000's)	$(19,988)							9.00
	Operating Revenue Per Revenue Mile	$3.04							5.00
	TOTAL FPI SCORE								45.00
CSI Excellence in Customer Service	Regional Transit Service	28.44							28.44
	Lift Line	0.31							0.31
	Batavia Bus Service	0.10							0.10
	Livingston Area Transportation Service	0.48							0.48
	Orleans Transit Service	0.10							0.10
	Seneca Transit Service	0.11							0.11
	Wayne Area Transportation Service	0.27							0.27
	Wyoming Transit Service	0.19							0.19
	TOTAL CSI SCORE								30.00
ESI Employee Success	Bus Operator Customer Service								
	Regional Transit Service	80.0%							2.66
	Lift Line	90.0%							0.06
	On Time % Lowest (20) Operators	60.0%							3.99
	On Time % Early	5.50%							3.99
	Call Center Staff Secret Shopper								
	Regional Transit Service	90.0%							0.51
	Lift Line	90.0%							0.51
	Regionals	90.0%							0.38
	% Achievement of Incentive Opportunities	75.0%							2.90
	Total ESI Score								15.00
CCI Connecting to Communities	% Growth in System-Wide Ridership	-0.1%							3.00
	% of Locally Generated Revenue from Partnership Subsidies	55.9%							2.00
	Fare Stability (RTS)	$1.00							1.00
	Customers Per Revenue Mile								
	Regional Transit Service	3.27							2.31
	Lift Line	0.12							0.68
	Batavia Bus Service	0.35							0.08
	Livingston Area Transportation Service	0.63							0.20
	Orleans Transit Service	0.31							0.11
	Seneca Transit Service	0.30							0.11
	Wayne Area Transportation Service	0.20							0.35
	Wyoming Transit Service	0.22							0.18
	Total CCI Score								10.00
TOPS Score									100

FIGURE 4-2

What would Moneyball look like for your local, county, state, or federal agency? Well, just as the fans at a ballpark have a scoring sheet to monitor performance of the game, you and your team need something very similar.

Figure 4-2 is a strategic metrics tool we created for the RGRTA called a *performance scorecard.* You use it to keep score just like a baseball fan would. A performance scorecard casts the organization's strategic and operational plans into a matrix that helps track the path toward realizing the success moment. More than that, a performance scorecard helps employees at all levels *measure what matters* by focusing on results rather than effort.

The scorecard's beauty is its elegance and simplicity: the organization's composite health is represented as a single, one-page chart. The scorecard is laid out horizontally and vertically in matrix form. Every metric is weighted in terms of its importance and presented accordingly from top to bottom in order of priority (in the RGRTA's case, the strategic pillars were long-term financial stability, excellent customer service, quality of service, and employee success, in that order). Within each strategy, an index is created that is composed of a series of specific metrics, which in turn are weighted to reflect their importance. Horizontally you see both goals and actual performance for each metric.

Using a performance scorecard, anyone inside or outside an organization can understand immediately what the organization is trying to achieve, how it has proposed to achieve it, the specific metrics that track performance against the objective, the relative importance of each metric, and, of course, how the organization is actually doing. There's no place to run, no place to hide: the full picture is right there in broad daylight, captured in carefully selected metrics to deliver success. You can spot the areas of performance in which the organization is strongest and those where more improvement is necessary. As a manager or an employee, you know exactly where to focus, and exactly what to fix. Packaging and presentation are critical to turn the complexity of a vast organization into a simple, intuitive system.

Packaging and presentation are critical to turn the complexity of a vast organization into a simple, intuitive system.

CREATING A PERFORMANCE SCORECARD OF YOUR OWN

Once an organization has been using a strategically aligned performance scorecard method of measurement and management, leaders begin to wonder how on earth they ever got along without it. But how do you begin to build one? There are eight steps, which I discuss in turn.

Step 1—Define Success

The first step is to *decide what you're trying to achieve.* What exactly constitutes success for your organization? I can't begin to tell you the dozens of times a senior executive has called our team and asked us if we can build them a performance scorecard so they can improve. "You guys have done some amazing things. I've read the results you've produced—lower costs, higher quality. Come help me do it here?"

Our response is always the same. "Sure, we can help you build a performance scorecard. No problem. What would you like to measure?"

"Well," the executive now says haltingly, "I thought you were going to tell *us* that."

We can only help organizations decide what to measure *after* they've clarified their intended goals. A scorecard begins at the top of an organization, with a careful assessment of the strategic pillars and their importance relative to one another (see chapter 2). An organization simply cannot know what to measure until it defines what success looks like. *That* is the foundation of measuring what matters.

> An organization simply cannot know what to measure until it defines what success looks like.

Step 2—Establish Output Metrics

Step two is to *establish metrics beneath each of the strategies.* We call this concept "strategically aligned metric management." A start-up company might choose monthly profitability as a metric to measure the success of its short-term financial strategy (short-term because the organization is untested and needs to build capital fast). As the company grows and establishes itself, it would likely choose a longer-term financial strategy, adjusting its measurement metrics to, say, a multiyear budget projection. A county might measure its percentage of debt compared to annual revenue stream. A school district might measure its cash on hand compared to its five-year capital plan.

Be careful to choose output metrics that reflect *results* rather than input metrics that merely track the *effort* of individuals and departments. We want people to actually pick up nails, not wander around aimlessly looking for nails on the ground. A school determined to raise student performance might choose test scores or graduation rates as output metrics. A police department wanting to improve community relations might track scores from customer satisfaction surveys or the number of people who feel community meetings are effective (remember, simply measuring the number of people who *attend* a community meeting is an effort-based metric). A hospital wishing to improve quality might track the number of complications arising from surgical procedures.

Step 3—Prioritize Metrics

Once you and your team have metrics in place below each strategy, step three is *prioritizing them*. Output metrics aren't created equal. Some metrics are more important than others to deliver success as it's been defined. For the Oakland A's, scoring runs was the most important metric. Other results mattered, but none contributed as much to their success. Which strategic pillar and corresponding metric will most directly enable *you* to deliver success this coming year? Allocate points to each strategy that reflect their relative importance. Within each strategy, you'll also want to allocate points to initiatives supporting that strategy in a way that reflects the relative importance of each initiative.

If you're a county health department whose most important (of four strategies is to improve public education about communicable diseases, you might have already allocated fifty points out of one hundred to that area of focus during the development of your Success Plan (chapter 2).

COUNTY HEALTH DEPARTMENT		
Strategic Pillar		Points
Improve Public Education About Communicable Diseases	Number of children who get inoculations	20
	Number of adults who have been inoculated	10
	% of residents who receive annual flu shot	8
	% of residents in quarterly survey who have seen PSA	8
	Number of residents who sign up for department Twitter updates	2
	Number of residents who say PSA caused them or children to get inoculated/flu shot	2

FIGURE 4-3

As your team is determining how to measure your success in the realization of that strategy, you establish six output metrics:

After a collaborative dialogue and debate, the team may decide that the most important measurement to deliver success in this strategic area is the number of residents who have been inoculated. The key here is that you've defined success, established output metrics to monitor progress toward the realization of success, and prioritized the most important metrics that you simply must get right in order to deliver.

We've all been to those dreadful meetings where an organization has three pages, single-spaced, of results to review. Where does everyone's eyes go? To the three metrics where the organization failed to meet its goal. But these might be the three least important numbers on the page. Or, they might be the most important. The problem is you're deciding their importance in the heat of the moment, when you're easily influenced by reporters, auditors, board members, elected officials, union leaders, and so on. It's vital that you prioritize at the beginning of the year, like Billy Beane did with the Oakland A's. That way, you'll stay grounded and attuned to what really matters throughout the year.

In early 2012, Detroit Mayor Dave Bing brought in our team to help repair the city's failing transportation system. Only 66 percent of scheduled buses were getting out on the road every single day. Can you imagine arriving at your local airport and, fully one-third of the time, having no plane pull up to the gate for you to board? Even worse, can you imagine that there was no way to know ahead of time whether the plane would show up? This was exactly the kind of chaos that existed on the streets of Detroit, even in the dead of winter. The city simply lacked the capacity to get residents to their destinations (including their jobs) dependably.

The first thing we did was work with staff at the agency to prioritize what was most important in order to deliver the desired output, i.e., on-time pullout of scheduled service. In this instance, because of the emergency circumstances, we didn't have time to go through the earlier steps in the process; we simply established the desired outcome of buses on the road. We then prioritized the cascading metrics to deliver that output, focusing everyone on what mattered most. The effort paid off almost immediately. Within three months, the agency was delivering 90 percent of its scheduled service. One month after that, the agency hit 99 percent and kept it there for the balance of the year. Customer service had improved (the inward-facing operational metrics), and so did customer satisfaction (the outward-facing impression metrics), the latter skyrocketing 44 percent by the year's last quarter. All this came from prioritizing the necessary metrics to deliver success, and from pushing aside far less important metrics that only served to distract.

Step 4—Define the Metric

With your metrics established, *define each metric in crisp detail and establish a clear information source.* If you're a bus company measuring on-time performance, what does "on-time" mean? Does it mean *exactly* on time? According to whose watch? Or does it mean within a particular window—say, between a minute early and three minutes after the scheduled time? If you're an airline measuring on-time performance, is that defined as the time when the airplane pulls away from the gate? When it takes off? When it arrives at its destination? Lacking precise definitions, you won't report data clear or consistently, and your metrics will lack accuracy. If an organization is to perform well, *everyone* must know exactly what constitutes the desired performance. Defining the metrics establishes whose watch we're going to use to monitor performance.

Step 5—Establish Ownership

Step five is to *determine which departments within the organization own which metrics. Someone* has to own a metric; you wouldn't send a ship to sea without a captain, right? If a school district wants to improve overall test results, one component of those test results—those relating to mathematics competency—might be owned by the chair of the mathematics department. The school district might in turn determine that inputs (step eight below) like student attendance, the number of homework problems assigned, the number of parent–teacher conferences held, or the number of hours spent on teacher training all help drive test scores (note that the school district would be better served by deploying output metrics, such as number of students with grades of "B" or better). The school district would then track these input metrics and hold the chair of the math department responsible for the team collectively attaining quarterly goals, so as to influence the broader output metric of student test scores. School district managers would also track whether the department is mobilizing the tactics (e.g., assigning more homework, performing more training, etc.) on schedule and on budget.

Step 6—Construct an Information System

The data must flow from somewhere. We're building a system that turns data into strategically aligned *information*, so that an organization can easily see which areas require celebration, adjustment, or wholesale change. In some cases, you'll already have the data for a metric like on-time performance in some corner of your organization, maybe without even realizing it. When RGRTA created its Customer Satisfaction Index, it was able to use data about the number of customers traveling on its buses that only a few people knew existed, and that had been squirreled away in a series of dusty binders on a low-level employee's desk. In other cases, you'll need to build an information system, investing in technology to monitor consumer behavior and impressions, harnessing data collected via the web, or hiring outside vendors to conduct customer satisfaction surveys and other studies. As a rule of thumb, *every metric* should be reported by either technology or an outside vendor.

The organization loses if it creates an opportunity to self-report and fudge the numbers. Just ask the former secretary of veterans affairs Eric Shinseki if he wishes he hadn't let employees report their own numbers to him. You will recall that the secretary, a retired general and decorated war hero, appears to have been misled by as many as two dozen administrators at VA hospitals about how long veterans were waiting to receive life-sustaining treatments. It seems administrators were cooking the books so that they could claim bonuses. Secretary Shinseki appeared before a Senate panel to express that he was "mad as hell," but sadly he had neglected to construct a quality-controlled information system. The issue was one of misrepresentation. Internal employees shouldn't touch output metrics. As Jim Collins says, we must "confront the brutal facts."[18]

Some agencies might find themselves swimming in too many competing information sources; in this case, they'll need to pare some back. When Chesterfield County, Virginia, implemented "Blueprint Chesterfield," its innovative planning and performance management, administrators attempted to address a "growing gap between organizational planning and budgeting fueled by a lack of easy access to the right information." Formerly, the county drew its information from five separate databases. Under Blueprint Chesterfield, one centralized database became the source of performance information. At last check, "over 80% of updated strategic measures have been defined and have a collection and reporting system in place along with a narrative on why the measure matters."[19] Chesterfield County offers a great example of how an agency at any level might collect and use data more thoughtfully and effectively.

Step 7—Set the Goals

Once we have established output metrics, we pivot to *set clear goals*. As mentioned, goal setting should be achievable, challenging, and collaborative (and you will recall that collaborative is far different from consensual). In chapter 5, you'll see that we need to build cultures of *ownership* within public organizations, cultures in which employees feel emotionally connected to their work and committed to organizational strategies. That can happen only if employees have a say in establishing what constitutes desired performance, as well as the inputs that drive results. Employees are on the front lines each and every day. They know as well as anyone how to produce results. If we simply impose goals on employees and teams, then they're not invested and they won't own the results. Not only that: if the results disappoint, employees will defend themselves by saying they never believed the goals were achievable, that they had never agreed to produce that level of result, and that no one ever asked them. Not a recipe for greatness.

MANAGEMENT PRINCIPLE #13
Goal setting is achievable, challenging, and collaborative

Former Notre Dame head coach Lou Holtz tells how he used to practice his team in August under the steamy, hot Midwestern sun. After several hours, when his players were starting to wilt, Coach Holtz would gather his team around and announce, "Men, I was just about to call an end to practice. You've all worked hard and I'm proud of you. But I just got off the phone with Bo Schembechler [Michigan Wolverines head coach and Notre Dame archrival] and he said his guys were still practicing. In fact, Bo just told me that his players were asking him to do two workouts today. So, I'll leave it up to you guys. We can wrap it up here, or we can double down and see if we can keep up with what the Michigan players are doing today. What do you men want to do?" As you might expect, taking such a collaborative approach got players' hearts and minds behind the extra practice. And that extra practice, as well as the approach Coach Holtz took to schedule it, undoubtedly contributed to Notre Dame going undefeated in 1988 and winning the national championship.[20]

In public organizations, we must also be sure to connect goal setting to operating and financial plans. If the average wait time in your call center is one minute and fifteen seconds, and customers don't rate wait time as an important part of customer satisfaction, it makes no financial sense to set a one-minute hold time as a goal the call center is trying to achieve. It's not easy getting wait times down; if the call center were to have any hope of succeeding, the organization would have to allocate resources (hire five more people to answer the phones). Yet doing so would yield little appreciable bump in customer satisfaction.

However, if customers *did* see hold time as an important part of customer satisfaction—if those extra fifteen seconds really mattered—then allocating the resources would be worth it, because the change could meaningfully improve customer satisfaction. Under this scenario, the organization would want to get the call center manager and her team to agree that with the new staff at their disposal, and perhaps some additional training on a new software system, they can hit the more ambitious goal of a one-minute average wait time.

It's one thing to set a goal, but we must always factor in what it will cost the organization to make that goal attainable, and the extent to which the goal carries strategic significance. Framing goals in the abstract and without employee participation quickly leads to confusion, misalignment, and substandard results. Organizations should also retain sufficient *tension* in the scorecard. If we only measure call center hold times and then tie an incentive to it, we're encouraging employees to answer the phone quickly to notch a good hold time number . . . and *then* ask customers to hold, so they can answer the next call. Hold times will decline, but customer satisfaction will, too, because customers are just stacking up listening to elevator music and wondering if anyone is ever going to come back to them. Incorporating a competing metric—for instance, "secret shopper" scores that measure quality—will properly incent employees to reduce wait times *and* ensure a high-quality experience.

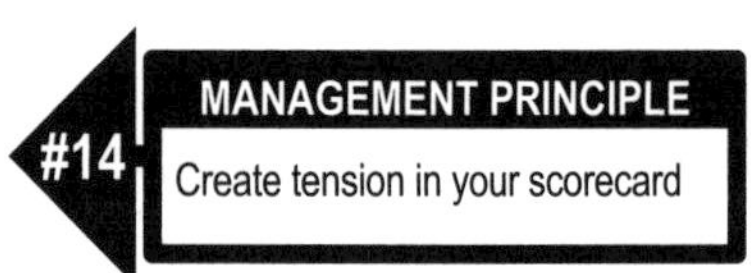

This entire structure is about delivering balanced success, that is, improving quality and reducing costs. It was precisely this model that helped us improve customer satisfaction for the City of Detroit's transportation department by 44 percent *and* save taxpayers more than $38 million in a single year. It's easy to go into any public organization in America and save money; all you have to do is cut services and lay off employees. It's also easy to go into any public agency in

> Sustained success requires that we achieve a balance, reducing the cost of government services while improving service quality. Prioritizing your scorecard and incorporating adequate tension in its metrics produces precisely these results.

America and improve customer satisfaction; simply spend more money, expand services, deliver more, and hire more employees. Sustained success requires that we achieve a balance, reducing the cost of government services while improving service quality. Prioritizing your scorecard and incorporating adequate tension in its metrics produces precisely these results.

Step 8—Establish Inputs to Drive the Output

Once the performance scorecard is fixed at the organizational level, *the process moves down to the individual departments charged with managing the organization's specific operations.* Here, we focus more on analyzing the inputs that create the desired outputs of the organizational performance scorecard. Managers in the departments perform the same process I've just described: defining and prioritizing a more granular set of metrics and ensuring that information systems exist to record and report. Managers will want to focus on those "department performance indicators" that have influence over the organizational results.

Think of how Billy Beane would have seen this. Organizationally, he was concerned with scoring runs; that was the output, or result. The inputs to that desired result were waiting until the third pitch to swing, increasing on-base percentage, and not being caught attempting to steal a base. In our model, we would weight those input metrics according to how important they are to delivering the desired output metric. That way, all team members might monitor what they are contributing to the team's victory.

Once the departmental process has been completed, the department produces scorecards that circulate at the organizational level to be united and synchronized with the wider scorecard. This ensures that department leaders agree with the scorecard's overall layout. It also gives the organization's management team a chance to identify blind spots departments may have overlooked.

MONEYBALL, GIULIANI STYLE

During the early 1990s, New York City was one of America's most dangerous cities, and Rudolph Giuliani's election as mayor in 1993 was widely regarded as a referendum on the performance of his predecessor, David Dinkins, whose term in office had seen only a meager decline in crime rates.[21] Giuliani's mandate from voters was unequivocal: reduce crime and improve the quality of life in New York.[22] Heeding that call, one of Giuliani's first actions in office was to appoint a new police commissioner, William Bratton.[23] At the time, Bratton was Boston's top cop, a position he had earned in part for his previous success in cleaning up New York's subway system as chief of the city's transit police.[24] Now in charge of the NYPD, an organization more than ten times the size of Boston's,[25] Bratton's first order of business was to clean up the department.

Bratton was a swashbuckling commissioner who had impressed Giuliani during early talks with his bold vision of reducing New York's crime rate by 10 percent in a year and by 40 percent over three years.[26] Once appointed, Bratton got to work doing just that. But he soon found that his task posed a much greater challenge than he had anticipated.

Bratton spent several weeks assessing the contours of New York's criminal landscape. He toured precincts, talked to commanders, and tried to figure out the nature, location, and frequency of crimes being committed in the city's boroughs. Bratton realized that despite the NYPD's ubiquitous presence in the city, commanders were unable to answer his most basic questions. They couldn't even give accurate crime statistics for the previous twenty-four-hour period. Bratton was stunned as well to learn that no system existed for recording or analyzing criminal activity.[27]

Bratton sought to change that. First, he gathered the department's top brass and announced his goal of reducing crime by 10 percent in a year. It was Bratton's success moment, and it aroused considerable shock. "Jaws dropped," one police official recalled. "Literally, mouths opened."[28] Next, Bratton and his advisers laid out an overall plan the NYPD would adopt in getting there: they would focus on "reducing crime, disorder and fear."[29] The pillars of that strategy were even more specific, and they would imitate the approach Bratton had implemented years earlier when leading the transit police. Crime fighting would henceforth stress "going after quality-of-life offenses, encouraging assertive policing, devolving authority to the appropriate level [of command],

and attending to officer psychology [or instilling the force with a much-needed dose of pride and confidence]."[30] At the department level, the strategies for combatting crime became even more granular, akin to what we have referred to as operational tactics. They included, in order, ridding the streets of guns,[31] reducing youth violence, driving out drug dealers, stopping domestic violence,[32] and reclaiming public spaces.[33]

Bratton knew that his strategy for achieving success would fail if the department had no way to measure, analyze, and adjust the department's performance. This wasn't a project—it was a new way of doing business. Over a period of several months, he and a crack team devised a system called CompStat to do that.[34] Bratton and his inner circle ordered precinct commanders to map out where crimes were occurring by date and type.[35] Commanders were expected to present those maps and data to the NYPD's leadership in high-profile meetings two mornings a week. Eventually, the city's seventy-six precincts were required to compile detailed statistics of the previous week's complaints, arrests, and summonses, as well as write-ups on the most serious cases, patterns, and the tactics used to combat them.[36] All of this information was entered into a database, analyzed week by week, month by month, and year by year, and then distributed to the department in real time.[37] Most importantly, precinct commanders were held accountable for their numbers by NYPD leadership in grill sessions before large audiences.[38] The commanders were given no more than a day and half notice.[39] In this way, ownership of results was ingrained and the practice of "CompStat-ing" filtered down to lower and lower levels of the force.[40]

At the end of Bratton's first year on the job, his results were spectacular. In 1994, New York's overall crime rate dropped 12 percent, an extraordinary change in its own right, but even more striking when compared to national crime rates, which went down a paltry 1.1 percent.[41] The individual rates of certain types of serious crime fell even more. Homicides fell 19.8 percent, robberies 15.6 percent, vehicle theft 15.2, burglary 10.9 percent, grand larceny 10.7, rape 5.4, and aggravated assault 4.8. In addition, shooting deaths had dropped 23 percent and shootings overall were down 16.4 percent.[42] Within a few more years, the NYPD under Bratton's leadership had brought crime in New York down to a level last seen in the 1960s.[43]

Information matters. And public organizations with disciplined approaches to collecting and using information can do incredible things. If your local government agencies have been fuzzy about performance metrics, or if they've neglected them entirely, you'll be amazed at the efficiencies and improvements they can realize by aligning metrics closely to strategies, creating reliable information-collection systems, and implementing a regular process to set and revise performance goals. At the NYPD, CompStat has for years now proven its worth as an indispensible part of the organization's success. The system remains in use today, and other cities around the country have crafted their own versions of this invaluable tool. Moneyball may have gotten its start in sports, but it isn't just for sports teams. It's for *any* team working to drive positive performance for its customers, its employees, and taxpayers.

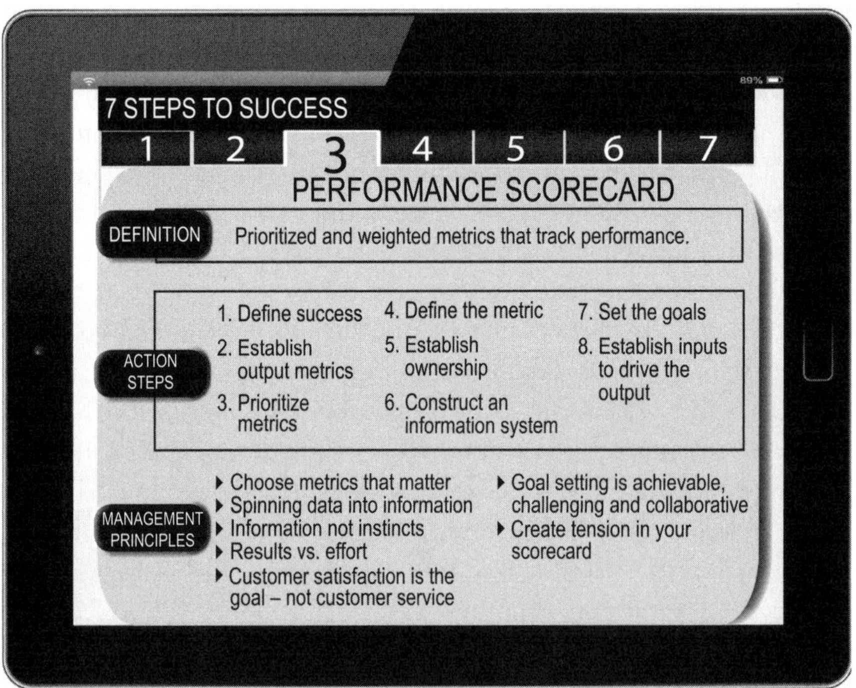

FIGURE 4-4

5

Build a Culture of Ownership

One beautiful Sunday morning in late July 2004, Cathy Clement, a pistol permit supervisor at the Niagara County Clerk's office in Western New York State, received an urgent phone call while sitting in her enclosed back porch. It was State Senator George Maziarz, her former boss at the clerk's office. "I've got a situation here," Maziarz said. "I know it's a Sunday, and I hate to do this, but I need your help."[1]

Maziarz explained that one of his constituents, Army Spc. John Pirinelli, had been shot and grievously wounded while patrolling in Iraq. Pirinelli had been sent to a military base in Germany for treatment, his life hanging in the balance. His brother Philip and sister-in-law Stephanie wanted to rush immediately to his bedside, but unfortunately they lacked passports. Maziarz had received a frantic phone call from John Pirinelli's aunt asking for help. There was no way Philip and Stephanie could wait days or weeks for passports; they needed to be on a plane the next day. "I'm working hard to find a way to make this happen," Maziarz told Clement. "Assuming I can find an office that will issue them a passport on the spot, could you help me get a passport application filled out for them?"

Clement had processed passport applications while working for Maziarz back when he was the Niagara County Clerk. Remarkably enough, she still kept extra application documents at home in case of emergency. She told Maziarz she thought she could help, but she'd have to call him right back. Hanging up, she asked her husband what she should do. Her father-in-law had died a few days earlier and her husband was still reeling with grief; she didn't want to leave him alone on a Sunday if she could help it. Also, she wondered if her current boss would be upset with her for helping Maziarz. She had been reassigned and no longer processed passports; the rules indicated she wasn't supposed to involve herself in it.

Clement's husband told her that none of this mattered; she should drop everything and go. "Our family was just destroyed by my father-in-law's death," Clement related, "but this was another family that needed help. And we were talking about a young man who was fighting for our country. My husband and I were both proud that I was in a position to do something." As for her boss, Clement decided not to contact him, mindful of a lesson she had learned while working for Maziarz. "George creates ownership. He showed me time and again how to help people. We don't have to be limited by rules that don't make sense; if there's a consequence for doing the right thing, we'll deal with it later. As a public servant, it's more important to do the right thing."

While Clement was deciding what to do, Maziarz was busy working the phones. Calling the Pirinellis' local congressman, he had learned of a U.S. State Department office located in Manhattan that would process passports on the very same day; if the Pirinellis went there first thing on Monday morning, they could catch a plane out of New York City and arrive at their family member's bedside the following evening. Yet a big roadblock was developing that Sunday morning: the Pirinellis were in the midst of an adoption proceeding, so their original birth certificates were sealed in a file in the Erie County Courthouse; it would take a judge to grant them entry. Maziarz called Judge Richard Kloch to get the documents unsealed, and to find out how on earth this growing posse being pressed into service could get their hands on the Pirinellis' birth certificates on a weekend. Kloch, who was cooking burgers at a big family picnic, dropped everything and started dialing himself. He tracked down court clerk Paul Smaldone, who was *also* hosting a family picnic and who *also* dropped everything to help. Smaldone in turn called another clerk, Cindy Gugino, who worked in adoptions. He had the key to the office and she knew where the birth certificates were kept and how they were filed. The two of them arranged to meet at the courthouse that afternoon.

The Pirinellis were in luck: sorting through files, the clerks found the correct birth certificates. Smaldone got in his car and rushed over to give them to Maziarz, meeting the state senator in a bank parking lot. "It felt like something out of a spy thriller," Smaldone told me. "Not how I thought I'd spend my Sunday. Here I am, breaking into the courthouse, tracking down documents for people I don't even know, and then meeting a state senator in a parking lot. I felt like I must have been breaking all kinds of rules!"

By late afternoon, Maziarz was back at his own office in Lockport, New York, with the birth certificates in hand. At around 5:00, Cathy Clement and Philip and Stephanie Pirinelli arrived; Clement had the application, and the Pirinellis had their passport photographs and all their baggage for the trip. The Pirinellis were understandably distraught, but Clement was able to take them quickly through the application process and get everything properly filled out and signed.

When the application was complete, Maziarz was ready to wish the Pirinellis luck and send them on their way. The congressman had advised Maziarz that the Pirinellis should arrive early at the passport office in order to claim a place in line. "The office opens at 8 a.m.," Maziarz told the Pirinellis. "And we're seven hours away from New York City by car. If you leave right now, you'll arrive early in the morning."

"Uh, okay," the Pirinellis said.

"I'd definitely go now—you never know what traffic will be like. And you know how to get there, right? What bridge to take across the Hudson?"

"Sure," Philip Pirinelli muttered. "Right."

As Maziarz told me, both Pirinellis were looking at him like he was from Mars. "Okay, what's up? Is there a problem?" he asked them.

"Well, we've never been to New York City before," Stephanie Pirinelli said.

It was clear that after all the effort a large number of people had put in to get the Pirinellis ready for the passport office, the frazzled couple did not know what to do next. If they got lost en route, they might not arrive at the passport office in time to be processed and still make their plane. It was then, at 6:00 p.m. on a Sunday evening, that Maziarz decided: he would drive these total strangers to New York himself. "I had cleared my Sunday schedule and was supposed to be with my family that afternoon, but there was no alternative," Maziarz said. "I had to drive them myself. So that's what I did."

Maziarz and the Pirinellis crammed into Maziarz's old Ford Taurus and started off down the New York State Thruway. It was a grueling trip fueled by Diet Pepsi and rest-stop food. Around midnight, they reached Albany, a bit more than halfway through the drive. Mariarz stopped there to pick up Mike Norris, one of his staff members. Norris had been preparing for his law school ethics exam and had been about to return home to Lockport when he had received Mariarz's urgent request to sit tight in Albany. Now Norris would drive them the rest of the way so Mariarz could take a breather and help keep the Pirinellis' spirits up.

The group arrived in New York at around 5 a.m. on Monday morning. At 6 a.m., they were in line at the passport office waiting for it to open at 8 a.m. Once the office opened, it became clear that despite everyone's efforts, the Pirinellis still might not get their passports in time. Others were in line ahead of them, and the line wasn't moving. Approaching the guard on duty, Maziarz identified himself as a New York state senator and said he needed special assistance. Maziarz recounted the Pirinellis' predicament and related all that had transpired during the previous twenty-four hours. The guard took a look at him—shorts, T-shirt, unshaven face, sneakers—and exclaimed incredulously, "*You're* a New York state senator?"

After a laugh, Maziarz pulled out his Senate identification. Without a word, the guard pulled the couple out of line. Forty-five minutes later, they had their passports. By late morning, they were on their way to John F. Kennedy International Airport to catch their flight to Germany. Upon reaching the gate, they called Maziarz to let them him know that they had received their seat assignments and were all set. Maziarz breathed a sigh of relief. "That was the signal I was waiting for. Now I knew we could all finally get some sleep."

The Pirinellis reached Germany in time to be with their brother. The presence of family in the room (the Pirinellis' parents had also made the trip) benefitted John Pirinelli; he began to respond almost immediately.

He wound up making it through several surgeries before transferring to Walter Reed Army Medical Center to continue his recovery. Almost a year later, he returned home to Western New York, and Maziarz was there to greet him at the airport. The Pirinelli family held a huge celebration to thank Maziarz and the troop of others who had helped them in their time of need.[2]

The Pirinellis' trip received national attention in the media, not only because it revealed the lengths Americans will go to support those in uniform but because it seemed to represent something extraordinary: a moment when public servants lived up to the true ideals of their calling. Clement, Maziarz, Norris, Kloch, Smaldone, Gugino: all had interrupted their weekends, dropping everything on a gorgeous afternoon to help the Pirinellis. Even the guard at the passport office had gone the extra mile so the Pirinellis could make their flight. Paul Smaldone summarized it well: "Everyone did their own little part to allow something great to happen. This is how government should work, and it made me proud to play my role. I've worked in government for thirty-eight years. You're here to help, not to create obstacles and hardship.... We are a nation of rules and laws, but we have to do it with some feeling and some heart. And that day we delivered."

Too often we talk about "holding people accountable," and many have lamented the lack of accountability in government. Yet the success of any organization hinges on something more: whether people on the front lines are willing to take personal ownership of their work, whether they care enough to go the extra mile and see something through to closure, especially in times of crisis. That kind of engagement is all too rare in both the public and private sectors. Instead, you tend to find people who clock in and out, doing the bare minimum stipulated by their contracts, performance reviews, or even their consciences. When a difficult or unusual task arises, they try to get someone else to do it. The result is those games of "hot potato" we've all encountered: you bring a problem to someone, and he immediately directs you to a different office. That office in turn directs you to a third office, and so on. The employee's goal, and that of the workforce collectively, is to get the person or situation off his desk rather than to actually solve the problem.

As the Pirinelli episode suggests, however, government doesn't *need* to work this way, and it often hasn't. A famous story, now lost to history, emerged from a visit President Kennedy took to the NASA space center in 1962. As the president toured the facility, he stopped to speak with a janitor he saw standing among other employees. He asked the custodian what he did there, and he received the following answer: "Well, Mr. President, I'm helping put a man on the moon."[3] *That* is what ownership looks like. It's an employee who sees himself in the delivery of the organizational success moment. Such an employee would never pass the buck to someone else, nor spend all day watching the clock. He is too aligned with the goals of his organization and takes too much pride in rendering service to others.

Once an organization has created a performance scorecard, the next step is to get people throughout the organization to own the results of that scorecard and to *care* about their individual and the organization's results. At the organizational level, we measure outputs, while at the department level we measure inputs. Employees need to see themselves in those inputs. It's about getting employees invested—both their hearts and minds—so that they go the extra mile and even suspend rules when necessary to get the job done. No amount of vision, no amount of planning will move a government agency ahead unless engagement and even a *culture of ownership* also exists. How do we build such a culture? How do we turn bureaucrats, who work inside a structure that encourages them to duck problems and play it safe to get to their pension, into purveyors of creative and thoughtful solutions? How do we spread the kind of ethos that drove Clement, Maziarz, Norris, Judge Kloch, and Smaldone to put personal prerogatives aside and make the rules work in order to help a family in need? How do we make that kind of commitment the norm, not the exception?

FOSTER OWNERSHIP, NOT ACCOUNTABILITY

Later in this chapter, I'll offer a series of actions leaders can take to inspire employees to become invested in what they do. First, we need to understand exactly what employee ownership is. As I've intimated, a culture of ownership is not the same as a culture of accountability. It's not that employees shouldn't be held responsible for their jobs; they should. In fact, our next chapter will address many ways to do exactly that. But there's a vast chasm between doing the discrete tasks you've been assigned and devoting yourself to achieving a specific outcome. Our goal is to create an environment where we *inspire* employees to deliver success, rather than *impose* it upon them. We want employees to own the results rather than simply feel accountable to an outside force (i.e., their bosses) for them. Compared with ownership, accountability is relatively easy to instill yet grossly insufficient to produce the high performance any organization needs to excel. As a management priority, accountability needs to come in a clear second—behind ownership.

Our goal is to create an environment where we *inspire* employees to deliver success, rather than *impose* it upon them. We want employees to own the results rather than simply feel accountable to an outside force.

Gerbil wheel employees put in lots of effort. They mow the lawn at the park once a week. They shelve their quota of five thousand books a day at the library. Round and round the gerbil wheel goes. One day, one week, one month closer to a rich pension. What's missing is an emphasis on doing the job *well.* Under the gerbil wheel system, employees often aren't required to know or even care about the actual results of their labors. They merely see themselves as responsible for doing the job that has been assigned to them. Think how limiting this is. If Cathy Clement and Paul Smaldone thought like gerbil wheel employees, they never would have helped the Pirinellis; that wouldn't have shown up in their performance reviews. Somehow, both had come to own the results of their labor rather than simply putting in effort.

The difference between accountability and ownership—between a culture of imposition and one of *inspiration*—was on full display recently when I picked up a few items at a convenience store near my house. Eight customers were in line, trying to spend money that in turn would pay salaries and keep the store operating. Four employees were on duty, only one manning the cash register. The other three were taking inventory. Why was this? Shouldn't one or two of them have joined their colleague at the register so that patrons wouldn't have to wait at what was quickly becoming an *inconvenience* store? They should have, except that management was holding these employees accountable for inventory. Managers might have talked about the importance of customer service, but they didn't have a culture of ownership in place that prompted employees to take *pride* in serving customers, such that if customers were waiting to spend money, the inventory could wait.

At the grocery store, a culture of ownership is the difference between employees mindlessly stocking shelves and doing it thoughtfully, to make customers' lives easier. It's the difference between the employee who, when asked where the ketchup is, points you to a location seven aisles over and wishes you good luck, and the one who tells you the location and cheerfully says, "Let me take you there right now." More generally, it's the difference between an employee who performs a task fully and intentionally and one who doesn't.

When it comes to customer service call centers, a culture of ownership is the difference between a "warm" transfer and a cold one. My assistant April taught me this; she was so good at warm transfers that we charged her with training our entire company on it. Let's say you have a customer on the phone, and you need to direct her to another department in order to resolve her problem. In a warm transfer, you get an employee in the other department on the phone—a real person—and explain the situation. Then you get back on the phone with the customer, explain that you're switching her to Beth in the other department, and that Beth knows what is going on and is ready to help solve the problem. You then complete the transfer of the call. Juxtapose that with a recent experience I had on United Airlines. Not only did the airline lose my luggage; employees there cold switched me between six departments. Every phone inquiry, after twenty minutes spent on hold, began with the employee requesting my reference number rather than my name—because I wasn't a customer to them, let alone a person. Keep in mind, I'm a Premier Access customer because I travel so often. Makes you wonder how they treat their non-VIP customers.

When a workplace starts to emphasize ownership over accountability, the transformation can be striking. At RGRTA, our underperforming call center (like the United one described above) delivered long on-hold times, negative customer interactions, and long response times to customer inquiries. Our unengaged call center agents spent more time in the bathroom than they did answering calls. However, when we established an average on-hold time metric, placed a large clock on the wall that reported this metric in real time, tied the results to everyone's performance review, and established a quarterly incentive for results that were better than the goal, things changed. The supervisor no longer had to chase people back to their desks all day long; employees *chased one another* back to their desks. They had taken ownership not just over their individual results, but the entire team's results. And those results saw unprecedented improvement. Our ridership grew three times the national average. Customer satisfaction shot up 26 percent. Employees earned their incentives and had more take-home pay. Customers won. Employees won. And taxpayers won.

To a large extent, our unengaged employees themselves had been victims. They were good people who wanted to perform good work, yet management had trapped them in a bad system. When the system changed, their true colors came out. They owned the results and delivered excellence. We didn't have to impose anything on them; we just had to construct the right structure in which they could do great work and be recognized and rewarded for it.

We didn't have to impose anything on them; we just had to construct the right structure in which they could do great work and be recognized and rewarded for it.

TELL PEOPLE WHERE TO GO, NOT HOW TO GET THERE

On Thanksgiving Day 1999, Admiral Thad Allen was sitting at home in South Florida, watching a Dallas Cowboys game and eating a turkey sandwich, when the phone rang. It was someone at the Coast Guard's regional command center saying that a Coast Guard vessel stationed out of Ft. Lauderdale had made contact with a fishing boat. The fishermen had stumbled upon a five-year-old boy in an inner tube, and the boy, who didn't speak English, was in bad shape, dehydrated and cold. The sailors wanted instructions on what to do.

At the time, official U.S. policy dictated that the sailors should send this boy back home to Cuba, since he faced no credible threat of political persecution. But this was a five-year-old kid. He clearly was not going to make it back, policy or no policy. As Allen recounted to me in an interview, he decided to follow his best judgment rather than the letter of the law. Protocol would have dictated that he set up a conference call with a whole series of bureaucrats in Washington to determine how to handle things on a case-by-case basis. That would have taken hours, even days. To Allen's mind, the first order of business was to get the five-year-old to a doctor, and that meant bringing him ashore.

Once you bring a Cuban refugee onto American soil, it's appreciably harder to return him back to Cuba. Indeed, the boy, Elian Gonzalez, ended up with relatives in Florida who wanted desperately to keep him from going back to his father in his home country. And so the ordeal that would later become national news—namely, Attorney General Janet Reno's decision to send Gonzalez back to Cuba—was spurred simply because a Coast Guard admiral watching a football game believed, rightly, that a child's health should come before the demands of any particular policy.[4]

Creating a culture of ownership entails a fundamental shift in organizational mindset, from an emphasis on policies and rules to an emphasis on judgment. If grocery store clerks and other entry-level employees are often disengaged, it's because they feel compelled to mindlessly follow rules above all else. Employees are driven by something negative, fear of the consequences that come with breaking the rules, rather than something positive, a genuine affection for their job, their organization, and the customers they serve. The effort they expend staying on the straight and narrow distracts them from what is even more important: personal commitment to the organization's mission and goals. The story of Cathy Clement and Paul Smaldone shouldn't astonish us; it should be the norm. We should expect people to energetically find solutions, not cross their arms, shrug their shoulders, and fall back on rules as an obstacle and an excuse.

Organizations should encourage employees to understand and respect the rules, but they should ultimately inspire them to exercise their own judgment in applying the organization's mission, vision, and goals to specific situations. When bosses express confidence that employees possess the independent judgment required to get a job done, they encourage them to "own" the result. If you're given the latitude to figure out *how* to solve a problem, you're likely to be far more invested in its resolution. General George Patton is famous for having recommended that fellow military officers encourage the exercise of judgment, remarking: "Never tell people how to do things. Tell them what to do and they will surprise you with their ingenuity."[5] It goes to the point I made earlier: establish the "what," and then empower employees in developing the "how."

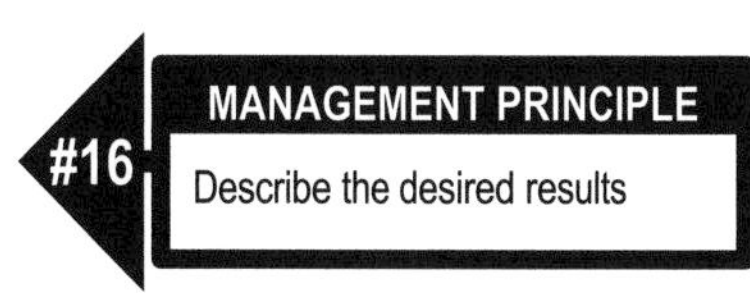

The importance of judgment has been amply borne out in the business world. As companies like Ritz-Carlton know, we get better customer satisfaction when employees are independent thinkers eager to keep the customer satisfied. Ritz-Carlton is famous for giving employees discretion to spend a certain amount of money to fulfill individual guests' wishes. If a guest feels miffed that she's had to wait too long for her car to arrive from the valet, the valet can waive the parking fee on the spot, without asking for authorization from a manager. Under this system, even the most junior employees aren't thinking simply about whether they've checked a box or completed their particular task; they're focused on the bigger picture—the output—namely, whether the guest is having a positive experience. Each employee's goals align with the company's broader vision of success. Rather than a workforce of Dilberts, Ritz-Carlton winds up with a company of superachievers.

Another company that stresses judgment over policy is Netflix. Whereas many companies institute formulas to determine how much vacation time an employee can take, Netflix has chosen *not* to promulgate a vacation policy. Employees can use their judgment in choosing when to take time off. They are held responsible for getting their jobs done, but beyond that, their time is their own. Similarly, Netflix doesn't have an expense reimbursement policy. Employees submit what they think is appropriate for work-related activities, and if it is indeed within reasonable bounds, all is good.[6] Think of the statement of trust Netflix is making to its employees. By treating employees like adults, Netflix is opening a space for them to feel a sense of ownership. A few employees might take advantage or show poor judgment, but most can and do rise to the occasion, revealing themselves as worthy of that trust. They not only get their work done, they feel more invested in the company that has let *them* decide how to work. It's worth noting that Sir Richard Branson has followed suit, doing away with vacation time at Virgin businesses, and that some technology companies allow employees to exercise discretion as to how they spend up to a fifth of their time.[7] At my company, TransPro, you got it: no vacation time. No sick time. No expense account rules. Employees use their judgment. It's the results that matter; how they achieve those results is up to them.

You might object that it's only private-sector companies that can encourage judgment; in the public sector we can't let employees do what they want when we're spending taxpayer money. I steadfastly disagree. We had exactly these kinds of policies in place at RGRTA. For example, while some administrators wanted to write pages upon pages of prescriptive rules about how and when an employee could work from home for the day, our "policy" simply said that employees and managers could work it out on a case-by-case basis. Juxtapose that with one agency I'm familiar with that has literally 150 pages of rules regarding travel, including which tickets and hotels are permissible and which ones aren't. Almost down to what kind of cheese on a hamburger is an appropriate expense, and which isn't. All this to save, at least in theory, tens of thousands of dollars a year. That very same agency spends tens of millions of dollars each year in highly inefficient service—that is just gouging both taxpayers and customers—and no one asks a question because it doesn't violate some policy. It's just stupid.

Nowhere was this better demonstrated than in St. Louis in December of 2014. Kelly Hahn, a preschool teacher at the Wilkinson Early Childhood Center had just been honored as St. Louis Public School Pre-K Teacher of the Year two weeks earlier. She was loved by her students and their parents. In December, a three- year- old preschool student was sent to school by his mother in a pull up diaper, a violation of school rules. (Yes ,they actually have a policy about the *kind* of diaper a student can wear.)

When Hahn discovered that the little boy had the "wrong" kind of diaper on, and that he had slightly soiled it, she left it on and called the parent immediately to let them know, instead of removing it as school policy required. One of Hahn's colleagues called the Missouri Department of Family Services to report this outrageous violation of policy and Han was terminated on charges of child neglect and endangerment. Even the mother of the little boy jumped into the fray saying "regardless of the policy, what happened is so minor, that it couldn't possibly warrant incriminating a fabulous teacher." After the state agency determined no indication of neglect parents confronted the St. Louis School Superintendent, coincidentally enough at an event he had sponsored on how the District was working to empower teachers, to express how absurd the District's policy was in this matter. The courageous Superintendent stuck to his policy, "That's the handcuffs that we have relating to personnel, we cannot discuss specific personnel issues" he said.[8] And then hurried back to describing how he was empowering his employees.

Infusing more judgment into public agencies is critical if those agencies are ever to get better. Taxpayers can't wish for Ritz-Carlton–quality performance from public-sector employees, and then not give them the same level of discretion that the valet parking staff at the Ritz-Carlton enjoys. And if we want employees like Paul Smaldone to go the extra mile for customers, we can't get upset when they occasionally use their discretion to break minor rules. Kelly Hahn clearly violated a rule. It just happened to be a foolish rule in this situation—and others were not willing to demonstrate some judgment because they allowed the rule to constrain them. So often, we say we want higher-quality performance, but then we gasp in horror when a reporter or auditor writes a story about how a Department of Motor Vehicles clerk broke the rules to waive a fee because a customer had waited in line too long. When the local TV station runs a sensational

Taxpayers can't wish for Ritz-Carlton-quality performance from public-sector employees, and then not give them the same level of discretion that the valet parking staff at the Ritz-Carlton enjoys.

story revealing that Paul Smaldone wasted $8 in electricity that Sunday by turning the lights on in the courthouse office, are you going to get upset, or will you applaud Smaldone's commitment to the customer experience? Stories like this get written all the time, and employees and their bosses frequently *don't* get cut a break, even when all they were doing was precisely what we should want them to do: showing judgment to get the job done right. Exactly the reason Kelly Hahn was Teacher of the Year.

Look, we're a nation of laws. Of course our policies matter. We can't let people fly to Germany without a passport, and we can't let everyone run to the courthouse on a weekend to get their documents. But in public administration we need to create cultures where employees mobilize their judgment. If retrieving a birth certificate or driving relatives to New York City or bringing these relatives to the front of a passport office line will help a critically wounded veteran, let's do that. The objective is to get the child's diaper changed—not how we go about doing it. Government needs rules, but government doesn't exist just to make people follow rules. Government exists to help citizens live better lives.

Government needs rules, but government doesn't exist just to make people follow rules. Government exists to help citizens live better lives.

OUR POLICY ON LEFT-HANDED LEPRECHAUNS

If employees at public organizations find themselves hemmed in by mountains of rules and regulations, it's often because of the way earlier crises at these organizations were handled. You see it all the time: one employee out of thousands at an agency does something wrong, and the leadership's unthinking response is to put yet another policy in place. Rather than training or terminating an offending employee, leaders limit thousands of others from using their common sense. It's gotten to the point where the media and even board members in the wake of any so-called scandal reflexively ask, "What's the policy on that?" And executives go around trying to find the policy—because even they don't know what it is—rather than terminating the employee if the misjudgment was egregious enough, or courageously saying to journalists, "Our policy is to empower our employees to use their judgment in these situations. In this situation, the employee used poor judgment, so we're going to train him and others on why that was such bad judgment and teach them what good judgment looks like."

So many agencies will boast that they have a "zero tolerance" policy for one behavior or another; they might as well say that they have a zero *judgment* policy. More than just overreacting to offensive behavior, taxpayer-funded bureaucracies often aren't able to handle it when something *good* is happening outside the norms of "standard operating procedure." If norms of behavior haven't been codified, bureaucrats feel compelled to write a set of rules to govern what's happening. And this can become the theater of the absurd in a culture that is policy focused when the taskforce charged with developing the new policy endeavors to imagine every scenario that might ever occur so they can write that into their restrictive policy. "So, if a left-handed leprechaun who was adopted on a Tuesday departs on an official trip on a day that is raining"—and then try to write a travel policy for that event—so they can defend their decision if and when a reporter, auditor, or board member asks a question about the agency's policy related to left-handed leprechauns. It is how the teacher of the year gets fired two weeks after the ceremony honoring her.

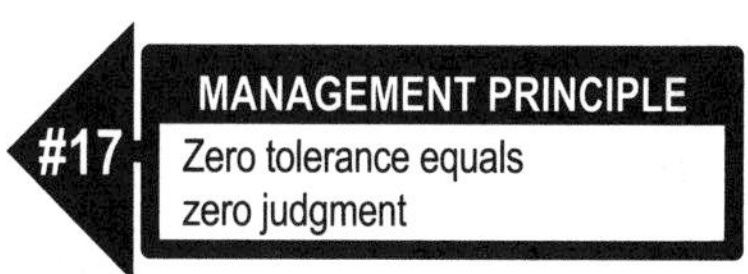

This usually undermines the sense of ownership that employees, operating out of common sense, might otherwise have felt. And the reality is we put all these restrictive rules and policies in place so we can catch people doing something wrong (as the so called whistle-blower at Kelly Hahn's preschool did)—and people still violate the rules. We get all the downside of disengaged employees who are rewarded for blindly following restrictive rules, using those rules to create obstacles in the customer experience, which obviously results in unhappy customers. Employees lose *and* customers lose.

HOW NOT TO HONOR OUR VETERANS

It isn't just public agencies that are beset by rules and a by-the-book mentality. Remember the effort George Maziarz and his public-sector colleagues went to on behalf of a wounded soldier and his family. Then consider the following story. In the fall of 2014, travelers were filing onto US Airways Flight 1930 from Portland to Charlotte. During the boarding process, a heavily decorated Army Ranger, Albert Marle, asked a flight attendant to keep his dress military jacket in a safe place so that it wouldn't get wrinkled, as he was heading to a job interview. She refused, saying that the closet was reserved for first-class customers.[9]

Predictably, in the age of social media, the entire episode went viral and US Airways had a public relations nightmare on its hands, with invective directed at the unfeeling flight attendant. But the flight attendant's decision said as much about the culture of US Airways as it did about the individual employee. US Airways had evidently imposed a environment in which rules trumped common sense. Employees felt prohibited from exercising their judgment, for fear of ignoring protocol. Even when faced with a challenge that any sentient being should know how to handle—whether to do a small service for an American hero—policy came before thoughtfulness. The flight attendant by all accounts had a bad attitude and was in serious need of some training, but if the airline had systematically encouraged judgment during its training sessions, rather than blind adherence to protocol, a more compassionate, cooler-headed colleague might well have stepped in to exhibit sound judgment, saving US Airways the bad media coverage. No colleague did, however, because in US Airways's eyes, the offending employee was doing "the right thing" by blindly following policy. It's very difficult for another employee to step in and demonstrate sound judgment when the offending, and in this case offensive, employee is actually following the policy she's been trained on repeatedly.

Leaders of large organizations often try to plan for every possible contingency (see left-handed leprechauns above); lawyers and executives sit in corporate suites developing policy books that employees are supposed to memorize and heed like robots. New hires are expected to sit through endless hours of "training" so that they can learn and follow all the rules the suits upstairs developed. All that effort goes out the door when a frontline employee leans in toward the customer, gives a knowing look, and whispers: "I agree with you, and I'd do it if I could, but our company policy says. . . ." Executives issue rules to mitigate risk, when in fact the greater risk stems from limiting employees' emotional ownership in the underlying enterprise. No single set of policy principles, no matter how comprehensive, will cover every possible situation. No compendium of best practices will prepare employees to handle every new challenge. And so, rather than imposing anticipatory rules *ad infinitum,* high-performing organizations focus on inspiring their employees to do what will most benefit the organization in the long run. Policies, as I've suggested, are guardrails; they shouldn't unduly constrain the delivery of excellence.

At the extreme, a mentality of blindly adhering to rules can alienate quality employees and even cause them to leave. I'll always remember a story I heard some years ago about an employee who stepped up for a big project that his company had won, volunteering to spend every week traveling to a city more than 1,500 miles away from his family so he could work on the project and contribute to the firm. Every week, the employee left Sunday night and returned home late on Friday night, usually after his kids had been tucked into bed. While he was on-site for the project, he was so dedicated that he typically put in twelve-hour days. One night, as he was leaving a business dinner, having worked a long day in this faraway city, he felt tempted to take a cab back to his hotel, but to save his company money he decided to walk. It started to rain, so he stopped at a newspaper stand to buy a cheap umbrella. He hurried back to the hotel, getting wet on his way despite the umbrella.

When he got back to the office, he submitted his expenses for the month: thousands of dollars in rental cars, hotels, airfare, and meals. Oh, and he also included a $5 receipt for his umbrella. Imagine his shock and dismay upon receiving an e-mail from accounting saying they were holding up his expense check until he removed his $5 umbrella reimbursement request, because it violated company policy. The bean counters even sent him a statement of the policy and highlighted it for him. To the employee, this was unforgivable. All these nights he had spent away from his family. And he had tried to *save* the company money by conscientiously walking instead of taking a $20 cab ride. The next month, the employee submitted his expenses just as he was supposed to. Only this time, he added a little note at the bottom of the expense statement: "Good luck finding the umbrella."

Once the message that "it's okay to think on the job" has been sent, there are three other steps leaders can take to spread the culture of ownership among line workers.

Meeting Cadence

First, break with the way most organizations traditionally distribute information. We all have a mental image, most likely derived from any number of television shows, of how police departments traditionally organize meetings at local precincts: at the beginning of each shift, line officers gather in an area that looks like a high school classroom. The commanding officer arrives to speak from behind a podium at the front of the room, and the officers listen attentively as they receive their instructions. They all then leave for their radio cars.

The problem with this model is that it treats those on the front lines—the uniformed officers in this example, but more broadly those working under a supervisor who controls their agenda—as cogs in a wheel. The mode of communication runs top down, from boss to employee. We are lecturing rather than doing what we should do: leading. The people receiving the instructions aren't being encouraged to think for themselves. By implication and often by design, those in the chairs are being told what to do.

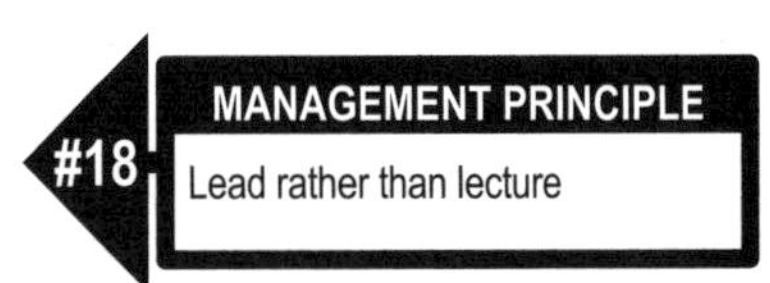

That's not what meetings should be. Interactions between members of any team should be empowering and energizing. By requiring open communication up *and* down the chain of command, those at the top can send a crucial message: ideas offered by those working the front lines matter. Workers aren't simply minions, but true decision makers. Remember, we said earlier that leaders have a responsibility to create a safe space for conversations. By the same token, it's the employee's responsibility to say the same thing in the meeting that she will later tell her family upon returning home. Now we have the recipe for a meeting!

It's the employee's responsibility to say the same thing in the meeting that she will later tell her family upon returning home.

As a meeting is wrapping up, I often put a decision on the table and say directly to participants, "Tell me why this won't work." I get immediate feedback that teaches me about my blind spots, and I give subordinates direct permission to challenge me. Equally important, if no one can argue why the potential decision I've put on the table isn't wise, the group now owns the decision every bit as much as I do. Employees and their teams will be that much more likely to execute properly, because they are invested in success.

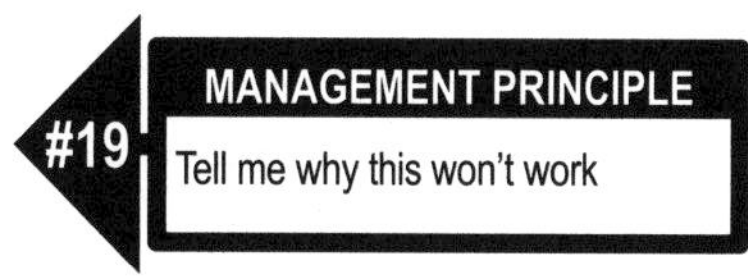

For too long, organizations have allowed meetings to become venues for discussing the latest distraction, a practice that amounts to organized squirrel chasing. To make organizations work most effectively, we must replace that impulse with a different norm of collaboration, guidance, and judgment. Focused meetings are about reviewing information related to results, not about the effort of individuals. We're essentially saying, "This is how we defined success. This is how your unit did, and this is how it compares to another unit." Think of the stats shared during halftime of a football or basketball game: time of possession, turnovers, yards rushing, and so on. That's what we're doing, offering a useful update on performance in relative terms.

If you want to know what a difference focused, two-way communication during meetings can make, just ask Jim Bennett, now the city administrator of Presque Isle, Maine.[10] One morning in the fall of 1996, he kissed his wife and two young children goodbye and settled into his new office in the town of Westbrook, Maine. Bennett had been a town manager in a municipality just a few miles away for the previous seven years, but he was excited to begin a new gig as town administrator. Because he had no real relationship with anyone on staff, he'd planned to spend the day developing rapport. Nature had a different plan. As Bennett drove to work, a storm began to dump a nearly unprecedented amount of rain on the surrounding area. In the end, nearly twenty inches of precipitation fell on the area surrounding Westbrook. Flow on the nearby Presumpscot River was 68 percent beyond what it had been at any point in the previous century, and peak flows in three of the river's tributaries were estimated to be so rare as to occur only once every five hundred years. The implications were dire. What the riverbeds couldn't handle began to pour out onto the roads and fields.

By late morning of that first day, it was clear to Bennett that the town was facing a major catastrophe. He began to call in his staff of new colleagues to assess what resources they had to deal with the flooding. As team members sat around a table at Town Hall, Bennett took the usual top-down approach, peppering his subordinates aggressively with questions: How many police officers were on duty? What sort of equipment did the fire department have at its disposal? Determined to take control of the situation and demonstrate his leadership as the new administrator, Bennett demanded immediate answers so he could issue directives from on high. His subordinates responded with suspicious glances and responses that were short, reluctant, and not especially helpful. Clearly, Bennett's approach wasn't working.

To his credit, Bennett switched gears on the fly, alternatively asking each department head how he or she would have handled the situation before Bennett arrived. The shift in approach—empowering the staff, rather than barking at them—encouraged individual members of the team to come forward with their solutions, many of which were more thoughtful than the team would have come up with had Bennett controlled the response.

By two in the afternoon, Westbrook was indeed facing a full-on crisis. The town had begun to lose culverts, and streets were flooding. By suppertime, many of the town's roads were entirely washed out. Most worrisome to Bennett personally was that he had lost contact with his family; he'd left his wife and two children at their condo in a neighboring town, which was being hit with many of the same conditions. It was only by catching a glimpse of his son on the local news sitting at the police chief's office in a nearby town that he learned they had, in fact, been rescued. A photo of their rescue by boat was later picked up in national news stories about the flooding.

By late in the evening, water was engulfing one of the town's most heavily trafficked bridges. Because those looking to travel from one part of town to another had few options but to traverse that particular span, many drivers were ignoring the barricades the town had erected to prevent their passage. Rumors swirled that someone from a town nearby had driven around the barricades, gotten caught up in the flow, and been washed away. Bennett and some of the town's other officials worried that the bridge itself would collapse.

At this point, Bennett made a risky decision. He issued an order to block the bridge with school buses commandeered from the nearby depots. It wasn't explicitly clear that Bennett had the authority to take the buses—he hadn't even been on the job a day—but he directed the police and public works departments to take them anyway. He figured he could worry about the consequences later (it seemed pretty likely at this point that there wasn't going to be school the next day). Once the town had taken possession, drivers used the buses to block the roads, preventing drivers from passing through and crossing the bridge. It was an ingenious solution for several reasons. First, the buses established an impenetrable barrier. But more important, having buses parked at either end of the bridge eliminated the need to place police officers nearby; with a larger stationary barrier now in place, a town already short staffed could deploy its personnel elsewhere.

Over the course of the day, the team that had come together in the morning made dozens of similar decisions. In the heat of the moment, they weren't consulting statutes or regulations passed down from decades before. Each member of Westbrook's management team possessed an area of expertise, and with Bennett's blessing, he or she did what needed to be done, regardless of the "policy." Bennett himself took care to avoid issuing heavy-handed directives, believing that in most cases those who had been on the job had a better sense of what needed to be done. Giving the staff latitude to maneuver established an unusual degree of camaraderie, effectiveness, and ownership.

Establish Expectations

The second step on the road to authentic buy-in from an organization's workforce is to have employees and their managers sign an annual Individual Ownership Agreement that specifies not which *policies* the employee agrees to follow, but the *outcomes* and *values* the organization expects the employee to meet and embody. Remember, we've already built a system to measure what matters at the organizational and department levels. We train people so that they have the skills required to deliver on those metrics (and recall, as well, the goals we set were achievable, challenging, and also collaborative). We also established owners: the one person responsible for delivering on a scorecard metric. Now we're putting that ownership down on paper and obtaining explicit commitments. So many organizations require that employees sign their employee handbook, which almost nobody reads. Did the employee really understand and assent to the myriad of policies established by the organization? How meaningful is such a signature, really? And how empowering is that to the employee?

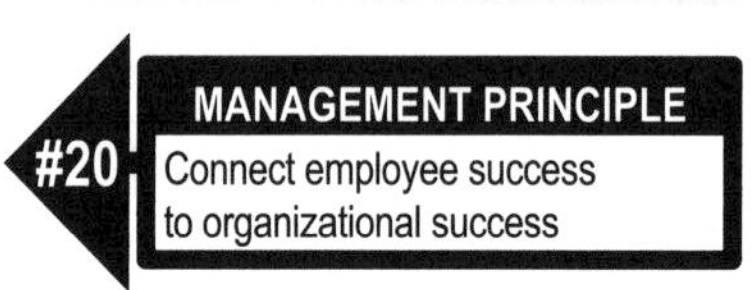

The goal here is to explicitly convey that employees can't thrive just by coming to work or completing a set of mundane tasks; they must buy into the organization's broader mission and approach challenges with a results-oriented mindset. It's crucial that employees sign these agreements at the beginning of each year so that they clearly understand their organization's expectations of them. Each employee's direct supervisor should draft and sign these agreements, with the expectation that the two will meet quarterly to discuss the progress made over the previous three months and to review what they still must accomplish in order to deliver success.

As figure 5-1 shows, the agreement should consist of three parts. The first is the most important: what constitutes the employee's "success moment." We want the employee to envision what exactly it would take for him to hit his mark for the year. The second and third parts are centered, respectively, around "organizational successes" and "personal values successes." The supervisor should make clear from the outset the percentage of an employee's year-end review that will center on objective or measurable standards and the percentage that will relate to management's more subjective assessment of how well he's embodied the organization's values.

The second section, focused on the more objective measurements, hinges on items an employee can track on her own: the number of sales she's completed; the feedback from customers she's collected; the outcomes

INDIVIDUAL OWNERSHIP AGREEMENT

NAME ______________________________

PERSONAL PERFORMANCE SUCCESS

ORGANIZATIONAL SUCCESS			QUARTERLY SCORECARD			
STRATEGIC AREA	Goal	Goal Points	Q1	Q2	Q3	Q4
Financial						
Customer Satisfaction						
Quality						
Safety						
DEPARTMENT SUCCESS						
Financial						
Customer Satisfaction						
Quality						
Safety						
INDIVIDUAL SUCCESS						
Financial						
Customer Satisfaction						
Quality						
Safety						
	Total Objective Score	100				

PERSONAL VALUES SUCCESS

	1	2	3	4	5	6	7	8	9	10
I am a team player.	❐	❐	❐	❐	❐	❐	❐	❐	❐	❐
I treat my colleagues with respect.	❐	❐	❐	❐	❐	❐	❐	❐	❐	❐
I arrive to meetings on time and prepared.	❐	❐	❐	❐	❐	❐	❐	❐	❐	❐
I meet deadlines.	❐	❐	❐	❐	❐	❐	❐	❐	❐	❐
I am courteous to my clients.	❐	❐	❐	❐	❐	❐	❐	❐	❐	❐

Total Values Score	100				

PERSONAL SUMMARY	GOAL	Q1	Q2	Q3	Q4
TOTAL OBJECTIVE SCORE					
TOTAL VALUES SCORE					
TOTAL EVAL SCORE	100				

INCENTIVE OPPORTUNITIES

Salary	Incentive Opportunities	Value of Additional Benefits	Total Compensation Opportunities
$xx,xxx.00	95% of goal – $xx,xxx.00 Goal – $xx,xxx.00 105% of goal – $xx,xxx.00	$xx,xxx.00	$xx,xxx.00

We have reviewed this Individual Ownership Agreement and are fully in agreement on the objectives, goals, and incentive opportunities outlined.

Employee Name (signature)______________________ Supervisor Name (signature) ____________________

FIGURE 5-1

of services she's provided. In each case, there is a certain standard against which the employee can measure her own performance; that way she'll be able to glean during quarterly check-ins whether she's exceeded, met, or fallen short of expectations. Remember from the previous chapter that all these goals were set collaboratively with employees rather than imposed.

EVAL® QUARTERLY SUMMARY OF INDIVIDUAL RESULTS

Success Moment	On Target Y/N	Year to Date	Projection

ANNUAL ORGANIZATIONAL GOALS	Goal Points	Actual Points	INCENTIVES		
			Goal	Overperform	Stretch
Financial			$xxx	$xxx	$xxx
Customer Satisfaction			$xxx	$xxx	$xxx
Quality			$xxx	$xxx	$xxx
Safety			$xxx	$xxx	$xxx
ANNUAL DEPARTMENT GOALS	Goal Points	Actual Points	INCENTIVES		
			Goal	Overperform	Stretch
Financial			$xxx	$xxx	$xxx
Customer Satisfaction			$xxx	$xxx	$xxx
Quality			$xxx	$xxx	$xxx
Safety			$xxx	$xxx	$xxx
ANNUAL INDIVIDUAL GOALS	Goal Points	Actual Points	INCENTIVES		
			Goal	Overperform	Stretch
Financial			$xxx	$xxx	$xxx
Customer Satisfaction			$xxx	$xxx	$xxx
Quality			$xxx	$xxx	$xxx
Safety			$xxx	$xxx	$xxx
TOTAL OBJECTIVE SCORE	80				

PERSONAL VALUES SUCCESS

Average Values Score	1	2	3	4	5	6	7	8	9	10
	❒	❒	❒	❒	❒	❒	❒	❒	❒	❒

	Goal Points	Actual Points
TOTAL OBJECTIVE SCORE	20	
TOTAL PERSONAL EVAL SCORE	**100**	

INCENTIVES EARNED

Organizational Contribution Incentive	Departmental Contribution Incentive	Individual Contribution Incentive	**Total EVAL Incentive**
$xxx.00	$xxx.00	$xxx.00	**$x,xxx.00**

FOCUS FOR NEXT QUARTER

START DOING	STOP DOING	CONTINUE DOING

FIGURE 5-2

The more subjective set of goals, designed to incentivize employees to embrace a certain set of values, are measured on a scale of one to ten. And organizations need to make the values clear and precise: "I am a team player"; "I am courteous to my clients"; "I treat my colleagues with respect." These are items that require managers to keep watchful eyes on each employee's performance. The point is not to spur managers to micro-manage; rather, it is to help mold the ways in which each team member approaches his job and interacts with colleagues. Simply hitting the objective goals won't suffice, if only because achieving measurable results with the wrong attitude can undermine the company's broader success.

The quarterly performance-review meetings are essential, because they occur with enough frequency to prevent employees from losing focus and to give managers an opportunity to steer wayward individuals in the right direction. After six or twelve months, employees can easily lose sight of how the organization defines true success. By ensuring that a review takes place every three months, organizations can help keep things on track. Supervisors will have a chance to provide honest and open feedback (the review of objective results really forces that), while employees can explain their challenges and frustrations. We actually use a quarterly tracking document that communicates clearly what we want an employee to start doing, what he should stop doing, and what he should continue doing. Having these items in writing means that no nasty surprises will pop up during the formal annual performance review.

Incentive Compensation

One of the strongest ways to build a deep culture of ownership in your organization is to tie compensation explicitly to performance. Some percentage of each employee's salary should correspond to how well she has done, how well the team has done, and how well the entire organization has done in meeting certain organizational success metrics. At TransPro, we created three incentive opportunities for most employees utilizing the following six-step structure:

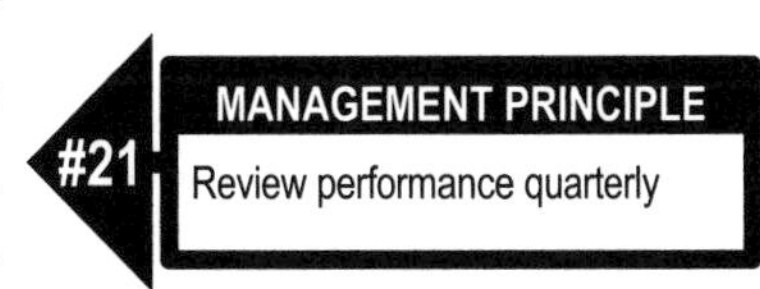

1. ***Set incentives at the beginning of the year.*** Just as we define success, prioritize performance metrics, and set goals for the organization before the year begins, so must we do it for members of our workforce individually. Setting incentives is a critical part of this. The process typically starts with the board or legislature setting incentives for the top executive. She in turns sets them for her direct reports, and this cascades throughout the organization. Obviously a wise boss sets employees incentives in ways that support her own. That is how we get everyone in the organization rowing in the same direction; individual incentives match up with the definition of organizational success. With this structure in place, every employee knows exactly what she must do to earn her incentive, and if she achieves it, what her benefit will be. *She* determines her compensation, not her boss.

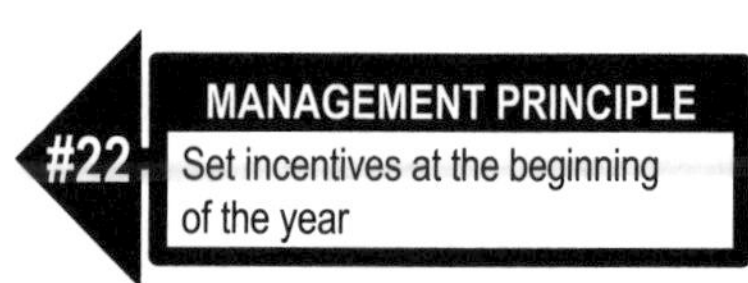

2. ***Set corresponding metrics for the organization, the team, and individuals.*** Establishing three kinds of corresponding metrics is what allows an organization to get employees behaving like that custodian at NASA, who said to the president of the United States that he was "helping to put a man on the moon." In chapter 4 we established a "stock price" for the organization, one composite number measuring organizational success. And, just like a publicly traded company with a real stock price, public organizations should report this number publicly every quarter. Senior executives should peg their largest incentive to this number, since they, logically, have the most control over and responsibility for organizational achievement. However, we want to peg some small part of a frontline employee's compensation to this number as well; this will help the employee to understand and appreciate the state of the organization's overall well-being. This, of course, would comprise the smallest portion of the employee's overall incentive opportunities, since he has the least amount of direct control or responsibility.

Both the senior executive and the frontline employee would also have a departmental incentive, comprising the middling portion of their incentives. The senior executive receives this because he is responsible for the overall leadership of the department, and the frontline employee receives it to incent him to encourage and lead colleagues to perform well as a group. You'll remember the old adage in sports, "There's no 'I' in team." This incentive is what helped prompt our call center staff to chase one another out of the bathrooms; employees had a shared stake in the *team's* hold-time performance.

And finally, there is an individual incentive, the largest for the frontline employee and the smallest for the senior executive. We design it this way because the senior executive has broader responsibility and authority, whereas the entry-level employee has a much smaller scope of responsibility for others and is largely responsible for delivering excellence for himself and a smaller team around him. At TransPro, we build a composite score for each employee corresponding to this incentive, rolling objective and subjective metrics into one number that in turn establishes the employee's eligibility for an incentive (think of the SAT score for students). We call this the "Eval Score," which I'll detail below in step four.

3. ***Set stepped-up goals: Goal, Overperform, Stretch.*** For each of the three incentive opportunities, we establish three levels of performance: Goal, Overperform, and Stretch. Imagine that the goal is a customer satisfaction rating of 80 percent (remember that customer satisfaction is made up of true operational performance on one side of the ledger and customers' impressions on the other). All employees would have an incentive associated with customer satisfaction at the beginning of the year; if we achieve the 80 percent goal, they would be paid a certain dollar amount. However, we want to inspire employees to exceed that goal. We don't want the nose of the football to just squeeze over the goal line; we want employees to run the ball in and spike it in celebration. So we establish an Overperform goal, perhaps 5 percent beyond the goal. Similarly, we might establish a goal that we all, at the beginning of the year, think we cannot attain. Our Stretch goal might be 12 percent beyond what the achievable goal is (you'll remember our rule that all goals must be attainable). If we were to realize that Stretch marker, the organization would pay an even larger incentive.

4. *Create an Eval Score.* As I mentioned above, the third incentive, the individual one for each employee, is based on a composite, SAT-like score we build for each employee. The combined incentive, distributed every quarter, indicates to all employees how well they individually are doing. They can either strive to replicate their success in the following quarter, or work harder to improve. They can also compare their Eval Scores with colleagues to get a better sense of how they did (much as students do with their SAT scores).

5. *Use an incentive pay cycle.* Paying incentives frequently is critical, particularly for entry-level and frontline employees, and particularly to reward operational performance. When we work with an organization, we create a structure so that the company pays its operational performance incentives quarterly and its financial performance incentives annually. We do this for three reasons. First, we want to remind employees regularly that they either did or did not achieve certain results, and that's why they are or are not receiving a check. Second, we want to compensate employees for achievement as close to when the accomplishment occurred as possible. And third, we pay financial incentives annually to help reduce the likelihood of "gaming" the system (an organization

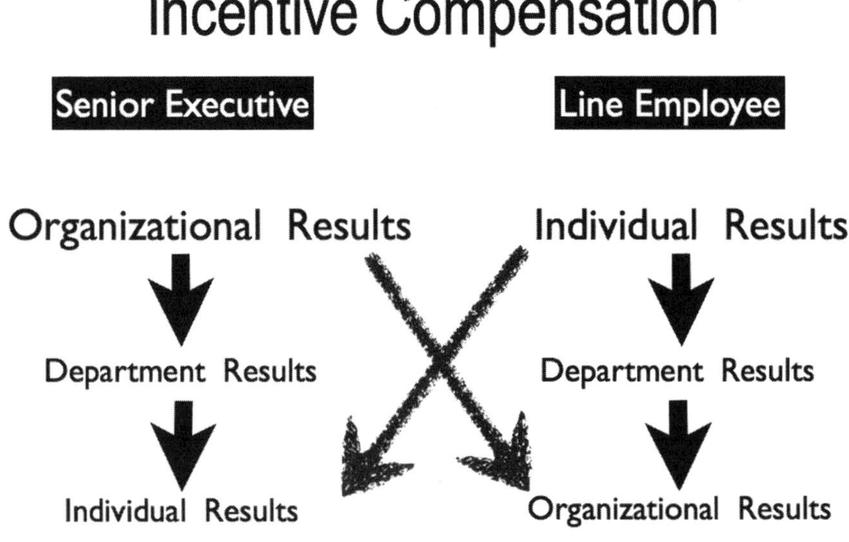

FIGURE 5-3

might delay paying some bills until the day after the quarter ends to make it look like the agency is in stronger financial position than they truly are).

6. ***Make incentives public.*** Finally, we encourage organizations to pay incentives in the course of presenting results in a group setting. We always gather the entire team together, reminding everyone how we defined success and how actual performance compares. One by one, we call employees up, hand them their incentive checks, and announce what they are receiving their incentive for. We don't share the dollar amounts publicly, but we do want people to directly connect organizational results and individual benefits.

Echoing the discussion in the last chapter, be sure you have the *right* metrics in place when crafting incentives, metrics that reflect results rather than effort.

Many Americans applaud when elected officials pound the podium and whip crowds into frenzies, calling on government to run more like a business. Those very same officials then criticize public agencies when they compensate employees in a manner consistent with private-sector principles—namely, paying incentive compensation in exchange for strong results. "That's their job," these officials say. "Why pay them a bonus to do it?" Well, it's also the "job" of people in the private sector. We're not talking about handing out "profitability bonuses," since government doesn't run up profits. But government *can* reduce its reliance on taxpayer dollars. It can improve efficiency and customer satisfaction. Shouldn't we compensate people for delivering real results rather than just punching a time clock to "do their job"? We shouldn't say, "We need to run government more like a business," and then fail to compensate employees according to the actual results they produce. It doesn't make sense.

Many public agencies we work with report that politics prevents them from building incentive compensation programs. Well, when do we stand up and say that we're going to set politics aside and make *performance* the gold standard? In this area,

> When do we stand up and say we're going to set politics aside and make performance the gold standard?

we need executives with the courage to lead elected officials, media, and taxpayers, helping them realize that proper compensation for results is *exactly* what builds high-performance organizations, just like in the private sector. When we get compensation right, when we encourage the right behaviors rather than encouraging people to play it safe just to get a pension, we'll truly have public-sector services rendered with a private-sector mindset. This is one of the big steps required to get the infrastructure of government right, so that we can improve the quality of the nation's infrastructure.

Thinking back to my time at the RGRTA, I am convinced that we produced such extraordinary results for two critical reasons: we had a clear performance measurement system that let us monitor both organizational success and the departmental inputs that would produce the desired outputs; and we built a compensation system that penetrated deeply into the organization, paying employees at all levels for results. At first our unionized employees resisted incentive compensation, preferring a one-size-fits-all approach. Over time, as we presented quarterly results and handed out incentive compensation checks in exchange for real results, unionized employees began to see that their work really mattered, and some of our unions elected to participate. When employees improved on-time performance and our customers said they had cleaned the buses better, our employees who did the work got checks.

It made no sense to pay me, the CEO, for better on-time performance; I wasn't driving the bus. It did make sense for us to pay the people who actually did the work. Compare this approach with that of so many organizations today, in which leaders at the top get fat bonuses while people who do the actual work get very little or nothing at all. This doesn't create a culture of ownership, but the exact opposite. Incentive compensation seeks to align everyone so they're moving in the same direction. Through compensation, we really *are* all in this together. If the organization wins, we all win. If it fails, we all fail.

New England Patriots coach Bill Belichick seems to get this. He has built the Patriots into a legacy team that has won four super bowls in fourteen years. When a player in the organization makes a mistake, Belichick doesn't single him out for punishment. The entire team does extra pushups, a practice that creates unity of purpose. Individual players have taken notice. In 2005, star quarterback Tom Brady stunned sportswriters by signing a six-year, $60 million contract. What was surprising wasn't that Brady's compensation was so large; it was that it was so little—in fact, $38 million less than what star quarterback Peyton Manning, then with the Indianapolis Colts, took home. Brady explained that he wanted the Patriots to have more money available to bring in other great players to produce team results. *Sports Illustrated* writer Peter King reported that he had never witnessed anything comparable, and, "if you think that plays well in the locker room, you're right!"[11] Brady's move reflects a strong culture of ownership. As we might expect, Brady has incentives in his contract to ensure that when the team wins on the field, he wins financially—and he *only* wins financially when the team wins.

EVERYDAY HEROES

If our first impulse in a crisis is to institute still more rules, it's time for us to take a step back. We might think more rules can prevent a flight attendant from refusing a hero's request to have his military uniform hung in the closet. But as I've argued in this chapter, rules and an ethic of mere accountability too frequently overwhelm what is even more important: good judgment. In any organization of a certain size, employees are regularly asked to make scores of decisions every day, from the mundane to the consequential. It's not possible for those sitting in an executive suite to anticipate every circumstance or prescribe a solution to every problem. Employees from the ground up need to take ownership of the challenges they will face, and management needs to either trust their judgment, give them a different assignment, or get them to the door.

It's not easy to instill a culture of ownership within an enterprise accustomed to simple top-down management, but the two core elements of the task—convincing managers to trust those on the front lines and demanding responsibility from those given additional authority to make their own decisions—are eminently achievable. I've had the good fortune to see over and over again just what's possible when line employees take full ownership of their jobs. One episode in particular sticks out. Early one morning in February 2008, I was returning from a conference in Phoenix, travelling to Dallas and then back to Rochester. The RGRTA was deeply immersed in the development of our annual Success Plan, and I was looking forward to spending seven hours of travel time marking up the first full version of the plan. The final version would be going to the board in just two weeks, and I needed to send in my comments on this draft by early the next morning.

Unfortunately, the file was too large, and I couldn't download it onto my computer. It was too late for me to have the file overnighted to me. On the way to the airport, I spoke to my assistant, April, and our communications team, expressing my frustration. We brainstormed ways they might get the file to me, and none of them would work. It seemed hopeless, and I resigned myself to losing a precious day of reviewing and commenting on this, our most important document of the year.

I boarded the plane for the quick flight to Dallas. Upon arrival, I didn't even make it up the gangway when I heard a woman calling my name. "Mr. Aesch? Mr. Mark Aesch?" She introduced herself as the executive assistant to the CEO of the Dallas Airport Authority. That is never a good sign. My face went blank. I could only imagine what awful tragedy she was about to share with me. She explained that April from my office had called her to explain the situation of our technological woes, and that April had sent her the file. This assistant had printed out the 250-page document, come to my gate, and was now personally handing me this massive document so I could review it on my five-hour flight to Rochester.

It was incredible: so many others might have given up in the face of the obstacles, but April had found her way to a solution. She had owned the fact that solving this was critical. She could have just thrown up her hands, blaming the situation on technology, in effect, passing the buck. But somehow she had tracked down the phone number for the Dallas Airport Authority, and had even thought of the right office to call. Then she had talked this woman, who was a total stranger, into being helpful and got her to hand-deliver it. April followed through, owning the situation from beginning to end and pulling off a miracle.

I spent my flight to Rochester marking up the document, turning it in as planned the next morning at 8 a.m. Two weeks later, our board passed the plan unanimously. Six months after that, we became the only transit system in America to reduce fares amidst a terrible recession. Senior leadership at our organization could have claimed ownership of that result, but in truth our success was owed to the heroic acts of everyday employees. It takes people like April—a whole organization of them—to pull off extraordinary results. And it will take people like April—tens of millions of them—to save America.

During his famous inaugural address, President Kennedy implored Americans to ask not what government could do for us, but what we could do for our nation. He was asking us to take ownership of our behavior, of our churches and streets—to do our part. Certainly we as citizens must do so, but as workers we must as well; and, just as crucially, leaders must guide us and set up structures so that ownership becomes both possible and prominent. But of course, that's not the end of the process by which we might rebuild America. Even with a vision, a plan in place, metrics to measure results, and employees invested in their work, organizations still must develop ways of making adjustments midstream to keep performance at its best. After all, as good as any plan might be, it cannot account for everything; some degree of adaptation and flexibility must be built into an organization's operations. How public agencies might do that is the subject of the next chapter.

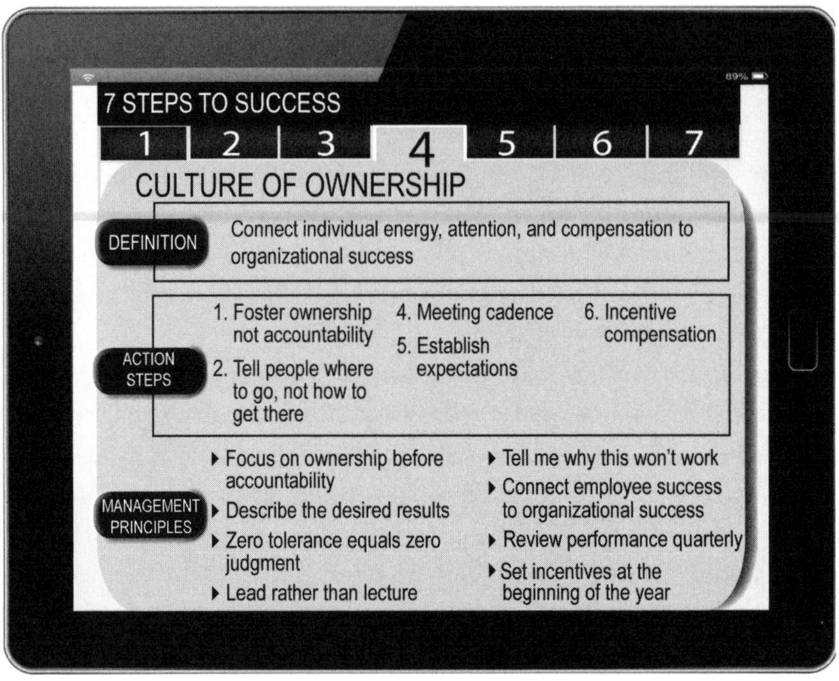
7 STEPS TO SUCCESS
1 2 3 4 5 6 7
CULTURE OF OWNERSHIP
DEFINITION
Connect individual energy, attention, and compensation to organizational success
ACTION STEPS
1. Foster ownership not accountability
2. Tell people where to go, not how to get there
4. Meeting cadence
5. Establish expectations
6. Incentive compensation
MANAGEMENT PRINCIPLES
Focus on ownership before accountability
Describe the desired results
Zero tolerance equals zero judgment
Lead rather than lecture
Tell me why this won't work
Connect employee success to organizational success
Review performance quarterly
Set incentives at the beginning of the year

FIGURE 5-4

6

Manage Results As They Come In

In the annals of the Second World War, one of the most famous assaults of June 6, 1944, or D-Day, took place at Pointe du Hoc, a promontory overlooking the coast in Normandy, France. In the initial planning for the assault, Lt. Col. James Earl Rudder wasn't slotted to participate. When he was told that he was too valuable to lead what would become renowned as one of D-Day's most dangerous operations, the young Texan responded with unusual candor. Rudder looked back at Lt. Gen. Clarence Huebner and simply replied: "I'm sorry to have to disobey you, sir, but if I don't take it, it may not go."[1]

The mission's objective was daunting. For months, the Nazis had been preparing for the Allied invasion they knew was coming. By the time the Allies launched Operation Overlord in early June 1944, the German military had fortified most of the French coastline. In many of the most strategically placed locations, they had built casements to protect the artillery they would use to repel any invading force. In Normandy, one such location was Pointe du Hoc, situated between Utah and Omaha Beaches. The German cannons there had the ability to pivot and could fire on both beaches within seconds, wreaking havoc on an invading force. Everyone knew that silencing those guns early would prove critical to the success of any invasion.

Achieving that goal was easier said than done. The cliffs below the Pointe were 100 feet high in places, and any unit attempting to scale them would be exposed throughout the climb to enemy fire. Nevertheless,

Rudder's assignment was to lead three companies of U.S. Army Rangers up and over the cliffs, defeat the German units assigned to defend the guns, and disable the cannons so that the troops arriving on the beaches below were spared their wrath.[2]

The landing was scheduled to begin at 0630 hours, after the three companies of men under Rudder's command had departed England in fourteen separate vessels under the cover of night. The men were thoroughly prepared, having trained for months for just this sort of mission. But almost as soon as the operation had begun, Rudder was forced to alter the carefully laid plan. Two of the group's ships sank while traversing the English Channel, diminishing the strength of the three companies attacking the Pointe. More distressing, when they reached the shores of Normandy, they realized that a strong tide had pushed their flotilla three miles east of the target. Now they would have to double back along the shoreline.

For the next thirty-five minutes, Rudder's men steamed back west, exposed all the while to incoming fire from the Germans on shore. By the time they finally reached the cliffs, they had missed the deadline before which they might have hoped to receive reinforcements. The companies of additional Rangers scheduled to join them would now have to join the assault on the beaches below. Rudder's men alone would have to make the assault on the cannons.[3]

Arriving at the Pointe, Rudder and his men again had to improvise. Because they had been pushed off course, all three companies were now on the eastern side of the cliffs, rendering obsolete the group's original plan to attack from both sides. In addition, the morning's aerial bombardment had made it impossible for the vessels on which they were riding to get close enough to the shore for the Rangers to climb directly up. That meant the whole group would first have to traverse the rocky and treacherous beach.

Finally, the choppy water had soaked many of the attendant ropes. Grappling hooks had been attached at the end of each line, and specially equipped rocket-propelled launchers were supposed to boost the hooks to near the top of the precipice. But the extra water weight now meant that the riggings wouldn't extend nearly as far. Nevertheless, Rudder's men forged ahead.[4] As President Ronald Reagan explained it on a commemoration held on the fortieth anniversary of D-Day:

> The Rangers looked up and saw the enemy soldiers at the edge of the cliffs, shooting down at them with machine guns and throwing grenades. And the American Rangers began to climb. They shot rope ladders over the face of these cliffs and began to pull themselves up. When one Ranger fell, another would take his place. When one rope was cut, a Ranger would grab another and begin his climb again. They climbed, shot back, and held their footing. Soon, one by one, the Rangers pulled themselves over the top. . . .[5]

That's when Rudder and his men were thrown the most puzzling curveball of all. Much to their surprise, after overcoming so many earlier obstacles, after fighting and climbing their way up a cliff while clinging onto a rope with one hand and a machine gun with the other, when they reached the inside of the Nazi fortifications, the guns weren't even there! The Germans had managed to fool Allied intelligence, replacing the cannons with telephone poles. Fortunately, tracks in the dirt suggested that the actual guns had been dragged further inland. And so, once again, the group was forced to deviate from the initial battle plan.

At this point, Rudder split his men into two groups. The first would stay near the Pointe, set up a command post, tend to the wounded, and repel any counterattack from the German forces. The second would set out in search of the guns. These amounted to some of the most treacherous moments for the Rangers, because German soldiers were mobilizing to retake the Pointe even as Allied shells flew overhead. The fighting that followed was both vicious and relentless. Rudder himself was shot in the leg and thrown by an errant British shell.

It wasn't until well after 0800 that two of Rudder's men finally came upon the original target. Five cannons sat in a field situated well behind the casements, each carefully hidden beneath camouflage netting. Oddly enough, the Germans had left the huge guns unprotected. Realizing that this was an opportune moment to strike, the Rangers placed silent thermite grenades at strategic points within the artillery, thereby melting much of the machinery inside. By 0900, and despite the myriad unexpected challenges that threatened to derail the Rangers, the mission had been accomplished. Almost nothing had gone according to plan, and yet the assault had achieved its objective. Success had been realized.

For Rudder's men, that success hardly marked the end of the battle. For nearly two full days, and despite nearly a half-dozen German counter-offensives, the Rangers held their ground without reinforcements, showing remarkable heroism. Rudder had held command over 225 men at the beginning of the battle; when the battle was over, fewer than a hundred emerged alive and uninjured. Still, their brothers in arms had not fallen in vain. Had the cannons stationed there been available to the Germans through the whole of D-Day, the carnage along Omaha and Utah Beaches would have been immeasurably worse.[6] Rudder would later receive the Distinguished Service Cross for his bravery that day, and he would command an entire infantry regiment later in the campaign. After the war, he would return to Texas, and eventually become president of Texas A&M University.[7]

It's impossible to hear the story of Pointe du Hoc without standing in awe of the Rangers' grit and determination. The image of soldiers struggling up ropes amid a hail of machine-gun fire defines courage at its root. But there's another essential point here: the importance of recalibration. What would have happened if Rudder hadn't steered the men back toward the cliffs, and instead joined the invasion on Omaha Beach? What if the group had given up when they realized that they couldn't position the boats close enough to the cliffs to make the climb directly? What if they had simply abandoned the search when they realized that the cannons were actually telephone poles? All the planning for the assault that had taken place for Pointe du Hoc was not enough to yield victory on a battlefield that was fluid and unpredictable. To succeed, Rudder needed dexterity, adaptability, and flexibility in the moment. In this respect, the assault on Pointe du Hoc illustrates a famous military axiom often attributed to Dwight Eisenhower: "No plan survives contact with the enemy."[8]

No business plan survives contact with reality, either. In both the public and private sectors, an ability to adjust midstream can strongly enhance performance, even making the difference between success or failure. It's one thing to have a goal or destination in mind, quite another to actually *get there.* Leaders must be able to adapt to new circumstances, and they need systems and processes in place that allow, encourage, and empower their organizations to change course midstream. The definition of success remains unchanged—we must destroy the cannons—yet the process of delivering success will evolve throughout the course of delivering it. The "what" remains rigid, while the "how" must be adaptive to the reality at hand.

The definition of success remains unchanged—we must destroy the cannons—yet the process of delivering success will evolve throughout the course of delivering it.

When there's a downturn in the economy, or a hiccup in the production line, or a massive spike in energy costs, or an unexpected spate of retirements in the ranks of an agency's middle management, those at the top need to be able to adjust accordingly. They need a mechanism for resilience. What exactly does this mechanism look like? And how might public organizations best implement it to help themselves run more efficiently and effectively, so that they can in turn deliver the agreed-upon results to service users and taxpayers?

THE PERILS OF INFLEXIBILITY

Most fundamentally, resilience in management comes down to attitude. Before leaders can institute any particular system of adaptation, they must be *willing* to deviate from plan and change midstream. History offers many cautionary tales of individuals and organizations that weren't willing to adjust, and that paid the price.

You may recall the film adaptation of Sebastian Junger's book *The Perfect Storm,* which hit theaters in 2000. The film's plot was based loosely on the story of the *Andrea Gail,* a boat that cruised into a terrible storm while fishing off the coast of Massachusetts a decade earlier. The boat's crew, frustrated by a lousy seasonal catch, set out late in the season to see if they couldn't snatch success from the jaws of disappointment.

In their daring, they tempted Mother Nature and wound up getting caught in an unusually fierce storm—the *perfect* storm. For those who have not read the book or seen the movie, I won't spoil the ending, but let's just say when a perfect storm arises on the horizon, you might want to get to safety as quickly as possible.

The crew of the *Andrea Gail* may have been ill advised to head out so late in the fishing season, but in reality (at least as depicted by Junger) the crew's fate stemmed not from their initial decision, nor even from the weather, but from the simple failure of those aboard the ship to adjust their plan as circumstances changed. The boat's crew could have avoided an unpleasant fate at any number of junctures if had it taken a different course of action. Had the crew been willing to sacrifice their catch when the *Andrea Gail*'s refrigeration unit broke, for instance, they would not have felt so compelled to steam to shore through the storm. Had the captain not chosen to speed over a cresting wave while racing to escape the tumult, the boat might not have capsized. The boat's final outcome owed to a series of relatively small decisions, not a single big one. The failure to change course, even when maintaining the mission, put the crew in mortal danger.

As a counterpoint to the case of the *Andrea Gail*, consider the story of Febreze, the spray-on liquid Procter & Gamble developed during the 1990s to help consumers eliminate unappealing odors. For years, scientists in P&G's research and development facilities had worked to create a simple product that would eliminate the bad smells that tended to seep into fabrics—the cigarette smoke that infused the jacket that someone wore to a bar, for example, or the cat odor that frequently clings to a living room couch. With the development of Febreze, many in the product development team thought they had emerged with a sure winner. And so, when the product launched, many of P&G's top brass expected a big return.

In the weeks and months after the launch, very few bottles of Febreze moved off the shelves. It wasn't for lack of marketing; commercials went up around the country showing women recommending the product to friends who complained about odors on their clothing. Many at P&G were shocked, having expected to win accolades internally for bringing a high-flying new product to the market. In the face of what looked like an abject failure, executives began to search for ways to understand the unexpected setback.

They didn't need to go back to the drawing board; the product itself worked quite well. Rather, they discovered where they had gone wrong upon interviewing a woman who lived with several cats in a rancid-smelling apartment. The woman had grown so accustomed to the smell that she had no clue how offensive it was to a visitor's nose. The power of habit, as *New York Times* reporter Charles Duhigg labeled the phenomenon, had diminished the product's appeal; because individual consumers did not perceive the nasty odors as offensive, they wouldn't consider buying a product such as Febreze.

P&G's developers suspected that small tweaks in their marketing of the product might well turn things around. Instead of selling Febreze as an odor neutralizer, they could sell it as a way to put the finishing touch on a newly cleaned room. That way, they wouldn't be asking consumers to establish a new habit but to reward themselves with a fresh new scent at the end of an *existing* routine. P&G adjusted the formula midstream so that the product's scent was just a bit stronger, and they altered the advertising campaign so that potential purchasers would imagine the charge they would feel when using Febreze after tidying a room. Guess what? These changes worked. The mission of creating a new, successful consumer product remained the same, but by remaining flexible and reframing the product in the consumer's mind, P&G was able to avoid a colossal shipwreck and build a household brand that is known to this day.[9]

KEEPING WATCH OVER THE FUEL GAUGE

P&G's managers succeeded because in the first instance they were monitoring closely how Febreze was doing in the marketplace. When Febreze was selling poorly, they knew that in time to take action. And when the product got back on its feet, they knew that, too. This, of course, presupposed that they had clear goals for the product's performance and were watching how the product was doing. We recognize a basic feature of any system of resilience: the ability to monitor performance data on an ongoing basis. You can't manage for results unless you're already *tracking* results in real time.

When I'm consulting with prospective clients, I often begin by asking a simple question: If we were to take a long road trip together, would they consider disconnecting the fuel gauge through the duration of the journey? Would they be happy to travel "blind," getting on the road and hoping for the best, not knowing how much fuel remains at any given point?

"Of course not," they say. "You need to know how much fuel you have left in order to prevent yourself from running out before you arrive at your destination."

"So," I say, "tell me this: Does your organization have the right information at its fingertips? Or is it traveling blind, too?"

Much of the time, organizations *are* traveling without the critical information they need to adjust to circumstances. Fortunately, the scorecard described in chapter 4 provides much of the information required. Often, when we work with a team, members thank us for the terrific scorecard that we've constructed for them and then inform us that they will just populate the scorecard at the end of the year so they can see how they did. *What?!* Can you imagine a football team waiting until the end of the season to unveil to players, coaches, management, and fans whether they won enough games to qualify for the playoffs? There's a reason that at the end of each game one team wins and another loses. Lose enough games in a row, and a team is going to make adjustments, like changing quarterbacks, running the ball more, acquiring a strong middle linebacker, firing the head coach. Regular monitoring of performance throughout the season is key. Public agencies need that same level of clarity throughout the year, for all metrics in their scorecard.

Yet that's only half of the equation. Remember those meetings we discussed in the last chapter? Only through routine discussions of the latest performance data distilled into information can organizations begin to process and understand the progress they're making toward the end goal. In the course of discussions, leadership teams can think seriously about how things are progressing. They can note what has and hasn't happened according to plan. Armed with this analysis, they can begin to divine why certain strategic elements haven't met expectations,

Data becomes information when we give it structure and sunshine; we need to talk about it, acknowledge it, and make adjustments to deliver our agreed-upon goals.

and they can consider adjustments. What can managers do to fix indicators that have fallen behind or to spread best practices to other areas of the organization? In the absence of the proper meetings, individuals will likely ignore the data, leaving the organization to plod ahead in what might be the wrong direction. Data becomes information when we give it structure and sunshine; we need to talk about it, acknowledge it, and make adjustments to deliver our agreed-upon goals. Football teams achieve this by huddling after each play and then making larger adjustments during the game's halftime. We suggest that organizations replicate this model with daily, weekly, monthly, and quarterly huddles.

Over time, persistent analysis of incoming data will yield something even more valuable: *predictive* analytics. When you've done the same hard analysis through several business cycles, you begin to distinguish seasonal changes and serious concerns. The year-end Christmas season tends to drive consumer sales beyond their likely first-quarter levels. Only by developing a real understanding of how much falloff an organization should expect can a company's managers gauge whether something is going awry in January, February, and March. Predictable benchmarks give companies an edge in adjusting to changing circumstances.

When establishing a system to derive predictive analytics, we use a formula that draws from three sets of data points. The first centers on the organization's performance for the year to date, the second focuses on the following quarter's performance from the previous year, and the third is a trailing twelve-month measurement. We weight the year-to-date metric in the formula more heavily as the year goes on; for example, after the first month's performance, we only weight the year-to-date metric at 8.3 percent, while after the eleventh month of the year we weight that same metric at 91 percent. This is because we gain higher levels of confidence of true performance as time passes. It's like a football team leading 40–7 with six minutes to go in the fourth quarter; you're pretty sure it will prevail.

The second formula input—the ensuing quarter's performance from the prior year—gives us a sense as to what will likely transpire based on seasonality and other factors. And finally, the trailing, twelve-month metric takes the results from the most recent twelve-month period, totals them up, and divides by twelve. This input smooths performance results and takes out all major bumps or drops accruing from seasonality, spikes in performance, and so on. This third input allows us to anticipate the Christmas rush while not overweighting it. The composite of all three inputs gives us the confidence we need to stand before a management team and essentially see the future. Trends emerge that suggest where any given metric will likely end up in the following months. And from there it becomes easy to understand whether the organization will likely hit any given goal. We can stand before a team and report that there's a 70 percent chance at this point in the year that they will realize their on-time performance goal. Or that there is a 40 percent chance that the students in third grade will realize their end-of-course exam goals. Or that there is a 90 percent chance that the county jail will exceed its overnight arrest metric.

Finally, effective use of predictive analytics requires a structured way to identify exactly what a team should most consider when making adjustments. We call this a FOCUS Report. You'll recall that in chapter 4 we prioritized all of our performance metrics, since not every metric was created equal, and some were more important to realizing success. The FOCUS Report is a quarterly presentation that maps the *likelihood* that any given metric will be met against the *importance* of that given indicator to the organization's overall success. A FOCUS report is the lynchpin for anyone considering whether and how to make adjustments, as it enables those running the organization to hone in on the metric results that most need improvement: those results that most affect the delivery of success yet that are most unlikely to meet the annual goal. This report tells leadership to repair its deficient bridges, check that the water supply is safe, and ensure that military veterans are getting quality health care *before* holding hearings on NFL team mascots. The FOCUS Report eliminates the risk that the organization will spend resources fixing problems that are of minimal importance, or gilding the lily on efforts already destined for success.

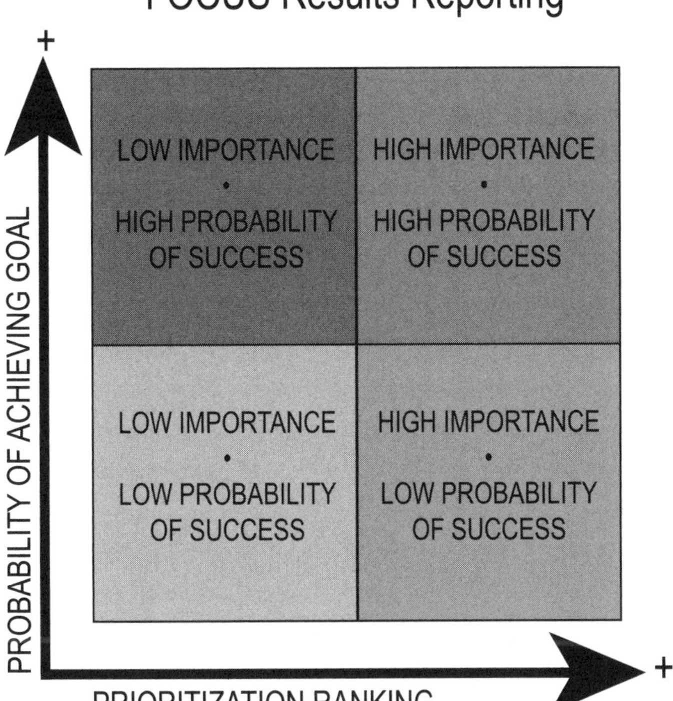

FIGURE 6-1

Using these three tools that spin data into information, management can take the famous lessons of Michael Lewis's *Moneyball* and apply them to whatever challenge an organization faces. Recall that Billy Beane, the Oakland A's innovative general manager, determined early on that the metric that mattered most to building a winning team was whether or not the team scored eight hundred runs during any given season. In Beane's analysis, that metric alone surpassed in importance the whole series of indicators on which scouts had traditionally trained their fixations. If the A's in any given year were on pace to lead the major leagues in errors committed, Beane could live with it, as long as the tradeoff helped his team meet its goal of runs scored.

The point, as we explored in a previous chapter, is to move beyond the misguided notion that "what gets measured, gets done." We know that's not true, because there are innumerable examples of measurable results going in the wrong direction: America's SAT scores have fallen for sustained periods of time, and yet efforts to lift them have failed to gain any real traction. For years, we've gotten reports that America's infrastructure is crumbing, but Washington has yet to address this extremely important problem. Predictive analytics reveal the dangers of old infrastructure in disrepair, and we know that Americans regard basic safety as important. It's not that we don't have data; it's that we don't pay focused attention on an ongoing basis to the most meaningful indicators, so that we can make adjustments. Properly constructed, a regime of results measurement and management provides us with the information we need to do exactly that.

Jim Collins, author of the book *Good to Great,* urged leaders to manage information rather than people. He believed the most effective managers were those who focused on their scorecards and determined how to handle their subordinates by diagnosing what had happened and why. Results management begins with the data, and it empowers those at the helm to keep mapping from there the actions they must take to deliver success. It's undeniably true, in business and in life: only those who can see the proverbial fuel gauge are able to plot a journey that steers them more pointedly toward their goals.

AN EMPTY CITY HALL

Government is all too often like the *Andrea Gail*: it tanks because leaders fail to make minor adjustments midstream. Recall the story of the City of Stockton, California, from chapter 3. Through most of the 2000s, property values were rising in Stockton, new housing was popping up around town, the economy was booming, and the surrounding region appeared finally to be benefitting from its relative proximity to Silicon Valley. These effects weren't lost on those in high political office; economic growth began to funnel money into municipal coffers.[10] Blessed with these newfound funds, city leaders made significant investments, often borrowing against presumed future tax revenue to get things moving. Ground was soon broken on a new marina, a municipal ballpark, and, most infamously, a new city hall.[11] At the same time, the city "sweetened" many of its employees' pensions, promising municipal workers lavish new benefits, including health coverage that would last through their retirement.[12]

Unfortunately, the city presumed that the gravy train would continue forever. From some angles, their thinking made sense: suddenly flush with money, leaders wanted to invest in the future and lay a foundation for future growth. But in their exuberance, they lost touch with reality, failing to protect against the possibility that the economy might not keep growing apace. So when the mortgage bubble popped and the bottom fell out of the economy in late 2008, the City of Stockton was entirely unprepared. It had taken on enormous fiscal liabilities—by 2012, the city was $1 billion in debt—and had very little wherewithal to make good on its obligations.

Some might argue that the bankruptcy that followed was inevitable. And by the time the city filed for Chapter 7 in 2013, there may well have been little else that those in positions of authority could have done. But that sense of inevitability looks at the problem through the wrong lens. Stockton *could* have prepared itself to weather the storm, making minor adjustments in order to hedge against the bursting of the housing bubble. Had leaders behaved more responsibly—had they deployed a more formal structure that allowed them to see the future with unvarnished truth—they might not have had to cancel their plans to move into their new city hall. As I've related, once the building was constructed, the city government couldn't even afford to move in and the new building was repossessed.[13]

Clearly, Stockton did not engage in the rigor of results management. Had leaders looked at revenues over a long period of time, they would have known that the growth they'd experienced was unusual and unlikely to continue unabated. Moreover, had leaders been meeting regularly to sort through the town's various metric performance goals, prioritizing those that were most important, they would have been expending energy only on the most important items. A city steeped in the routines of predictive analytics would have been able to modify the new city hall, scaling the project down, putting it on ice, or renting the space to a company in the private sector. Instead, the city was caught flat-footed amid a national crisis. We need more agencies capable of adjusting nimbly *before* a crisis.

Why do failures like Stockton keep happening? It's not that government lacks a mechanism for collecting data, or that policies established by public agencies are set in stone. The problem is that ongoing self-analysis within taxpayer-funded organizations focuses much more squarely on issues of budgeting than performance. As a result, the feedback loops that would spur public bureaucracies to achieve their goals often don't function. Those who have worked for the taxpayers know the annual drill. Departments are given money at the beginning of any given fiscal year, and they aim to spend it, regardless of whether their plans become obsolete at some intermediary point. The institutional fear is that if you fail to spend what you're given, your budget will be cut in the next cycle.

The purpose of any given department shouldn't be to spend down its kitty; it should be to perform according to its mandate. Public works agencies should be maintaining a region's infrastructure; social service bureaus should be caring for those in need; education departments should be schooling area kids. In each and every case, managers have ways of tracking the effectiveness of the department's efforts, beyond how money is being spent. When they fail to do so, they inevitably waste taxpayer dollars.

When I arrived at RGRTA, the agency suffered from a glaring inability to monitor its own performance. The only data set we tracked was financial: how much money we spent, and how much we took in. Many other indicators might have told us how we were delivering against our mission and how we might have improved our performance: how frequently our buses arrived on time, for example, or how full each coach was on any given route. Paying attention to such data points would have allowed us to change the way we did business. We might have chosen to put more coaches on one route and fewer on another. We might have chosen to establish new routes connecting commuters' homes and offices more efficiently. And so, when our team took over the agency, we began figuring out how to use strategically chosen information points to adjust the way we did business, all focused on delivering success. In our case, this meant enabling ourselves to do the unthinkable, reduce customer fares.

In Washington, the only consistent reporting comes from the Congressional Budget Office and the Office of Management and Budget, departments geared to track money more than anything else. Various inspectors general perform occasional audits of government functions, as does the Government Accountability Office, which acts as Congress's investigative arm. But scathing reports of mismanagement or bureaucratic failure substitute poorly for ongoing analysis of indicators. Only the latter allows a bureaucracy to adjust midstream. Government needs more leaders who display the kind of productive paranoia Jim Collins talks about in *Great by Choice.* When everyone else is celebrating, the productively paranoid leader only sees thunderclouds. Because he sees them, he can guide his organization around them, so that the organization never winds up caught up in a storm. Ideally, public administrators will become paranoid enough that, rather than chasing headlines, they will productively delve into the data, adjusting as necessary to point their agencies toward blue skies.

Ideally, public administrators will become paranoid enough that, rather than chasing headlines, they will productively delve into the data, adjusting as necessary to point their agencies toward blue skies.

Just because an agency has information at its fingertips doesn't mean that the agency will make the necessary adjustments. As I said at this chapter's beginning, information is only half the equation; we need structure to make the necessary adjustments. The institution has to be willing and eager to match new information with ways to improve performance—and not just financially. Once data is streaming in, regular discussions of what that data means have to become part of organizational life, and leaders must use more sophisticated number crunching—predictive analytics—to address problems even before they arise. But the broader point remains the same: to achieve a public agency's mission, the bottom line can't focus just on money but also on the service being provided. Is the infrastructure sound? Is the transit system efficient? Are the needy being helped out of poverty? A public works, transit, or social services agency's spending of its budget does not necessarily correlate with whether the agency is completing its mission. In this case, the numbers really do tell the most meaningful story.

Information is only half the equation; we need structure to make the necessary adjustments.

REINVENTING GOVERNMENT...AGAIN

Some agencies have begun to use nonfinancial data to help shape their operations. By some standards, the movement to make government more responsive began in earnest during the Clinton administration, when Vice President Al Gore took up the cause of "reinventing government." After an initial survey, the National Performance Review issued a series of recommendations about how to improve the workings of government, and then saw these recommendations through to implementation. More than 425,000 federal jobs were eliminated, 640,000 pages of outdated regulations were rescinded, and 2,000 obsolete field offices were closed. As a result, taxpayers saved hundreds of billions of dollars.[14]

At the federal level, results management spread during the Bush years before exploding under President Obama. Brookings Institution scholar and former Republican congressional aide Ron Haskins explained in a *New York Times* article how the Obama administration was using evidence to shape policy: "About 700 programs around the country are being required to evaluate their work. The evaluations have to be part of the budget, they have to be high quality, and they have to happen on a continuing basis so staff and administrators know whether they are producing impacts." And the White House is hoping to expand the imprint, asking for more money for evaluation and creating incentives for federal money to flow to programs that work in a demonstrable way.[15] That's important progress.

In some cases, we've seen results management deployed at the state and municipal level. New York City's CompStat system embraced the ethos of predictive analytics by identifying where the next crimes were most likely to occur, enabling the NYPD to deploy additional officers to the most problematic neighborhoods. Likewise, when Martin O'Malley became mayor of Baltimore and then governor of Maryland, he applied the same management practice to fighting crime and then to all areas of government service. He tracked potholes and blight in the way New York had tracked muggings, and to much the same effect. By 2003, after several years as mayor, he estimated that CitiStat, as his system was called, had saved Baltimore's taxpayers $100 million. When he became governor, he used StateStat to clean up and preserve the Chesapeake Bay, giving Maryland the ability to respond to local incidents *before* pollution seeped into the wider landscape.[16]

Even with such progress, significant opportunities remain. Those who benefit from the traditional gerbil wheel system fight tooth and nail against reforms, and understandably so: by evaluating the effectiveness of such systems work, reformers expose those who work within them to potential criticism. Consider education reform. Studies have shown that tracking an individual teacher's progress—and, maybe more importantly, tying that teacher's compensation to his performance—is among the best ways to improve educational outcomes. One pilot program in the District of Columbia found that rigorous evaluation often compelled poor teachers to leave the profession, ensuring that the next year's class of students wasn't forced to suffer with the same lousy classroom teachers. If districts around the country deployed similar programs, it would almost surely help greatly to address the crisis of quality in American education.[17]

Teacher evaluation faces stiff resistance, most notably from teachers' unions themselves. Falling back on a host of rationales, union leaders decry the imposition of standards, claiming that the results are too subjective or demeaning to teachers. Is it fair, they ask, to hold teachers responsible if children can't learn because of bad conditions in their homes? In some cases, teachers have become so incensed that they have ousted union leaders who haven't fought the imposition of standards vociferously enough.[18] This has sadly led many not-so-courageous politicians to think twice about championing teacher evaluation as part of their educational agenda.[19] Of course, such a reaction is not unique to teachers nor to education. We see it everywhere in the public sector, from policing to health care. And, of course, more broadly, we continue to spend tens of billions of dollars on pet projects of elected officials that are of questionable value, even as a quarter of our bridges are deficient and tens of millions of Americans drink substandard water.

In addition to transparently providing the right data, agencies need to construct an accompanying structure that incorporates data *analysis* into their operations. They need to spend time understanding how the data aligns with what they want to accomplish, and then adjusting to improve performance. Only then can we turn data into information. It's not hard to imagine what proper performance management might look like in the federal government. What if, rather than using cabinet meetings as opportunities to spout political rhetoric for television cameras, the president took the opportunity to closely inspect each bureaucracy's performance scorecard, updating agencies on where they stand in achieving their goals, discussing what's working more or less effectively, and developing ways to make improvements? What if the president did all this publicly and online, in such a way that Americans could see their government working to get things done against quantifiable preestablished goals?

The president might call on the secretary of agriculture to discuss which farmers were doing well during the course of any given harvest season, and which were having a tough time. They might then discuss which crops the nation ought to be producing, and which were of a lesser priority. They would then look at that data: How have the subsidies the federal government provides affected the various crops? And finally, they would consider what needed to be adjusted to improve the picture. Are some subsidies not working in the national interest, and if so, how would those resources be better invested?

Every department would perform a similar exercise, repeating it again and again on a regular basis. Moreover, the White House staff would keep track of decisions made in the meetings for everyone's benefit. Inevitably, politics would begin to interfere: lobbyists would try to protect less effective ways of governing, and members of Congress would object to changes that negatively affected their biggest donors. But at least we'd be having this conversation in public. With the facts in hand, maybe more narrow-minded, interest-driven objections would lose favor. Even if that wasn't quite the case, we would still begin to weave into routine government business the expectation that data-driven, midstream adjustments were important.

THE BELL TOLLS IN NEW HAMPSHIRE

Ronald Reagan's 1980 presidential campaign represents one of the clearest examples we have of results management at work. When the campaign hit full swing, few doubted that former California governor Ronald Reagan wanted to be president, and that he would be a top contender. Reagan had been a torchbearer for the Republican Party's more conservative wing for most of the previous two decades. In 1976, he had almost snagged the nomination from the sitting Republican president, Gerald Ford. Unfortunately, Reagan's front-runner status didn't confer a pure advantage. Voters seem to hold candidates at the head of the pack to a higher standard, and when these candidates lose a debate or other skirmish, their invincibility can be punctured. Reagan's campaign operatives, therefore, had a tough decision to make at the start of the primary season: whether or not to compete in the Iowa caucuses. And, as is typical in high-stakes political campaigns, Governor Reagan's aides split into two camps.

The first camp, led largely by Ed Meese, was situated in Los Angeles. Meese had come to know Reagan as a member of his gubernatorial staff, where the young lawyer had risen to become Reagan's top aide. Over time, Meese had become an indispensable advisor. He believed that Reagan ought to head to the Hawkeye State and take his message directly to the electorate, contrasting himself with George H.W. Bush, the Republican establishment's favorite. Meese was less concerned that trying to win could jeopardize Reagan's perch. John Sears, who was running Reagan's national campaign from Washington, felt differently. Sears was an old hand at political warfare, serving as a conservative strategist for campaigns throughout the 1960s and 1970s. He was intimately connected to the world inside the proverbial Beltway, and he believed Reagan was such a favorite that he should eschew any real engagement with his adversaries. In Sears's view, it was beneath Reagan to appear on stage with Bush, Howard Baker, John Connally, and the other candidates competing for the nomination. Better for the governor to stand alone and aloof.

Sears won the day. Reagan did not travel to Des Moines or Sioux City. The decision proved to be a grave error: Bush upset Reagan in the caucuses, making Reagan appear like anything but a sure bet.[20] No one knew whether Reagan would survive the setback. But what was clear was that the nomination would not be handed to him; he would have to fight hard for it.

The next primary contest took place in New Hampshire, and the scene that played out there only days later marked one of the most consequential political pivots of the last several decades. Reagan traveled to the Granite State to meet voters, shake their hands, and answer their questions.[21] He also agreed to appear in a debate moderated by the *Nashua Telegraph,* and to underwrite the costs. Arriving at the debate venue, Reagan found only two chairs set up, one for him and another for Bush. Reagan protested, arguing that the other nominees should have a chance to engage as well. The moderator responded by telling the technical staff to turn the governor's microphone off. Reagan had none of it, angrily retorting, "I am paying for this microphone." (the moderator's name was actually Jon Breen).[22] In a single, memorable sentence, Reagan had distanced himself from John Sears's entire strategy. Far from remaining aloof, the front-runner appeared entirely engaged. Not only was he taking on his opponents in the flesh, he was illustrating that he would not be pushed around, much to the audience's delight. Reagan revealed himself as exactly the sort of strong, engaging leader the Republican electorate wanted from their standard-bearer. From that point on, the governor never looked back. He won the nomination later that year and unseated President Carter in November.

Reagan's goal remained consistent: to win the nomination and become president. But given the data he garnered from his defeat in Iowa, Reagan made a modest but important adjustment to his campaign strategy. On the day he won the New Hampshire primary, Reagan institutionalized the shift, firing John Sears. And the rest was history.

Results management may not always have such a dramatic impact, but it remains essential. Organizations cannot thrive without goals or a plan for achieving success, but no plan is perfect, and in the course of any effort, organizations need to adjust. The only way to do that is to keep track of what matters and how circumstances are evolving in real time. To turn our public agencies into centers of excellence, we need to do the hard work of entrenching performance management more deeply. Your local school district or fire department may not be charged with

To turn our public agencies into centers of excellence, we need to do the hard work of entrenching performance management more deeply.

taking an enemy position, like the brave soldiers were at Pointe du Hoc, but if they are to achieve their important goals, they, too, need to constantly monitor how they're doing and modify operations accordingly. At all times, the definition of success remains unwavering. It is a clear stake in the ground. As President Kennedy set the goal: "before this decade is out, of landing a man on the moon and returning him safely to the earth."[23] However, the path to get there is constantly changing; no strategy or plan survives contact with the enemy. Eisenhower's wisdom remains true today.

As I've suggested, none of this is easy. It takes discipline on the part of leaders, and, ultimately, real courage. Someone has to stand up to entrenched interests inside and outside the organization, especially when the picture the data paints isn't so flattering. In fact, much of what we've discussed in our Seven Step plan requires deep commitment, a willingness to take risks for the public good, and even, on occasion, a willingness to risk one's own career. When leaders in the public sector show this courage, the results are nothing short of inspirational. All too often, courage *isn't* in evidence, and opportunities to reform and energize our public agencies come and go. As I argue in the next chapter, we all need to look deep inside ourselves and do what it takes to effect positive change in our government. We need to call upon our better natures, and remember the reasons we got into government in the first place. Saving America requires real leadership, the kind I used to read about when I was doing book reports on Nathan Hale, William Dawes, and Paul Revere in the frigid upstate New York winter. The time for that leadership is *now*.

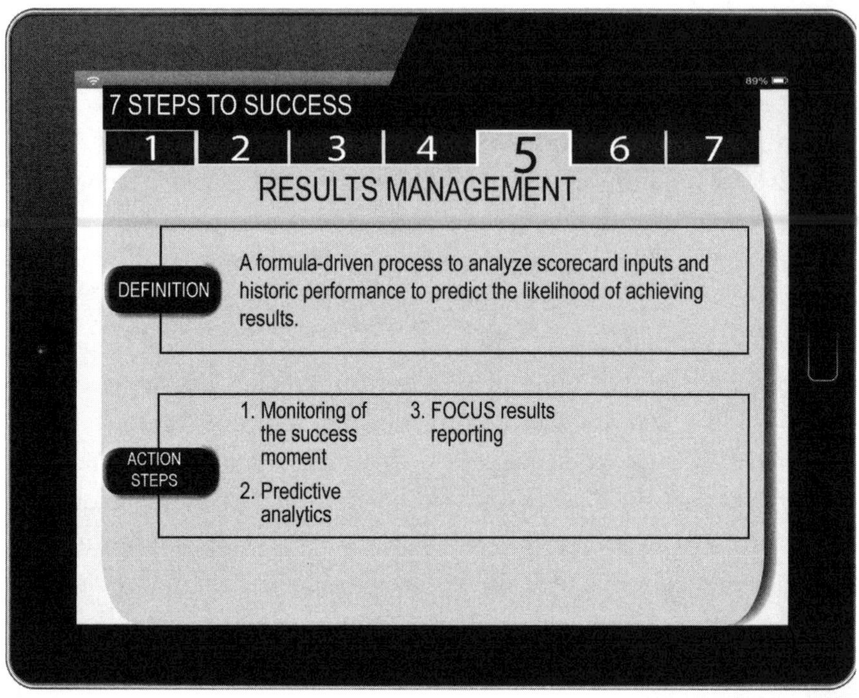
7 STEPS TO SUCCESS
1 2 3 4 5 6 7
RESULTS MANAGEMENT
DEFINITION
A formula-driven process to analyze scorecard inputs and historic performance to predict the likelihood of achieving results.
ACTION STEPS
1. Monitoring of the success moment
2. Predictive analytics
3. FOCUS results reporting

FIGURE 6-2

7

Courage and Decision Making

It was the middle of the night of May 1, 2011, and Rob O'Neill had been in this situation dozens of times—at this point, maybe even hundreds.[1] Seated aboard a helicopter flying close to the ground, he counted to himself from zero to one thousand, and then from one thousand to zero. Then he did it again. He didn't do this out of fear, but rather as a way to keep focused. You see, this wasn't just any helicopter, and he wasn't sitting among strangers. This was a high-performance, combat-ready U.S. Navy Blackhawk copter. To O'Neill's left and right were fellow members of Seal Team Six, the navy's most elite counterterrorism unit. Some of the men are napping, others are listening to their iPods. Their objective on this particular mission, code named Neptune Spear, was to kill or capture Osama bin Laden. In less than an hour, Rob O'Neill would come face to face with America's most wanted enemy.

The two helicopters ferrying the Seals to the compound had taken off from an air base in Afghanistan and headed due east. Midway through the flight, the pilot had come on the intercom to announce the ominous news that they had entered Pakistani airspace. United States military leadership had not notified their Pakistani counterparts that the helicopters were coming. As a result, they could have been regarded as hostile attackers and shot out of the sky at any moment. A tense hour and a half later, the two Blackhawk helicopters came upon the compound they'd been studying for days. As O'Neill would later explain: "We knew every single part of the exterior: every opening; every garden;

every path; how high the walls were."[2] The men also knew of the intense danger they would face upon their arrival. Most of the Seals expected this to be their final mission, and not because they were planning to retire. Intelligence suggested that bin Laden's compound would be heavily fortified or booby-trapped. They expected some of the people defending him to be fitted with suicide vests, designed to kill anyone who came near the al Qaeda leader. O'Neill was so convinced he would perish that he wrote farewell letters to his family and called his father to say a final goodbye.

The operation plan had specified that one helicopter would deposit several of the Seals outside the compound's exterior walls so that they could deal with any threats coming from there. The helicopter would then lift off and drop the remainder on the roof of bin Laden's house; that way, the soldiers could jump down onto a balcony and descend through bin Laden's house from the top down. The second helicopter would leave a second team just outside the house's front door, assaulting the same building from the bottom up. The two teams would meet in the middle.

Things began to go sideways right from the start. The second helicopter, designated to hover beside the house throughout the assault, stalled out due to heat reflecting up from the enclosed space beneath. For those monitoring the mission from Washington, it seemed for a moment as though all might be lost. Little more than thirty years earlier, President Jimmy Carter had sent a team of commandos to rescue fifty-two American hostages held at the U.S. Embassy in Iran. The failure of that mission claimed the lives of eight American servicemen and doomed the hostages to 444 days in captivity. Now those in Washington feared this nightmare scenario might repeat itself.

This night in Pakistan, the Blackhawk's pilot managed to save the mission by gently crashing the struggling chopper lengthwise across the compound's thick outer wall, setting the nose onto the ground inside the perimeter and breaking its tail over the back. The Seals hopped out without casualties. The pilot of the other helicopter—the one in which O'Neill was riding—reacted without hesitation. Determined not to risk a similar fate, he abandoned the plan to hover atop the roof of the house and instead landed his chopper on the ground just outside the compound's exterior wall. He then directed O'Neill and his team to get out and join the team massing inside the exterior wall. Once a member of the other team opened the gate, the group got back to the business of hunting bin Laden.

Authorities in the White House's Situation Room were overcome with relief and then incredulity. The Seals had survived a particularly inauspicious beginning to the mission. And once they were massed outside bin Laden's front door, they knew exactly what to do. They formed a single line and blasted through the door. The first soldier stormed into the building, charging through as the Seals behind him peeled off successively to secure each successive room. O'Neill, far from being the first in the line, fell into a slot near the end.

The Seals cleared the first and second floors in a matter of minutes, and the soldier nearest the front of the line decided it was time to move onto the third. He motioned for O'Neill, now one of the few Seals not clearing a room on the first or second floors, to follow him up. After climbing the stairs and pulling back a curtain, the lead Seal jumped on top of two women positioned right in front of him, expecting them to martyr themselves with a suicide vest. O'Neill, following just behind, turned to his right, and there, standing in front of him, tucked behind a woman, was the face he'd seen a thousand times. In a split second, Rob O'Neill fired three quick shots, and Osama bin Laden crumpled to the ground, dead.[3]

The courage of Seal Team Six was on full display that evening. Every member put his life on the line. Yet those thousands of miles away in Washington showed incredible courage, too. Days before Rob O'Neill had found himself face to face with the world's most wanted terrorist, the president of the United States had made one of the most difficult decisions of his career. Armed with the intelligence that bin Laden *likely* resided in Abbottabad, Barack Obama could have chosen simply to bomb the compound, killing everyone inside. But beyond robbing the American public of any surefire confirmation that bin Laden was dead, a bombing would have taken the lives of innocent children housed within the complex. Obama also could have ordered the military to launch missiles into the building. But what if they failed to kill bin Laden, enabling him to escape capture, as he had years earlier in the mountains of Tora Bora?

In the end, President Obama chose an option with the starkest possible downside. He ordered a unit of commandoes into the sovereign territory of a (sometime) ally, authorizing what was by most standards an act of war. The Seals who went on the mission were aware that if they were caught they would likely have spent the rest of their lives in a Pakistani prison. Obama knew that if the mission failed—if any of the Seals perished, or if bin Laden escaped alive—his political career might well end early, much like President Carter's, whose reelection bid was certainly not helped by the crashing of American helicopters in the desert and the death of those eight American servicemen. But Obama sent in the Seals anyway. When it really counted, he made the call, demonstrating the courage required to let Rob O'Neill and his colleagues do what they were trained to do.

The great stakes of the president's decision are evident in the famous photograph taken of President Obama's national security team in the White House Situation Room the night of the raid. Squeezed into a cramped space, aides at the end of a table monitored the mission in real time. The snapshot catches Obama glaring at the screen, worry painted on his face. Secretary of State Hillary Clinton clasps her hand over her mouth, betraying a nervous calm. Others stand and sit attentively, grimly aware how fraught the mission was. The monitors allowed them to have some sense of what was happening, but no one could say for sure whether bin Laden would in fact even be present. After watching the first helicopter crash and then standing by as the Seals secured the first and second floors, they could do nothing but wait. And then the call came. A few moments after O'Neill pumped those three bullets into bin Laden's head, word was relayed back to the White House: "Geronimo, Geronimo, Geronimo." This was the verbal signal to confirm that the Seals had indeed gotten their man.

The Seals spent the next several minutes collecting whatever they could harvest from the computers and files scattered throughout the house. Then, after sealing bin Laden's corpse in a body bag, they piled into the helicopters and raced back to base. After an eighty minute trek to the border, the pilot announced: "Gentlemen, for the first time in your lives, you're going to be happy to hear this: welcome to Afghanistan." Now the men could begin to celebrate their accomplishment. A decade after 9/11, the world's most wanted man had been brought to justice.

Few of us will ever partake in the heroics of a Seal Team Six. Still, in any professional environment, a willingness to take risks and face danger when it would be easier to avoid them is utterly crucial. To perform the steps laid out in previous chapters, leaders and employees up and down the organizational chart need ample amounts of courage. Every step, after all, requires that an organization break from established practice to do things differently—and better. At every step, the potential exists for resistance and blowback, from both inside and outside the organization. Public agencies can't hope to make any headway if leaders aren't willing to burn bridges with their decision making and even, on occasion, to put their careers on the line. No matter where we are in our organizations, we can't wait around for others to act. If we're going to save America, we need to be heroes ourselves.

Public agencies can't hope to make any headway if leaders aren't willing to burn bridges with their decision making and even, on occasion, put their careers on the line. No matter where we are in our organizations, we can't wait around for others to act. If we're going to save America, we need to be heroes ourselves.

TAKING ON THE MTA

What defines courage and heroism, exactly? It's important to realize that courageous decision making doesn't relate to the *outcome* of a decision; it's about the decision itself. President Obama's decision to send in Seal Team Six worked out, and thank goodness it did. But even if it hadn't, the decision would have been equally courageous. During the 2015 Super Bowl between the New England Patriots and the Seattle Seahawks, Seattle coach Pete Carroll took a chance at the end of the first half. With only five seconds left and his team in field goal range, conventional wisdom said that he should bring out his kicker and try for a field goal. Carroll opted for a pass to the end zone, which resulted in a touchdown. Analysts lauded his courage, but only because it worked! At

Elements of a Courageous Decision
1. Success is clearly defined.
2. It is focused on delivering success.
3. There is a clear and achievable plan to deliver the decision.
4. It is organizationally focused, not self sustaining.
5. It has the potential to succeed.
6. It is judged not by the outcome but by the elements contributing to the decision itself.

FIGURE 7-1

the end of the game, Carroll made a similarly risky call and it failed; the Patriots intercepted a pass on the goal line and won the game. Analysts decried this call, when, in fact, it was equally courageous.

You might interpret my definition of courage to imply that leaders can do anything and be judged courageous, since, after all, the results of the decision don't affect its degree of courageousness. Not at all. Courageous decisions are not the same as brash or uninformed ones. To act courageously, one must understand the risks and benefits of a course of action as completely as possible, and make a responsible choice. That's the key word: *responsibility.* Leaders who make brash or uninformed decisions are abdicating the responsibility vested in them. As a leader, your *job* is to apply all of your experience, wisdom, and intelligence to evaluating the potential risks and benefits of the choices at hand so as to arrive at the best one for your organization. That "best" choice might entail a significant amount of risk and therefore require considerable courage to make. But this is well-considered risk, not foolish risk.

That "best" choice might entail a significant amount of risk and therefore require considerable courage to make. But this is well-considered risk, not foolish risk.

However you define courage and related terms like valor and heroism, it's pretty clear that they aren't present in overwhelming quantities in the public sector. Most people associate courage with the military and with first responders, but it usually ends there. That county administrator who appears before the media making excuses for year after year of deficit spending, or that slow-moving clerk at the Department of Motor Vehicles who refuses a reasonable request for help from the mother with three kids in tow because she didn't fill out form DD-221-b in blue ink instead of black—how heroic are they?

Courage does exist in the public sector. Consider the story of Nassau County Executive Ed Mangano. Located just beyond New York City on Long Island, Nassau County is one of the largest suburban municipalities in the United States, boasting a population that dwarfs that of nearly a dozen states.[4] Because Nassau County is situated within the Big Apple's greater metropolitan area, many of the county's residents depend on the region's powerful transit agency, the Metropolitan Transportation Authority (MTA), which runs buses both within Nassau County and between Nassau and Manhattan. Just after Mangano's election in the fall of 2009, the MTA decided to play hardball with the residents of Nassau County. Facing its own budget shortfall, the transit agency told the county that unless it was willing to pony up an additional $30 million in annual subsidies, the MTA would cut service within the county by half. The ultimatum immediately put Mangano in an untenable position: to comply, he would have had to raise taxes, cut services, or abandon the buses that allowed millions of commuters to get to work—exactly the opposite of what he had promised during his campaign.

Mangano suspected there was a better way, and he was right. It turned out that at least half a dozen private companies were in the business of providing "public" transportation. And many of them held out the promise of offering a higher-quality service for lower cost. Having learned of the work I'd done in Rochester, Mangano asked TransPro to help him determine whether his county could realistically provide the same or better service while paying less than the ransom demanded by the MTA's brass. We quickly concluded that he could; by contracting with a private provider, he could deliver on success as he had previously defined it.

Few could have anticipated that Mangano would look so far afield for alternatives. And when it became clear that he was seriously considering firing the MTA, everyone with a stake in protecting the existing system came out with their knives drawn, including MTA executives, unionized employees, rider advocates, and others. If you can believe it, Mangano began receiving death threats. Even more significant, the county was hit by a major public relations blitz. Reporters were spoon-fed an unflattering narrative about Mangano by the MTA's media spin-meisters. According to this narrative, Mangano had only been narrowly elected to office, and now he was taking on one of the state's most established bureaucracies. He was proposing something entirely new, and they suggested that he was way out of his league.

Mangano could have folded to the pressure. The headlines were blistering. The unions were picketing. He could have made excuses and done nothing. But he knew he was right, and he was determined to act. Two years after the MTA had presented Nassau County with its ultimatum, Mangano presented his proposal to end the MTA's monopoly to the county legislature. The opposition was organized and came out in force. In a public hearing focused on the new contract, a circus atmosphere pervaded. Parachuting into the scene, an outsider knowing nothing about the practical realities would have likely assumed that the county's residents were united against Mangano. Beneath the swirl, however, the facts spoke for themselves. The Nassau County Legislature was about evenly divided between Democrats and Republicans. Such an emotionally fraught issue might have spurred debate and divisions among the members, but in this case the choice was clear: the MTA was offering an inferior service at a premium cost, while Mangano's alternative offered an improved system at a deep discount. Despite the vociferous opposition, the legislature voted unanimously to support Mangano's plan.

As of 2015, few can argue with the results. By firing the MTA, the county saved tens of millions and prevented the citizens of Nassau from having to make further sacrifices. Every eligible MTA employee whose job was eliminated in the transition was hired back by the new service provider. And when the MTA subsequently raised fares system-wide, Nassau County managed to keep prices down. After all the gnashing of teeth, the people who mattered—the customers and the taxpayers—won without question. Maybe most revealing: when Mangano ran for reelection against the same opponent he'd squeaked past in 2009, he prevailed by a decisive eighteen point margin. Voters evidently know a courageous—and smart—public official when they see one.

A LEADER WHO BACKS YOU UP

Employees also know a courageous leader when they see one in action, as a story from the Hurricane Katrina disaster illustrates so well. During the first week after this ferocious hurricane had hit the Gulf Coast, Admiral Thad Allen (yes, the same one from the Elian Gonzalez story from earlier!) spent much of his time helping New Orleans piece together some semblance of order. Then he was asked to fly up to the joint operations command center in Baton Rouge to plot the next stages of the recovery. When he arrived, Homeland Security Secretary Michael Chertoff announced abruptly that he was relieving the incumbent director of FEMA, Michael Brown, of any responsibility for the federal government response, and promoting Allen in his stead. "Brownie," as President Bush had called him, had been a disaster; the federal government's response to the situation in New Orleans was being panned across the board. Allen knew that many of the federal employees who had been working twenty-four-hour days for the past week were making enormous progress that deserved to be celebrated. But a brief conversation with a FEMA worker he'd run into on the way into the meeting—someone proud of the work she was doing but hurt by the public criticism—had convinced him that one of his primary responsibilities was raising morale.

When Chertoff left the room after the announcement, an obvious question was in the air: "So what happens now?" Allen responded by directing his staff to immediately convene a meeting of everyone in the building—some 2,500 people. The federal government had established its joint operations command center in a shuttered Dillard's in Baton Rouge, a cavernous space with rows of computers and telephones. The arena was filled with federal officials representing a range of agencies, few of whom had any statutory responsibility to heed Allen's directives, since at this point local governments were in charge. Somehow, the admiral had to inspire them to follow his lead and work together by convincing them that what they were doing was important.

When everyone was assembled, Allen climbed up on a desk and raised a bullhorn to his lips. His remarks were brief, but resolute. The message was simple. He told the people who had gathered that they should treat everyone they were trying to help like they were members of their own families. And he explained that he was issuing that directive for two reasons. First, if people were working to help members of their family, he knew that inevitably they would err in each situation on the side of doing too much, which was precisely what he wanted them to do. But the second reason was even more important: he wanted employees to take that approach because it meant that if anyone in the local, state, or federal bureaucracy had a problem with what they decided in any individual circumstance, their problem wasn't just with the person who had made the decision, it was with Allen, because *he'd* told them to take initiative. Allen was, in effect, telling those 2,500 people that he had their backs. At that moment, many of the people gathered to listen began to weep.

As Allen told me, the episode was a pivotal one in his career, and perhaps in the careers of those in attendance. On a number of occasions, strangers have approached him to say that they had been present at this speech, and that they still remembered how the barometric pressure in the room had instantly changed. A group of individuals who had been demoralized by the media's criticism now felt empowered to use their own judgment, rather than follow byzantine rules that tied their hands, when trying to speed the recovery, because Allen had courageously stepped up and explicitly promised that he *personally* would back them up. That's courage in leadership. Admiral Allen knew that in empowering FEMA employees to use their judgment and take ownership he wouldn't agree with every decision they made, and he knew that his hastily assembled team wouldn't necessarily achieve the desired outcome. However, he had confidence that by asking employees to behave with familial compassion and cut through interagency and cross-jurisdictional rules, he would improve the situation on the ground, whether it changed media impressions or not.

THE LAST KODAK MOMENT

As organizations deploy our Seven Steps framework, not every decision leaders face will be "tough." Yet failing to do the right thing at those few critical junctures is sometimes enough to ruin everything. Windows of opportunity open and close. Leaders must call the right play at precisely the right time. Think of Kodak, the corporation that dominated the world of photography for more than a century. Many people believe that the invention of digital cameras drove this fabled company into bankruptcy, but that's not so. One of Kodak's own engineers, Steve Sasson, actually invented the digital camera in the mid-1970s. Kodak's top brass refused to bring digital technology to market, allowing companies like Canon and Nikon to exploit an opening in the market. Why did Kodak's leadership fail so miserably? Simple: they lacked courage. Much like those with a traditional bureaucratic mindset, they sought primarily to protect the status quo.

Failing to do the right thing at those few critical junctures is sometimes enough to ruin everything. Windows of opportunity open and close. Leaders must call the right play at precisely the right time.

As Sasson has explained, when he presented his invention to Kodak executives in the 1970s, he drew blank stares from the top brass.[5] The company chose not to embrace the technology because its executives feared that digital photography would eviscerate the cash cow it had cultivated by dominating the market for film. Many of the company's decisions seemed rational. If Kodak executives had embraced the digital revolution in the early 1980s, it would have appeared as if the company was abandoning its core competency, and maybe even preparing to lay off longtime Kodak employees who produced, marketed, and sold film for a living. Embracing digital photography might have cued potential competitors into an unexploited market for a new type of photography. But even after digital photography was clearly reshaping the market, Kodak's leadership still refused to shed the less profitable parts of the company so as to keep the firm at the vanguard of technology. Had the top brass admitted to themselves that disruption was inevitable, they could have begun to reimagine and retool the company to become a leader in the digital revolution. But they didn't. They lacked the requisite courage (not to mention vision). As a result, nearly all of Kodak's tens of thousands of employees went down with the ship.

WHAT *NOT* TO SAY

You might wonder why employees at certain organizations seem to display more courage in decision making than those at other organizations. To some extent, the disparity may reflect the behavior of those at the top of the organizational pyramid. If those in positions of power set a strong example, they lay the groundwork for their subordinates to perform their jobs courageously. In addition, executives can help inculcate Ed Mangano's brand of smart risk taking by moving toward more collaborative environments. You'll remember the distinction we made in chapter 2 between collaboration and consensus. Collaborative environments spur individuals with established points of view to talk through their differences. Even if collaborators don't end up seeing everything eye to eye, they still take advantage of information they glean from their colleagues. In seeking consensus, by contrast, people easily abandon their beliefs and principles in order to arrive at decisions that most people will accept without complaint. Organizations that encourage true collaboration by inviting *all* voices to become engaged implicitly encourage employees to step up and to take risks. Empowering individuals from the top down invites courage from the bottom up.

Organizations that encourage true collaboration by inviting *all* voices to become engaged implicitly encourage employees to step up and to take risks.

Throughout my tenure at RGRTA, I called upon one of my bosses, our board chairman John Doyle, whenever I got stuck trying to figure out how best to tackle an incoming challenge. I would ring John up on the phone and nearly every conversation unfolded in the same way. I would explain the nub of the problem, doing my best to put only facts on the table, and then express that I was just kind of stuck, really uncertain and confused as to how best to handle the situation. John would ask a series of clarifying questions in order to better understand the issue in front of us. Then he would pivot, asking me another series of questions about the inputs I was contemplating as well as the variables that would affect my decision. He'd ask me which factors were most important, and which were less so, pushing me, in effect, to make sure I wasn't missing anything crucial in the decision-making process. Once we'd gone through this process of questioning, he'd almost always simply say: "Seems to me you're thinking about all the right things. I'll be interested to hear what you decide. Let me know. Have a great day."

By concluding our conversations in this way, without dictating or even suggesting a particular course of action, John was providing me with something more valuable than advice; he was inspiring me to behave courageously without ever saying so explicitly. He was conveying that he *trusted* me, that he felt comfortable letting me make the ultimate decision. He was providing ample space for me to use my *judgment.* I should add that I have learned so much from this more open, collaborative approach than I would have if he had told me the answer. I knew I could put real problems in front of him and not have to pretend that I had a handle on everything, which of course no executive ever does.

John's brand of collaborative, courage-inspiring leadership is too frequently the exception. Some might argue that an experienced and knowledgeable leader would do better by mandating that her subordinates always do *exactly* as she says. But as we established in chapter 5, that's exactly the dynamic leaders ought to avoid. Remember Jim Bennett, who in the middle of an historic storm unleashed his team to show their own judgment and to propose their own solutions. As that episode suggests, the truly courageous, righteous, and practical thing for leaders to do is to help their people develop confidence, the notion that they *can* do it and should not be afraid to make bold decisions.

STAY NORTH, YOUNG MAN

In my discussion thus far, I've spoken of courage in the context of specific business decisions leaders and employees are called upon to make. We should also keep in mind that leaders and employees alike can show courage in a slightly different way: by making high-minded decisions about how they pursue their careers. In any organization, individuals

The principle of courage dictates that you always choose the higher path and prioritize the organization. If you're a leader, the example of your behavior will naturally cause others within your organization to show courage as well.

will inevitably experience situations in which they must decide whether to act on something that might benefit them personally but would detract from the organization's broader mission. Perhaps you've faced such a quandary yourself. Do you look out for "number one," or do you do what's best for the organization? The principle of courage dictates that you choose the higher path and prioritize the organization. If you're a leader, the example of your behavior will naturally cause others within your organization to show courage as well.

Consider a terrible career quandary I faced while serving at the RGRTA. For years, our organization had taken something of an ad hoc approach to technology acquisition. Like most public agencies, we were constantly approached by private-sector companies proposing piecemeal improvements to the way we did business. Vendors hawked a new way to maintain our fleet of buses or collect fares from our customers. Some of the proposals made sense while others did not, and we had to sort these out. We then had to fashion rules and requirements, writing hundreds of pages of byzantine specifications, to assure (at least in theory) that we got what we needed from our vendors.

There was one problem. At any given time, our employees were spread thin trying to manage dozens of separate contracts. Each of these contracts made sense on its own, but together they gave rise to a mishmash of confusion. We might simultaneously have been engaging in negotiations to install a state-of-the-art GPS system for our buses and a separate state-of-the-art website for our customers. But if the systems weren't able to talk with one another, bus riders wouldn't be able to use the website to know if our service was running on schedule. We were finding it very difficult to integrate our various IT systems.

We decided to take a whole new approach to technology acquisition: rather than enter into negotiations with our partners on a piecemeal basis, we would compile all our technological needs into a single all-encompassing contract. Then, issuing a new, comprehensive "request for proposals," we would select a single partner to take responsibility for handling all of our IT needs, at enormous cost savings to the department. We took another unconventional step: we didn't write the traditional burdensome specifications documents. We simply instructed the vendors as to *what* the technologies must do when fully installed. And we invited them to astonish us with their ingenuity. They got to determine the "*how.*" We solicited bids from several potential vendors, chose a partner, had a big news conference, had our board approve the deal, and began negotiating the contract's specifics. That's when things began to turn sour. Individual items within the $25 million scope of our request emerged as sticking points, and our first-choice partner wouldn't sign a contract consistent with what it had promised in its proposal. This had been a very public process, we had taken a lot of risk with our highly nontraditional procurement approach, and everything was falling apart.

At roughly this same moment, RGRTA was in the midst of tense negotiations with our county government over a $230 million infrastructure project. A dispute arose because we didn't believe the project could be completed with the allotted budget. The incumbent county executive was running for reelection, this project would create thousands of jobs, and her staff was eager to announce that the project had been green-lighted. But I simply wouldn't budge; the math was the math. Many people were furious over my intransigence, and some suggested I be shown the door. It was an unpleasant time, to say the least.

To make matters worse, a group of disability activists chose this very moment to renege on an agreement we had with them to expand transit access to a much broader range of disabled riders. And if all *that* wasn't enough, our federal regulatory body, the Federal Transit Administration (FTA), had just written us a letter three weeks before school started saying that we should "cease and desist" from picking up any students and taking them to school that fall. We had picked up students for years, but the FTA now believed that a new arrangement we had entered into with the school district to pick up public school students at the beginning and end of each day violated federal regulations. The FTA was adamant—cease and desist aren't exactly the opening terms for a conversation—and in three weeks time, students were going to have no way of getting to school.

So there I was, in the midst of a firestorm of controversy on multiple fronts. On the same day we received the letter from the Federal Transit Administration, I was headed to the airport. After noticing the progress I'd made at the RGRTA, a headhunter had approached me about leading the transit agency in Tampa, Florida. I tried to block all of the turmoil back home, flew to Florida for a day of interviews, and, as though God was intervening to pluck me from the eye of the hurricane, the board in Tampa voted to hire me as the transit agency's new CEO. The pay was significantly better, not to mention the weather, and I would enter with none of the liabilities that hung over the RGRTA. It wasn't exactly a tough decision, since there was a decent chance I was going to get fired back in Rochester.

However, what *did* make this an especially difficult decision was the board members and senior team at RGRTA. They had stood right next to me as we defended our math on the construction project with the county, putting their own reputations on the line. Our board leadership was so convinced we were headed in the right direction (despite the pretty miserable month we were having) that they offered to match the compensation the folks in Tampa were offering me and sign a long-term contract. That's when my own underlying sense of courage kicked in. Although I felt I'd do well personally in Tampa, jumping ship at this juncture would have sent my colleagues in Rochester reeling. We were caught in a war, battling on several fronts simultaneously, and it would likely prove devastating to morale if the leader took this opportunity to walk off the battlefield and save his own skin. So I made the unexpected decision to decline the job in Tampa; I passed on the offer of additional compensation in Rochester until we had solved some of the major battles in front of us, and I committed instead to finishing the job with RGRTA.

As many of my colleagues later told me, this was a key turning point for the organization. Once my team members realized how much I'd given up personally to see our mission through, they became doubly committed to what we were trying to accomplish. We eventually signed a deal to integrate our technology with a different partner, beginning a collaboration that would establish RGRTA as an industry leader, with IT systems that were years ahead of those at agencies three times our size. The county executive stepped in personally, and we collaboratively redesigned the construction project to fit the financial limitations. We pushed through our supplemental service program for disabled riders, and it has subsequently served thousands of additional customers. And we took the FTA to court, were issued an immediate stay so we could pick up school students on the first day of school, and five months later celebrated with all of our employees a decision from a federal judge essentially approving our plan to expand service to even more schoolchildren.

I might have done well myself had I chosen to move to Tampa, but for my team in Rochester, sticking together made all the difference. As a mid-level guy in our IT department, Mark Hoffman, said, "Mark's decision to turn down more money and a lot more sunshine suggested to all of us that we needed to step up our game. If he was going to take that kind of risk, we knew we needed to work our piece of the business to be a little sharper. A year later, almost to the day, we became the only transit system in America to reduce fares."

> We simply can't hold our heads high as leaders if we aren't willing to put our personal survival at risk in order to establish organizational success.

We simply can't hold our heads high as leaders if we aren't willing to put our personal survival at risk in order to establish organizational success. We should take comfort in knowing that the broader effects of individual sacrifice are well worth the price. Organizations thrive when those working on the front lines know that the people in positions of power are unselfishly invested wholeheartedly in the organization's march to success.

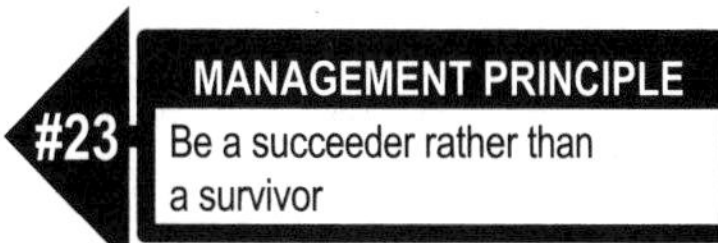

BURNING THE BOATS

Courage sometimes isn't so much about taking personal risk as it is about having the fortitude to make decisions that are emotionally gut wrenching, yet that the leader knows are absolutely right for the organization. As I observed in my previous book, these decisions are sad ones, but they're not intellectually tough decisions, since the way ahead is clear, with success as well as a plan to achieve it explicitly defined. It's absolutely essential that leaders of public agencies follow through with these decisions, even if their hearts pull them strongly the other way. If they do, they'll frequently find that they will take comfort over the long term at bringing about a greater good: the organization's own health and vibrancy, which, after all, they are charged with protecting. Invariably, the leader's own chances of survival in turn increase as the organization's success becomes more likely.

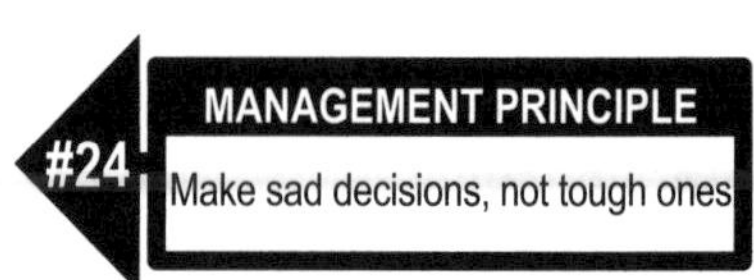

Scott Leonard arrived at his post as a senior executive at the Texas Department of Transportation (TXDOT) during a moment when the agency appeared incapable of meeting its statutory responsibilities. TXDOT was an old, lumbering bureaucracy, and the agency's board had tasked Leonard with shaking things up at the core. Realizing that organizations frequently take one step forward and two steps back while trying to turn themselves around, Leonard figured that the best way would be to craft a strategy for the organization that would leave no real options for turning back. This is what we might call the Hernán Cortés approach. Upon arriving in the "new" world, Spanish conquistador Hernán Cortés grew concerned that his men wouldn't fight to conquer the natives, so he decided to do what some thought was unthinkable: burn the boats that had transported the entire cohort across the ocean so that there was no way to turn back. As a result, Cortés's men became entirely invested in the mission's "success."

At the time of Leonard's appointment, estimates suggested that TXDOT needed $15 billion annually to operate its system, and it had only $10 billion at its disposal. It fell to Leonard to make up the difference. As a first step, he searched both for ways to increase revenue and cut expenses. The department sought additional funding through a statewide ballot initiative, and it reformed the way it deployed service vehicles (after selling off more than a third). It installed more exacting standards in personnel performance evaluations and updated protocol for procuring new capital. All of these important steps delivered real results, contributing to TXDOT's definition of success. But the gauntlet was laid down with the department's IT system.

For many who have worked for big, public bureaucracies, TXDOT's technology story is likely familiar. The department had failed to invest properly in its IT systems for years, and the costs born of that failure were quickly coming due. Roughly 450 customized applications were in operation across the bureaucracy, many of them created and maintained by computer technicians inside the building. The software used by the finance system was thirty years old! Those who knew how to run the software were retiring in droves, and the technical knowledge needed to keep "feeding the beast" was so obsolete that younger computer engineers didn't have a clue about it. As a result, the old system left the doors wide open to cyber attacks.

Despite these dire circumstances, the culture inside TXDOT made the idea of radical reform almost entirely unpalatable. Old-timers considered the agency a "family," and switching systems threatened to imperil peers whose jobs were as obsolete as the old system. Most insiders weren't too worried; they suspected that any ambitious plan to trim the system down could be slow-walked to death. Aware of this tactic, Leonard concluded that to change the system, he had to burn the boats. He led a rigorous procurement process and signed a contract with an outside technology partner to outsource the department's IT capacity, thereby making it impossible for the agency to cling any longer to the old way of doing business.

As Leonard told me, the decision aroused real sadness in him. The department would have to terminate nearly three hundred members of the TXDOT "family," and no one relished the pain their families would endure. But the organization's best interests were clear. Everyone, including reluctant members of the state legislature, knew that there was little else to be done. To his credit, Leonard did what he could to make the transition less heart wrenching. He guaranteed that no one would lose his job or be pinched for salary during the first six months after the transition. And he wrangled a commitment from the outside technology partner to ensure that those losing their jobs would get a fair shake when TXDOT in turn hired again. In the end, roughly 90 percent of those offered new jobs by the technology partner accepted them. Not everyone was happy with the shift, but the results spoke for themselves: soon after making the change, the cost of the department's IT systems plummeted and performance improved. Leonard had dug deep and made the "sad" decisions required to bring the department back in line. TXDOT was now on a path to future success.

IN PRAISE OF DISSENT

Why aren't such displays of courage more common in public agencies? Why don't we hear about them happening every day? Why are people so driven to protect the status quo? An important reason has to do with the *fear of failure* many employees in public agencies experience, thanks to the very structure of public bureaucracies that I've described. In the private sector, successful risk taking frequently yields bonuses, promotions, and accolades for employees. But those paid on the taxpayer's dime rarely see a similar upside. The big question at a department of motor vehicles isn't how heroically a clerk serves a citizen in a unique circumstance, but how many drivers' licenses that clerk can process in a given period of time. Individual workers aren't incented to anticipate problems that will arise down the road, only to execute orders without unusual delay. Moreover, inspectors general, media coverage, and legislative oversight panels are all designed to point out problem areas, not to point out what's going right. The feedback loops ensure that things keep humming along; rarely do they celebrate efforts employees might make to improve operations.

In the private sector, successful risk taking frequently yields bonuses, promotions, and accolades for employees. But those paid on the taxpayer's dime rarely see a similar upside.

I'm not suggesting we should reward courage per se; what matters are results, and courageous decisions, as we've seen, sometimes fail. Yet because public bureaucracies generally don't reward results, public employees become more inclined to *always* make safe, box-checking decisions. Initiative, imagination, and boldness just aren't in employees' job

Because public bureaucracies generally don't reward results, public employees become more inclined to *always* make safe, box-checking decisions.

descriptions. And we shouldn't expect government employees to take risks, demonstrate courage, and fight for substantive change when all the systems reward the opposite. Take a risk and wind up testifying before Congress. Show some well-intended judgment and wind up the lead story on Channel 2 news at 6:00 with a breathless reporter explaining some alleged "misdoings." There's very little upside to venturing outside the box, and lots to lose.

The Partnership for Public Service, a private nonprofit focused largely on this problem, recently commissioned a survey that asked federal employees whether they could raise a violation of law, regulation, or ethic without fear of retribution. Dispiritingly, almost half said no. In response, the Partnership for Public Service created an award of its own, called the "Sammie," to celebrate public-sector employees who do good work by taking real risks. As the Partnership's president and CEO Max Stier told me, "We started the Sammies to share the positives with the people. We've found that it's even more important to share those positives within government. People inside don't know about the achievements of their colleagues, and that's even more harmful than the lack of public recognition. You need the inside people communicating to get the public recognition."[6]

One "Sammie" went to an employee of the National Institute for Occupational Safety and Health who worked across federal agencies to establish standards for ambulances in order to reduce injuries in the event of a crash.[7] Another went to an FBI agent who brought to light abuses by prison guards other agents might have chosen to overlook.[8] In however limited a way, the Sammies recognize courage within the ranks of public service. Agencies from the federal level on down need more and similar efforts, particularly awards within organizations that recognize employees.

Several years ago, the America Foreign Service Association set up a series of awards, presented annually in the Benjamin Franklin Diplomatic Reception Room at State Department headquarters, to individuals who have displayed the fortitude "to take an unpopular stand, to go out on a limb, or to stick his/her neck out in a way that involves some risk."[9] In 2013, for the fifth time in seven years, the association wasn't able to identify a single senior American diplomat worthy of such esteemed recognition. With similarly worrying frequency, the same group has been unable to find anyone deserving from the lower ranks of the State Department's employees.[10] Courage, it seems, is becoming increasingly rare, likely because many inside the walls of government have gotten the message that higher-ups don't exactly welcome dissent. These awards must continue, and we must add to them measures at every level of government to applaud courage. It will be hard work, but over time, if we change the calculus of incentives and disincentives attached to courageous conduct, courage can become the default setting of public employees, instead of what it is today: a rare exception to the rule.

If we change the calculus of incentives and disincentives attached to courageous conduct, courage can become the default setting of public employees.

STAYING STRONG IN STORMY WEATHER

During the darkest days of World War II, the Nazis controlled most of continental Europe. The only real hope the Allies had of winning the war hinged on the coalition's ability to open up a western front by landing a contingent of soldiers across the English Channel and then marching toward Berlin. The supreme Allied commander, General Dwight Eisenhower, had spent months planning what was known as Operation Overlord. The entire plan hinged on the Allies' ability to establish a foothold in the northern French region of Normandy.

By the first week of June 1944, Eisenhower and his team of advisors were utterly exhausted. They had worked to prepare for every possible contingency, but while they had tentatively set the date for June 5, they were aware that circumstances might compel them to push the invasion back.[11] Weather forecasting played a crucial role because the plan to storm the beaches of Normandy depended largely on the ability of American paratroopers to cut off supply chains linking the German lines with the rest of France. For those paratroopers to succeed, they needed to drop through the sky on a clear night. Unfortunately for the Allies, the English Channel was hit by terrible weather, including the worst storm it had seen in two decades, and so they chose to push the invasion back by at least a day.

Meteorologists in the mid-1940s had few of the tools available today, and so those advising Eisenhower had trouble giving him an accurate readout of when the storm might break. Indeed, forecasters offered conflicting reports. Those who feared bad weather suggested that Eisenhower delay the invasion even further, but that recommendation came at a risk. The longer Eisenhower delayed, the higher the likelihood that the Germans would learn of the Allies' plans. And if the Allies didn't invade on June 6, the entire operation would need to be shelved for another two weeks on account of the tides.

At 4 a.m. on June 5, Eisenhower called together his senior staff, the generals and analysts who had created the plans for Overlord, to make the final decision about whether to set the plan into motion.[12] Even as the troops were all loaded up in their boats, ready for the green light, this small group conferring on whether to pull the trigger huddled together in the converted library of a country mansion located near the channel-side city of Portsmouth.

Southwick House had a stately feel about it, but the room where Eisenhower had convened his advisors was heavy with tension; everyone knew the decisions made there that morning would affect the war's outcome. Blackout curtains covered the windows, and very little hung on the walls save a map of Europe. Wind and rain from the storm that had already delayed the invasion beat against the windows, offsetting the crackling of logs burning in the library's fireplace.

When the discussions began, a Scottish meteorologist explained that in his opinion, there was a good chance that the bad weather would break for thirty-six hours on June 6, providing the slightest window for a successful invasion. He explained the variables that contributed to his prediction, and after the group peppered the meteorologist with questions, Eisenhower went around the room soliciting views from the distinguished group of warriors whose opinions he valued.

This was hardly the first time Ike had convened this sort of meeting. He had a long track record of pulling together this group of thoughtful and independent thinkers, asking for their honest input even if it cut against his own preconceived preference, and then taking the totality of views into consideration. Ike's subordinates took comfort in the knowledge that when he nodded at them with his chin, he wanted their honest opinion, not their easy acquiescence.

Had Eisenhower wanted at that moment the comfort of consensus, he would have been disappointed. His advisors held a range of opinions, with some arguing that the Allies should move ahead on the sixth, others suggesting that the risk was too severe. After hearing the various points of view, Eisenhower paced in silence for several minutes, his brow furrowed as he sorted through the various bits of information. And then finally, a calm washed over him. He looked up, turned to the men reporting to him, and ordered the invasion to proceed.[13]

Eisenhower knew full well the risks he was taking. Indeed, he returned to his quarters later that day and scribbled a note taking responsibility in the event the invasion failed. In Eisenhower's own words:

> Our landings in the Cherbourg-Havre area have failed to gain a satisfactory foothold and I have withdrawn the troops. My decision to attack at this time and place was based upon the best information available. The troops, the air, and the navy did all that bravery and devotion to duty could do. If any blame or fault attaches to the attempt, it is mine alone.[14]

Eisenhower's gut-wrenching call represents the height of courage in decision making. He had empowered his own subordinates to speak their minds. He had successfully created the model to lead in a collaborative manner, rather than simply seeking consensus. Taking the information he had available, he used his best judgment, adjusting the changing circumstances even as the goal remained the same. And most importantly, he subordinated his own interests to that of the mission; if the mission failed, he would go down in history as a failed leader—a courageous leader, perhaps, a noble leader, but a failed one. The Allies' effort to stop Hitler hinged largely on Eisenhower's decision that early morning. And far from shrinking away from the responsibility, Eisenhower stepped up.

All the planning and vision in the world can't compensate for the absence of courage. If you don't have the stomach for making gutsy calls, don't start on the other steps outlined in this book. You'll raise the hopes of those in your organization, only to see them dashed when you fail to make the sad decision at a critical moment. Indeed, to a large extent, we can understand America's plight today as deriving precisely from our nation's lack of principled leadership at every level. It's much easier to do the safe thing and not rock the boat, and all too often, elected officials and bureaucrats do that. But when those at the top of any enterprise put everything on the line, and when they do it again and again, incredible things can happen. Evil can be defeated, and terrorists can be killed in the dark of night. Entire organizations that once seemed hopeless can rejuvenate themselves.

With the proper leadership, organizations that follow the first six steps in my framework will find themselves realizing transformational shifts in performance. How you solidify those shifts and pave the way for further change is simple: you take stock and celebrate. You understand what worked and you spread it further through the organization. Bringing the process of organizational change to a proper closure is the vital seventh step in my framework for saving America.

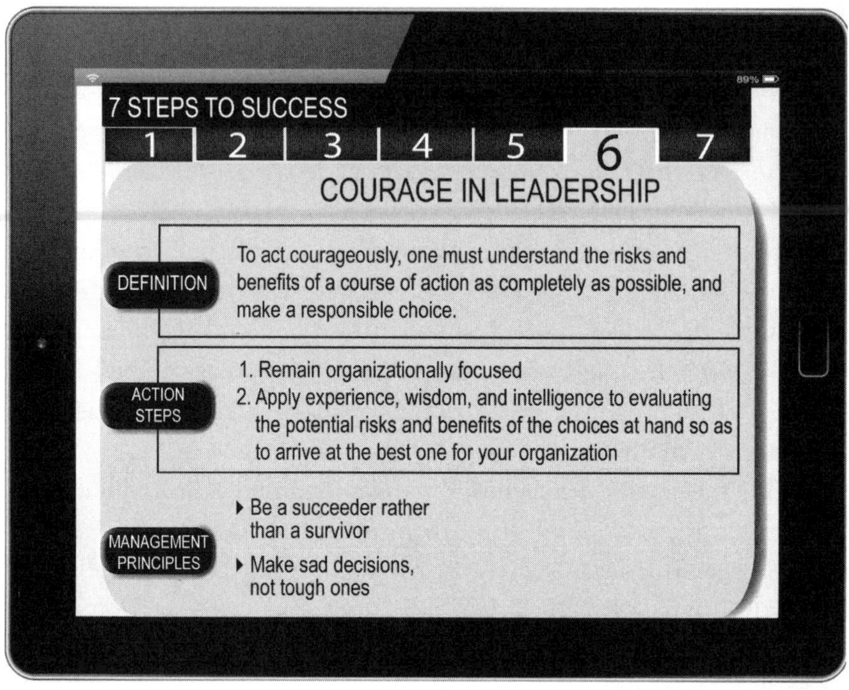
7 STEPS TO SUCCESS
1 2 3 4 5 6 7
COURAGE IN LEADERSHIP
DEFINITION
To act courageously, one must understand the risks and benefits of a course of action as completely as possible, and make a responsible choice.
ACTION STEPS
1. Remain organizationally focused
2. Apply experience, wisdom, and intelligence to evaluating the potential risks and benefits of the choices at hand so as to arrive at the best one for your organization
MANAGEMENT PRINCIPLES
Be a succeeder rather than a survivor
Make sad decisions, not tough ones

FIGURE 7-2

8

Honor the Results

It was June 12, 1987, and President Ronald Reagan's motorcade was speeding along the streets of West Berlin on the way to the Brandenburg Gate, the iconic structure set in the middle of the nearly ninety mile–long wall running between East and West Berlin. Reagan had come to speak at an event celebrating Berlin's 750th anniversary. With little more than a year and a half left in office, the president was focused on his historic lifelong task of destroying communism. Nothing represented the scar left by the decades-old rivalry between the Soviet Union and the United States more vividly than the Berlin Wall.

Throughout the 1980s, the Reagan administration had pursued a comprehensive, two-part plan to win the Cold War. The plan called for a much stronger American military presence, doubling of the country's defense budget, and aggressively investing in a missile shield program called the Strategic Defense Initiative, known colloquially (and sometimes derisively) as "Star Wars." This sent a clear message to the Soviets that the free world was intent on negotiating from a position of strength.[1] At the same time, the plan called for Reagan to work equally hard developing a personal rapport with the reform-minded Soviet leader Mikhail Gorbachev. Reagan hoped that warmth between the globe's two most powerful leaders might help draw the Soviets away from communism.

At Reagan and Gorbachev's first summit, held in Switzerland in 1985, Reagan had interrupted a large bilateral meeting, suggesting to Gorbachev that the two of them leave their table of advisors and take a walk, one on one. They strolled down to a small pool house by Lake Geneva where they had what Reagan would come to call a "fireside" summit. Seated in plush leather chairs by a fire, the two leaders spoke frankly. Gorbachev made clear that the Soviets felt threatened by Star Wars, expressing his concern that the emerging American technology would allow the United States to attack without fearing Soviet reprisal. Reagan countered that the missile shield was simply protection for America in case relations between the two countries someday took a turn for the worse. Although unable to come to any agreement on the issue, the two leaders pulled back from further confrontation and vowed to meet again.[2]

In the months that followed, Reagan stuck to the same basic strategy—strength coupled with rapprochement. And then in September 1986, Gorbachev sent a six page letter requesting, at the end, "a quick one-on-one meeting, let us say in Iceland or London" to deal with arms control. The two leaders agreed to meet over the weekend of October 11–12, 1986, in Reykjavik, Iceland. Their advisors had spent six months preparing for the Geneva summit, but this time they had only twelve days. In very personal conversations conducted in Hofdi House, the leaders of the world's two superpowers nearly reached a grand deal on nuclear arms reduction. At the last minute, though, Gorbachev demanded that the United States abandon any field testing of Star Wars technology. True to his principles, Reagan refused. His strategy was to negotiate from a position of strength, and he had no intention of giving up on what he saw as America's most crucial defense.

Some months later, when the invitation to speak at the Brandenburg Gate arrived, Reagan's aides fiercely debated what he should say. Arms-control talks were gaining momentum; in this context, how confrontational a tack should Reagan take at the podium? Hawkish Defense Department officials thought he should speak his mind, taking a hard line on communism. Pro-democracy movements were beginning to build steam within the Soviet-dominated Eastern Bloc, and a rousing call for reform might spark a new wave of liberalization. Senior officials in the State Department, the National Security Council, and even the White House felt that the president should avoid such incendiary language. They feared that the Soviets would view any explicit call to reunify Germany as a provocation, prompting Gorbachev to back away from reforms already in progress across Eastern Europe, and dooming the arms talks.

As Ken Adelman, the director of the U.S. Arms Control and Disarmament Agency for the Americans, and author of the book *Reagan at Reykjavik*, shared with me, Secretary of State George Shultz sought an arms control deal in 1987 that he could sign before his term in office expired. "We needed the Soviets to turn around on their traditional approach, and we needed the help of Gorbachev to push a deal. So the idea was not to be provocative. At Geneva and Reykjavik, a personal rapport between Reagan and Gorbachev had been built up. The logic was 'let's not bash the person we're trying to get concessions from.' "[3]

This internal war raged on through early June. Even in the backseat of Reagan's car, as he made his way to the Brandenburg Gate, Deputy Chief of Staff Ken Duberstein took one more run at him, once again raising the question of the wording of the speech.[4] But Reagan knew exactly what he wanted to say. Back in April, when he had first called his speechwriters in to discuss his remarks, he had asked them to draft a hard-line speech. And now, flipping through his printed remarks, he turned to Duberstein and quietly said, "It's gonna drive the State Department boys crazy, but it's the right thing to do."[5]

At the Brandenburg Gate, West German Chancellor Helmut Kohl introduced Reagan to the crowd of 45,000 West Berliners. With flags flying, Reagan, in his booming voice, delivered a rhetorical flourish that many consider to be the turning point of the Cold War: "We welcome change and openness; for we believe that freedom and security go together, that the advance of human liberty can only strengthen the cause of world peace. There is one sign the Soviets can make that would be unmistakable, that would advance dramatically the cause of freedom and peace. General Secretary Gorbachev, if you seek peace, if you seek prosperity for the Soviet Union and Eastern Europe, if you seek liberalization: Come here to this gate. Mr. Gorbachev, open this gate. Mr. Gorbachev, tear down this wall."[6]

Not since President Kennedy had stood in a similar setting more than a quarter century earlier and declared, "Ich bin ein Berliner" had a single sentence spoken in Germany captured so much of the world's attention. And just as Kennedy had evoked a success moment of sending a man to the moon by the end of the 1960s, so Reagan defined a similarly clear success moment: toppling the Berlin Wall, destroying communism, and providing freedom. And on November 9, 1989, less than a year after Reagan left office, the Berlin Wall did indeed fall. East Berliners, for decades trapped on their side of the divide, were finally able to travel freely into the West. Not long thereafter, Germany itself was reunited and the Soviet Union disbanded.

On November 9, when news of the wall's fall spread, the world celebrated. Policymakers, diplomats, and political operatives who had been part of conceiving and achieving President Reagan's strategy—many still serving in the ranks of government under President George H.W. Bush—took time out to take stock of what they had accomplished. Ken Adelman, now out of government, remembers where he was when he first learned what had happened. He had departed from Dulles for Budapest on November 9 to attend a conference on nuclear armament. Arriving on November 10, he went straight from the airport and took a walk through a downtown square before meeting the deputy foreign minister of Hungary for lunch. His longtime colleague, and now friend, greeted him with tears in his eyes and asked what he thought of the news. Adelman looked at him quizzically, having seen no news since his departure. The minister told him that the wall had fallen. "I simply couldn't believe it," Adelman told me. "I was euphoric." The minister related that members of his parents' generation had suffered from a spiritual malaise; they had been thwarted in life and unable to make the most of their talents. "And now his sons and the sons and daughters that followed would be able to go as far as their talents would take them."[7]

More than two million people from East Berlin poured across the wall into West Berlin that weekend. In the words of one journalist, it was "the greatest street party in the history of the world." But the celebration didn't end there; indeed, it continued in different ways and different venues for years. On April 12, 1990, almost three years after Ronald Reagan's call to Mikhail Gorbachev to "tear down this wall," a section of the wall was presented at the Reagan Presidential Library in Simi Valley. With more than one thousand people on hand, President

Reagan jokingly said that his 1987 speech "wasn't merely a polite suggestion."[8] A few short months later, members of the old Reagan team gathered at the library for a conference to recognize this tremendous achievement in their lives, for their administration, for America, and for the world. Key players like Ken Adelman, George Shultz, Richard Perle, and Frank Carlucci spoke and raised a glass to some of the extraordinary people who had caused the almost unimaginable circumstances to occur. As Ken Adelman departed the library, he stopped to look at that huge hunk of spray-painted Berlin Wall that used to sit so oppressively half a world away. On this evening, he watched the sun set over it, dipping into the Pacific Ocean, thinking, "We won, they lost."[9]

When they achieve victories or sustain failures, organizations are frequently tempted to move on to their next challenges almost immediately. It's an axiom of effective management that you should always be looking forward, not back. But, in my judgment, that's a mistake. In the absence of a clear and unambiguous understanding of what has just happened, organizations can't grow, improve, or change course. Leaders have to bring ongoing projects to closure. They must sit down with stakeholders, including employees, board members, and the management team, and remind them of the initial definition of success and how their actual performance stacked up. They need to publicly laud accomplishments and acknowledge shortcomings. This is not about giving every employee a gold star. It's about realistically and productively coming to terms with what happened, so that the successful organization can consolidate its gains and increase them even further going forward, and so the unsuccessful organization can learn from its mistakes. The last step of any comprehensive transformational program to achieve success is to pause, take stock, and honor the result.

This is not about giving every employee a gold star. It's about realistically and productively coming to terms with what happened, so that the successful organization can consolidate its gains and increase them even further going forward, and so the unsuccessful organization can learn from its mistakes.

THE WHEELS ON EVERY BUS GO ROUND AND ROUND

I recounted earlier how the reform-minded Detroit Mayor Dave Bing, when he took office in 2009, inherited a transit system that was a nightmare for those who depended on or wanted to use the bus to get around town. One of out every three buses scheduled to run a route each morning failed to leave the depot, often because of broken equipment. Detroiters weren't getting where they needed to go; they were quite literally left out in the cold. In December of 2011, knowing that something drastic had to change, Bing hired TransPro to help him. His goal was to get every scheduled bus out of the depot and onto the streets. At the time, after a decades-long history of Detroit government failures, that goal seemed about as impossible as getting the Berlin Wall to fall.

The next few months were exhausting. Every day, twenty transit department managers and members of the TransPro team gathered on the third floor of the Soviet-looking building that housed the agency's headquarters. The building represented the worst of Detroit, situated as it was right next to the municipal mortuary and the refuse incinerator. With scents of diesel fuel, formaldehyde, and torched waste wafting through the hallways, it was not the kind of place where you brought your lunch to work. Nevertheless, at ten each morning, while sipping lukewarm coffee from Styrofoam cups, we'd gather to pore over results from the previous day's service. We tried over and again to impress upon the agency's managers that the printed bus schedule was, at its root, a contract between the people who worked for the city and the people who rode the bus. Management needed to face up to the fact that they, and now we, were breaking that contract every single day.

At those morning meetings, we got into the nitty-gritty of operations in each of the city's two bus garages. We asked the questions that mattered, starting with outputs: What percentage of buses did we get on the street at the scheduled time yesterday? Then we moved to the inputs: What percentage of buses was *ready* to go out, and what percentage of drivers showed up? We went through dozens of other statistics, relentlessly tracking the numbers, working to produce a comprehensive picture of the barriers impeding our goal of getting every single scheduled bus out to the city's ridership.

Over time, we uncovered a host of problems plaguing the system. As I highlighted in a previous chapter, we concluded that the city's fleet had not too few but rather too *many* buses. The number of broken buses overwhelmed the maintenance department, and because mechanics were spread so thin, they weren't able to get enough buses in working condition before each shift. Mayor Bing was courageous enough to accept our recommendation that the city sell off a portion of its fleet, and the decision proved to be an important element of our effort to turn things around.

But the problems went beyond the city's large bus fleet to include the bureaucracy itself. Those tasked with getting the buses out evinced an utter lack of ownership, and a silo mentality existed throughout the organization, with departments toiling in isolation. Most employees wanted the agency to succeed, but a culture of mediocrity had taken over and most everyone felt embarrassed that the public so reviled their organization. Some employees even told us that they lied to their neighbors about where they worked. These were good people trapped in a bad structure.

To help them, we made a number of changes, altering elements of the agency's standard operating procedures, rewriting schedules, expanding our inventory of spare parts, and so on. For two long months, the results at the 10 a.m. meeting remained unchanged. Scheduled bus service actually on the streets saw a modest improvement from 64 to 66 percent, but then sank back to 61. We were nibbling around the edges, and many around the table were becoming frustrated. We were *talking* about results, but nothing was shifting on the street.

Then something did change. Team members started to become more emotional about the challenges we faced. Without realizing it, we had forged deep relationships with one another over our cups of stale coffee, and we began to express what we felt more freely, calling one another out if we felt we weren't living up to the agency's mission. One woman, who had been with the agency for years, had largely given up on her job, but these meetings were giving her a breath of fresh air. She didn't begin to speak her mind all at once, but as she saw she was on solid ground, that we were there to truly help, she lit the place up, challenging her colleagues when they came back with bad results, had made up data, or even if they came strolling in late. She even lit into me from time to time, bringing rounds of laughter to others in the room. It was no longer my people and the agency people grappling with problems, it was *us*.

That's when things really began to turn around. People who used to come into these meetings and glower suspiciously broke out in smiles one day when we got 70 percent of the agency's scheduled service onto the street. Then we jumped to 77 percent. More changes. More tinkering. Louder discussions. Some impassioned yelling. We were finally moving the needle. By March we were at 90 percent and smoking. And the next month, we reached our goal: a full 100 percent of the agency's scheduled buses were put out for service and on the street! It was amazing.

The next morning, our team was all smiles and high fives. Managers who had been at the agency for more than two decades noted that never before had they managed to get every single bus into the community—and now *we* had. All our hard work had paid off. It really was both an exciting and emotional meeting.

At this point, we made a potentially controversial decision. Typically, in a cash-strapped environment like Detroit's public transit system, where customers had come to think, quite reasonably, that they aren't getting their money's worth, administrators shouldn't spend taxpayer dollars on anything but improvements visible to the community. The press loves to present scandalous stories of bureaucrats lavishing public dollars on themselves. But at a moment of monumental success like the one Detroit was then experiencing, we felt we needed to do something to celebrate. Failing to commemorate perfect service deployment would send a deeply destructive message to those working toward a goal: that achievement wasn't particularly meaningful to those keeping track.

To be sure, we all have a right to be angry when we learn that administrators have spent millions sending employees to conferences that are little more than paid vacations—as the federal government's General Service Administration did for many years.[10] But we must allow government to celebrate when a certain threshold of performance has been attained. The employees who did the actual work—those who designed the plan, kept track of the progress, managed the results, and took risks along the way—need to know that their supervisors value their success. They also need to know that the lessons behind their success will carry over to future endeavors, shared among their peers as a model of "best practice." Absent that sort of recognition, it becomes less likely that employees will take ownership over their next assignment.

And so celebrate we did. Our team announced at our morning meeting that we were ordering lunch for the employees at both of the agency's large garages. Nobody could believe it. Granted, our firm was paying for lunch, not the taxpayers, but the effect was the same. More importantly, Mayor Bing, who from the beginning of his administration had been embarrassed by the department's performance, held a news conference at one of the garages lauding the achievement. Employees were beaming. They'd worked hard, achieved their goal, and now were reaping their deserved recognition. And we stepped back, and made sure they took the bow.

If an organization has completed all the steps laid out in this book—defining success, establishing a culture of ownership, instituting a system for measuring performance, adapting to new circumstances as they arise, and encouraging courage in decision making—they are likely to hit their marks. But unless there's a built-in feedback mechanism that allows them to mark their achievement and prepare for the next one, they're less likely to show the same sense of determination going forward. Celebration of success allows the momentum gained by meeting a goal to propel employees forward and creates a culture of sustained excellence. Have you heard of the Lambeau Leap? Following a touchdown, members of the Green Bay Packers leap into the stands at Lambeau Stadium in Madison, Wisconsin, in shared celebration with their fans. Well, the leap really works! Because once you've done it once, you want to do it again. It is the capstone and continuation of sustained excellence.

THE RENAISSANCE THAT WASN'T

Of course, not every carefully laid plan concludes successfully. When a team or organization fails, the principle of "honoring the result" requires us to acknowledge that, too. I alluded earlier in this book to an unpleasant experience I had when I was CEO of RGRTA: a large and complex public development project we'd been working on fell apart because the mayor of Rochester suddenly changed his mind. When the city council voted to effectively kill the entire project, our leadership team was bitterly disappointed. We'd spent $25 million in taxpayer dollars designing a massive building that included a new educational campus, transit center, and performing arts center in a dilapidated section of Rochester. We'd secured approval of more than $100 million more in federal funds for construction and were convinced that the project, called Renaissance Square, would have sparked exactly that: a renaissance for our inner city. We'd spent years on this project, galvanizing the entire organization behind it. And now we had nothing to do show for it. Our efforts had failed.

Still, we had an important task before us. We had to gather our larger team and deliver the grim news. By midafternoon on the day we learned of the decision, it had already been an emotional day. Our senior executives had been communicating news of the project's death to all our partners. As I rode the elevator down to the first-floor conference room, I began to tear up. I was about to face people who had spent years working nights and weekends to bring the project to life. They were as emotionally invested as any group of employees could be, and now their cornerstone project was dead in the water. Not one dilapidated building knocked down. Not one job created. Just millions of taxpayer dollars flushed down the bureaucratic drain. And tens of millions more sent back to Washington, D.C., to create jobs in other cities.

When I stood up in front of our team, I was heartbreakingly honest. I explained that we had set out to achieve something great and had nurtured it until it was well within our grasp. No matter where the fault lay, we as a team had failed. We were not going to build the project. I thanked our employees profusely and expressed my appreciation for the fact that they had done their jobs beyond even the high expectations that I, the board, and our community had set. This failure didn't reflect poorly on them as individuals, yet we needed to acknowledge that collectively, we'd come up short.

After I'd said my piece, there was total silence in the room. Employees looked back at me with blank faces, almost as if they'd received the news that a close friend had succumbed unexpectedly to illness. Now, nobody wants to be bearer of bad news. Certainly no one wants to hear it. But the act of acknowledging what had happened gave meaning to the efforts the team had put into the project. Had Renaissance Square fallen apart without our official acknowledgment, we would have been implicitly communicating that the time and energy they put into their jobs didn't really matter. But it did matter. And by facing the honest truth, everyone understood that, despite the disappointment.

Fortunately, we had the weekend to lick our wounds, and on Monday, our team came in and just double-clutched and refocused themselves in being great at what they did every day. They built the American Bus Benchmarking Group, so we could transparently compare our performance against a dozen others in our industry and compete against them. They worked even harder to improve on-time performance and drive customer satisfaction even higher. When public revenues dried up, they went out and replaced them with private sources of revenue. And when they read national clips about transit systems across the country raising fares—often repeatedly—they made certain that our recently *lowered* fare was going to stay right where we had cut it.

When an endeavor fails, employees often move to distance themselves from it. They might have owned the project before, but they don't want to own the failure now. Perhaps they feel embarrassed, perhaps they fear repercussions for their career, perhaps it's wise politics. Whatever the case, leaders must work doubly hard to make sure no one abandons their sense of ownership. If leaders do take time out to mark the failure, they can actually *intensify* team identity and individual ownership, setting up the team for future victories. By honoring the results, we empowered our team to fight another day. And fight another day we did. In November of 2014, a transit center almost precisely like the one the mayor had spiked opened in exactly the same location in downtown Rochester.

SAVED BY A SAUSAGE SANDWICH

When organizations fail to honor results, they not only diminish ownership, they also decrease the odds that the organization will learn anything from its failures and change what it does. A year after the horrific collapse of the I-35 bridge in Minnesota, two contractors from the Pennsylvania Department of Transportation decided to stop to buy a couple of sausage sandwiches for lunch. They parked under one of the fifteen bridges located within the City of Philadelphia that support the nation's most important highway, I-95. These workers turned off the ignition, got out of their truck, locked the door, and began making their way to the restaurant.

Then they saw something that stopped them dead in their tracks. One of the columns holding up the highway bridge had a huge gash in it several feet deep and a few feet wide. The column appeared on the verge of collapse, and if it did collapse, the whole span above it would fall as well. Aware of the catastrophic consequences of *not* closing a dangerous bridge, the engineers decided to pass up their sausage sandwiches (at least for the moment) and sound the alarm. Once others confirmed their fears, authorities closed the massive roadway atop the bridge for a few days to reinforce and protect the column with steel plates. Asked about it years later, then-Pennsylvania governor Ed Rendell speculated that, but for their taste for sausage sandwiches, the bridge would eventually have collapsed. It was, in his mind, "a tragedy waiting to happen."

That was years ago. And yet, despite the nightmare that befell those driving across I-35 and the near miss on I-95, America has failed to learn the underlying lesson. These incidents should have spurred leaders to gather the nation together to take stock of what went wrong and to focus on specific measures to fix the problem of failing bridges. It didn't; our leaders didn't honor the result. And not surprisingly, nothing has changed.

The federal government still deems roughly sixty-five thousand bridges nationwide as "structurally deficient," meaning they need to be replaced or drastically upgraded. That's one of every nine bridges. As a 2014 report on the news program *60 Minutes* noted, a small train bridge over the Hackensack River in New Jersey just happens to be the busiest train bridge in the western hemisphere. On a single day, as many as five hundred trains transverse that span of the famed Northeast Corridor running from Boston, through New York, and on to Washington, D.C.

The bridge has begun to malfunction, and everyone knows it. And yet the bridge, which was constructed more than one hundred years ago, has yet to be repaired or replaced. It's not for a lack of planning: engineers have developed a complete design for a replacement bridge, so it's "shovel ready." Yet the project hasn't yet received a green light.[11] It's almost as if thirteen people hadn't lost their lives crossing a similar bridge on the Mississippi River on August 1, 2007. At least it's on a list. God forbid someone hold a news conference the day after.

You may recall the story I told of Tiffany Lawrence, a West Virginia House of Representatives delegate who nearly lost her eyesight after being poisoned by chemicals that had seeped into the drinking water near the state capital.[12] It was only after five days in a hospital and fifteen rounds of antibiotics that a staph infection in her eye was brought under control. When she returned to the floor of the state legislature, she vowed never to let a similar environmental disaster plague the people of West Virginia. It was only during the weeks and months that *followed* the disaster that the government vowed to fix the problem.

This response is a case study in subpar management—not just because a government led by Tiffany Lawrence should have acted *before* the disaster in 2007, but because at a minimum Lawrence and her peers should have used the occasion of the drinking water disaster to internalize the reasons for the failure and apply it to *other* areas of government oversight. If this had happened to their drinking water, what else was in danger? Could authorities analyze why the public had been left vulnerable and use that to improve performance in other areas, such as in the state's mines, utility companies, or their railroads? To turn any organization around, we have to extract the broadest lessons possible from a failure and apply them to other areas under our

> What if we passed a law requiring that an even bigger sign with their name in even larger font go on either side of every bridge in their district that is rated as structurally deficient or obsolete? What if we made them put their names on signs in front of the Veterans Affairs hospital where forty veterans died last month while waiting for a doctor's visit? Maybe, just maybe, we would see a focus on performance rather than projects.

span of responsibility. We simply can't do this unless we have acknowledged to the fullest extent what has failed and why.

Elected officials are far too quick to emblazon their name on a sign next to a bridge or building and proudly crow their accomplishment. What if we passed a law requiring that an even bigger sign with their name in even larger font go on either side of every bridge in their district that is rated as structurally deficient or obsolete? What if we made them put their names on signs in front of the Veterans Affairs hospital where forty veterans died last month while waiting for a doctor's visit? Maybe, just maybe, we would see a focus on performance rather than projects.

Public officials and public-sector managers fail to honor results for a whole slew of reasons. We hear all the time about managers who can't take action against flailing employees because of civil service protections—the red tape that, at least in theory, prevents politicians from hiring their friends for jobs in the bureaucracy—that make it too difficult to reprimand those on the public payroll. The hassle of *trying* to discipline employees leads many managers to simply shift work to more productive employees. And so, just as they refrain from celebrating successes, they choose not to acknowledge in any real fashion when their employees fall short.

Because of too many public administrators' perpetual failure to honor organizational results both positive and negative, our agencies tend to celebrate dates on the calendar regardless of whether they're aligned with success or failure. Bureaucracies can get away with having an annual barbecue or a "holiday" party, even as they're loath to celebrate big accomplishments or face up to their failures. The effect is readily apparent: the gerbil wheel spins one year closer to retirement with the passing of another calendar-driven party. Instead, organizations should invest in honoring results—good or bad—and acknowledging progress. Showing up isn't worthy of a celebration—success is.

Our agencies tend to celebrate dates on the calendar regardless of whether they're aligned with success or failure.

Showing up isn't worthy of a celebration—success is.

HOUSTON, WE HAVE A PICTURE

On March 12, 1994, when I was little more than a kid working for Bill Paxon, my local, upstate New York congressman, I awoke to news that a 3.6 magnitude earthquake had hit the tiny hamlet of Cuylerville, New York, in our district. While people felt the quake up to three hundred miles away, no one died, and despite some damage done to a bridge across a nearby river, it seemed like a largely inconsequential event. I checked in with a few local town supervisors, each of whom confirmed that there wasn't much Congressman Paxon could do. So I set the issue aside and headed out to enjoy the rest of my weekend.

Over the next few weeks, some odd things began to happen. We began to get reports that sinkholes were popping up without warning all around our county. In many cases, the holes were imperiling the foundations of houses and barns. On April 6, a sinkhole two hundred feet in diameter and twenty feet deep appeared, and on May 25, another sinkhole two hundred feet wide and fifty feet deep developed, swallowing seventy-foot-tall trees.[13] Other people reported that their wells were going dry. Farmers showed photographs of hip-deep cracks that were growing in their fields. Methane gas was seeping out of the ground and had to be corralled and ignited in flares. People were frightened, and they wanted to know what was causing it and when it would stop.

As geologists and other experts began to explore the issue, they discovered that the initial theory—that the region had been affected by shifts in the Earth's tectonic plates—was just plain wrong. There had been no earthquake at all. Instead, more than a thousand feet beneath Cuylerville, a portion of a mine larger than the field at Yankee Stadium had collapsed.[14] The region had a long history of salt mining, with the original shaft dating back to 1884. Over more than a hundred years, the local salt mine had grown to become the largest in the United States and the second largest in the world, producing the kind of salt spread on roads up and down the Eastern Seaboard during winter months. By the 1990s, this mine encompassed an underground area of more than six thousand acres.[15] And on March 12, the roof had collapsed in one of the cavernous, underground rooms that miners had dug, just a few months after workers had stopped mining in that area.

Beyond the surface dangers that had emerged, the mine had begun to flood, with more than twenty-two million gallons of water a day flowing in. While geologists predicted that the number of new sinkholes would taper as a result, water levels at local aquifers were declining, and many throughout the county began to worry about something else: the loss of the salt mine itself. Scores of local businesses producing everything from chemicals to beans used the same railroad that carted salt out of the mine to bring their products to market. If the mine closed, the railroad would almost surely shut down, forcing those unrelated businesses to move or close up shop. In addition, 325 jobs would disappear in the mine itself and more than 100 at the railroad. The economic blow to the region would total $70 million, a big deal considering that upstate New York's economy was suffering disproportionately from unemployment and lack of growth.

As rumors of the mine's impending closure circulated, citizens grew angry, frustrated, and scared. It wasn't clear to them what was going on. Yet a ray of hope emerged when the company that owned the mine announced its desire to dig a new mine. It needed government support at all levels to make this happen. Of course, local support was no problem. A citizens group collected ten thousand signatures supporting the construction of a new mine. The board of supervisors was unanimous in its support of a new mine. The State of New York began to step in with tax incentives to get the company to stay and reinvest. A big problem emerged, though: nobody knew where the water gushing into the old mine was coming from. Until engineers figured that out, it seemed foolhardy to build a new one.

One Monday morning, a day after the *New York Times* ran a piece detailing how NASA had installed new equipment on the space shuttle that could peer beneath the surface of the Earth, I got a call from an executive at the salt mine company. While managers there were sorting out building a new mine, they needed to find a new place in the existing mine to center their operations, a spot set apart from the mine's flooded portions. Could Congressman Paxon get NASA to use its new outer space equipment to survey the area around the mine and identify the source of the water?

I called Paxon and explained the request, which to my ear sounded fairly far-fetched. The space shuttle had launched a few days earlier. This company that was literally sucking the water out of the ground of our constituents wanted to know if the office of a single representative from upstate New York could get the space shuttle rerouted for a little extracurricular photography. But my boss didn't hesitate. He was all in. "This is your project," Paxon said, creating ownership. "Do what you have to do. Just keep me informed." And so I jumped into the fray.

The first thing I discovered was that the people at NASA were incredible. To a fault they were thoughtful, helpful, resourceful, and imaginative. They were willing to consider lending a hand and showing off their new fancy camera; in fact, they were eager to do it. We went back and forth dozens of times, zeroing in on what would be most helpful to the team on the ground that was exploring how to save the mine. After several days, I came into the office, and a NASA representative was on the phone, indicating they had rerouted the space shuttle to fly over upstate New York on several orbits in order to grab the required images. It was beyond amazing to think that we had played a role in altering the path of the space shuttle so it could take pictures for us. The administrator of NASA went so far as to hand deliver the photographs to Congressman Paxon.

This just bought the company time, however. The mine was still going to flood. The company's strategy was to build a new mine shaft a few miles away. And in order for the new plan to work, they would need to make many adjustments. First, they would have to set up a new processing facility, something they could do largely on their own. But to transport the salt excavated from the new shaft to market, they needed help extending the railroad line. This was no easy task: the railroad extension would have to run over several farmers' fields, cross a river, which required the construction of a new bridge, and then pass under an interstate highway.

At this point, we ran into our next bit of good fortune. Decades earlier, during construction of a major interstate highway that ran up through western New York, an engineer deep in the state bureaucracy had foreseen exactly this type of circumstance. He had worried that generations later the salt mine might have a need to construct a new shaft on the *other* side of the interstate, and that trains *might* need to run underneath it. He had believed so much in the mine's importance and taken such ownership of the project that he'd designed one of the openings beneath the interstate to be tall enough to accommodate a train beneath. And wouldn't you know it, when we looked to extend the railroad, we discovered that standard-size trains, while snug, fit perfectly. It was an example of incredible ownership from decades earlier paying off handsomely today.

In the end, every level of government and all sorts of competing private interests—companies, labor unions, farmers, environmental groups—had a hand in the project, and we had to address their respective concerns. After two years of sometimes agonizing work, everyone did come together to save the salt mine as well as the thousands of jobs that depended on it. A new mineshaft was built, a new processing facility was constructed, and the railroad was extended. Our team at Bill Paxon's office had accomplished what it set out to do. And working with our colleagues at all levels of government, we had collectively saved the county from becoming another victim of industrial decay.

To celebrate this victory, the community held a huge event at the County Office Building, expressing appreciation to all who had helped save the mine. More meaningful to me was the private celebratory dinner Congressman Paxon held for those of us who had driven the project as his representatives. It's not often that a member of Congress creates the opportunity for his staff to own such a large local project, but our boss had trusted us, and he had wanted to encourage us to take similar ownership of the next challenge. I'll always remember the toast he offered us. The congressman tipped his glass in the air and said, "This was a big deal—a really big deal. Quite simply, I'm proud of you all."

We went around the table that night sharing war stories from our journey through adversity, growing closer as a team. The process had encompassed all the steps outlined in this book. We had defined success, developed a plan, established a way to measure our progress, inculcated a culture of ownership, managed the results, demonstrated courage in decision making, and now we were honoring the result. We had experienced a lot of tense moments, and yet, they had been worth it. I became energized to get back to work and try to achieve even more. And I learned the lesson that the congressman had taught me, carrying it with me to organizations that I ultimately had the opportunity to lead: that celebration is not trivial, as some may think. To save America, to rebuild our decaying infrastructure, by breathing new life into the infrastructure of our government institutions, we need to honor the results of our effort. It empowers those around us, and our organizations, to rise to the even bigger challenges of tomorrow.

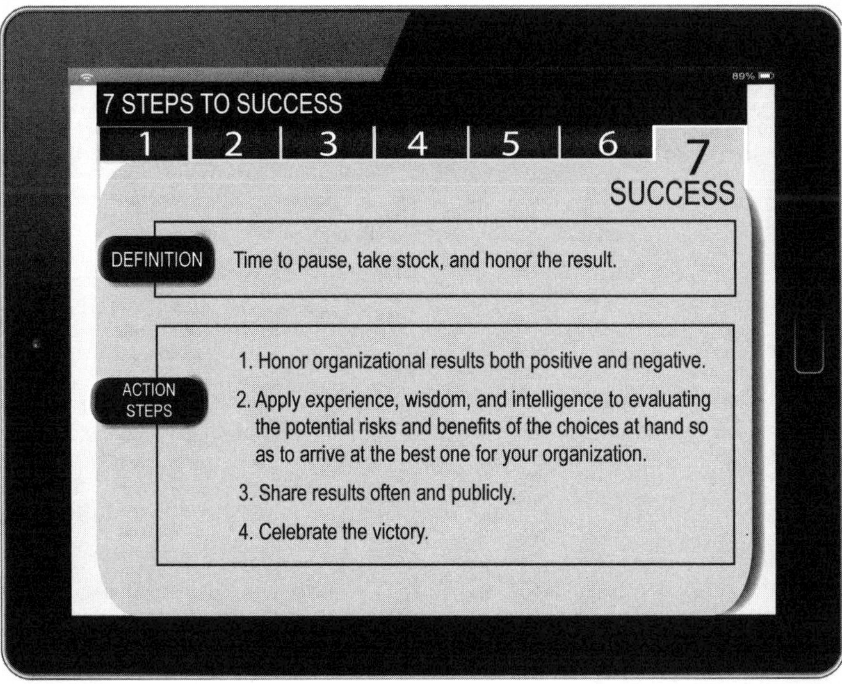

FIGURE 8-1

Epilogue

Our nation's history is replete with heroic individuals and groups who dreamed big dreams, defined success, and then did what it took to make success real. Think of the pilgrims who struggled through early winters and celebrated their success at our nation's first Thanksgiving. Or the sons of liberty that I used to write book reports about in fourth grade, whose revolt led to the establishment of a nation where citizens could govern themselves as they saw fit. Or President Roosevelt, who galvanized a nation and its allies to defeat tyranny.

Americans *can* rise to a challenge when history demands it. And today, history is certainly demanding it. Our infrastructure is teetering on the brink of collapse and our national rankings in many important health and quality-of-life indicators are lagging. Five or ten years from now, if nothing is done, we might well witness the utter ruin of our economy and way of life. What would happen if an entire major metropolitan city lacked clean water to drink? Or if highway fatalities were triple what they are now? Or if our entire electrical grid was suddenly taken out and damaged beyond repair by a cyber attack? Or if one of our faulty nuclear plants became another smoldering Chernobyl?

Tens of thousands of good people work today in government jobs, while hundreds of thousands, maybe even millions, of patriotic Americans remain committed to protecting and furthering our democracy. Sadly, though, so much goodwill and effort of these everyday heroes is lost because they find themselves trapped in failed bureaucratic structures. These structures reward the status quo, longevity, box checking, and rule following rather than actual results and the behavior required to achieve them. My goodness, the U.S. State Department has a coveted reward for demonstrating dissent and can't find anyone worthy of it!

This book has laid out the framework we at TransPro have used many times to reduce costs while improving customer satisfaction. None of the elements of this framework are entirely new; as we've seen, leaders across the political spectrum have embraced some or all of my principles—figures such as Presidents Kennedy, Reagan, and Obama, City Administrator Jim Bennett, Deputy Court Clerk Paul Smaldone, and Coast Guard Admiral Thad Allen. What we have done with this book, however, is package these principles in one unified system to deliver excellence. We have designed a new structure for both people and performance to thrive. If you work in government, whether at a small local agency or a mammoth federal one, I hope you'll deploy the Seven Steps to Success within your organization to deliver excellence for taxpayers, customers, and yourselves. And if you're a concerned citizen, I hope you'll use the Seven Steps to demand excellence in your government, to know definitively if your agencies and elected officials and executives are providing value, and to push for positive change.

Package these principles in one unified system to deliver excellence. We have designed a new structure for both people and performance to thrive.

Years ago the foundation of change that saw the creation of our nation was led by our leaders themselves, courageous individuals like Nathan Hale, Paul Revere, and William Dawes. Today, far too many of our nation's leaders are nothing more than followers, conducting focus groups and polling to decide what they "think" about a particular issue and then simply parroting that back to the masses. Today, the leaders who save America must be us, rather than our leaders themselves. And this book is designed to empower people like us to become those successful leaders of tomorrow.

Today, far too many of our nation's leaders are nothing more than followers, conducting focus groups and polling to decide what they "think" about a particular issue and then simply parroting that back to the masses.

The American Revolution found its tipping point in our forefathers' fury over taxation without representation. Today, we are at a tipping point for taxation without performance. We pay taxes for police forces, yet watch dozens of small businesses get burned down by rioters in places like Baltimore. We pay taxes to educate our children, yet watch Latvia's youngsters improve at a rate three times ours. Today, millions of Americans live in communities that contract for private security. Even more Americans send their children to private schools. These citizens have in effect "contracted" with the government to deliver those services, yet wind up paying for them twice. We would never accept such failure from a private company. No one in her right mind would have two lawn-mowing services. Yet we somehow throw up our hands and accept such abject failure from government.

The American Revolution found its tipping point in our forefathers' fury over taxation without representation. Today, we are at a tipping point for taxation without performance.

It's easy to lament the signs of America's collapse, easier still to let ourselves become distracted by relatively inconsequential issues like abortion, gun rights, global warming, and the mascots of NFL teams. Sure, we can and should address those issues, but let's do it once our food is safe, our children are properly educated, we have enough firefighters so they can show up promptly at fires—and drive their trucks across bridges that are safe—and sinkholes *aren't* routinely appearing due to aging water pipes. For now, we would be foolish not to commit ourselves to the hard work of building structures of excellence in our public agencies. Those agencies that already are producing extraordinary results reveal that American government *can* be great. They also reveal what greatness requires: leaders courageous, persistent, and determined enough to remake entire processes. We need structures that encourage clear definitions of success, that measure performance, that recognize and reward courageous decisions, that empower employees to demonstrate sound judgment, and that compensate employees for results rather than effort. We also need structures that honor results—good or bad—and galvanize employees to push progress ever further.

If we are to make our government great, our national leaders must first stop debating tactics and start debating success. What does success look like for America? Let's agree upon that. We will be number one in education in the world by 2020. We will reduce the number of bridges that are rated as deficient by 50 percent by 2025. We will prevent any American from being the victim of terrorism. Once we have defined success, then, and only then, can we transition to debating *how* we will deliver success. For a municipal administrator, school superintendent, or toll roads executive, the process is the same. Define success first, then build a plan, and then use our available revenues to invest in delivery of that plan.

For the line employee working in a government call center, mowing lawns in a park, or driving a bus, I encourage you to take ownership in your daily work. Be that grocery store clerk who walks the shopper to the item he wants to buy. Take that extra minute to answer the phone with a smile in your voice. Help that working mother with a stroller board the bus. Deliver satisfaction, rather than simply service. As for the rest of us, let's all pay more attention to our government, ignore the campaign rhetoric, and above all, vote for candidates who delivered results compared with what they promised. As Max Stier of the Partnership for Public Service reminds us, "The biggest thing missing [in politics today] is a constituency that cares about the effectiveness of government. Part of our engagement with government ought to be that whatever government is doing, it's doing it well. People lose sight of what we can achieve collectively through government."[1]

My parents recently sold our family farm of nearly eighty years. No one in the family wanted to take on the high taxes and government regulations that saddle such enterprises today. So just like that, another family farm has disappeared from the American landscape. Yet my parents have identified a new goal for themselves. They are building a home for their golden years on a small hill across the road. All of us in America need to ask ourselves: What does *our* shining city on the hill look like? Let's define it, and let's go deliver it. We can do it—our history confirms this. Other generations have risen to the challenge of establishing, building, and protecting America. Let us be the generation that saves it.

ABOUT TRANSPRO

I formed TransPro, a public-sector management consulting firm, in 2011 to support public-sector organizations and their leadership in their drive to improve performance. TransPro's objectives are threefold: to transform leadership behavior among executives; to provide them with tools to transform the organizations they lead; and to mobilize the first two objectives so as to produce extraordinary results for those who utilize their services and the taxpayers who fund those services. TransPro provides services across four primary market segments: local government settings such as cities and counties; entire state agencies; school districts; and transportation entities like transit systems, toll roads, and rail systems.

Across those four market segments, our team provides tools in four key areas for boards, executives, and employees to improve performance while reducing costs:

- **Plan:** Through our Seven Steps to Success performance management process, we bring strategic plans alive and actionalize them.

- **Perform:** With the plan in place, our performance measurement scorecards at the organizational, department, and unit level allow employees, taxpayers, customers, board members, and management to monitor the implementation of their plan.

- **Evaluate:** Through predictive analytics, FOCUS reports, and our innovative Eval tool, we make information-based decisions on objective analysis related to organizational performance and employee evaluations.

- **Leadership:** Through our Executive Leadership Academy, we provide one-on-one, group, and podcast training opportunities to leaders across the country. And GovReporter.com provides a platform to webcast a bi-weekly news program for public agencies and leaders to communicate directly to their communities in the same proactive manner as the weekly White House radio address.

Since its formation, TransPro has helped dozens of organizations and hundreds of public-sector executives reduce costs, improve quality, and provide taxpayers and consumers with measurable performance. While our focused work is in public-sector management, and while so many claim that we must get government to run more like a business, we have worked with private entities across America as well, supporting their efforts to get their business to operate more like a *government*! This demonstrates that sound management principles are effective whether they originate in the public, private, or not-for-profit sector.

ACKNOWLEDGMENTS

With tremendous support from so many I do believe we have succeeded in the bold challenge to balance the inspirational with the instructional to build, lead and manage government agencies that actually deliver results.

My Mom and Dad, Richard and Sandra Aesch have been steadfast in their love, ideas, and encouragement. So many lessons of leadership from that little family farm in upstate New York.

Jacqueline Halldow provided love, space, and a fantastic sounding board for ideas. There were dozens of sacrificed meals, Saturday afternoons, and experiences missed as the team built the foundation for the book. I will always be grateful for more than her understanding, but her encouragement to deliver.

To my deep thinking friends Hal Carter, John Doyle, Ray Melleady, and Seth Schulman, each of whom have invested dozens of hours talking and thinking through management principles and organizational structure with me. Their thinking through the intersections of organizational success and leadership maturity immeasurably strengthened the quality of this book.

U.S. Ambassador Ken Adelman, U.S. Coast Guard Admiral Thad Allen and NYS Senator George Maziarz all provided new, fresh information on their experiences in government, and provided fantastic stories to illustrate several of the seven steps that make government agencies deliver real results.

To my fellow current and past TransProvians, Shelly Dinan, Aimee Harrington, Cole Hoopingarner, Ryan Gallivan, Barbara Lyons, Julie Pope, Lyndsey Scofield, Randy Weaver you have each demonstrated time and again that government actually *can* be done great! It is remarkable to watch you inspire others and provide the tools that make employees stronger, taxpayers win, and quality of services to improve for customers.

To early readers of the manuscript Slater Bayliss, Hal Carter, Justin Day, Mike Merrill and Randy Weaver who provided great critique and significantly strengthened the final version I am grateful for your time, commitment, and the seriousness with which you took your work.

My Young President's Organization (YPO) mates, Henry Brown, Lenny Castiglione, Doug Davis, Jamie Harden, Michael Hemsey, Michael Morales, and Shilen Patel lived this process from beginning to end and were always there to push, identify blind spots, and also provided some very insightful strengthening of the final manuscript.

Seth Schulman was my editor on this project, as he was for *Driving Excellence.* Seth is able to make a page come alive and took every story, every concept, and every element of the book and made it sharper and added more vividness to every story. His creative collaboration has been a gift as we worked through the delicate balance of inspiring with instruction.

Christine Allen was steadfast as a research assistant, sorting fact from fiction and ensuring the strength of our arguments.

My old boss, former United States Representative Bill Paxon taught me so many lessons in how to get public organizations to perform. It is not by mistake that the closing story in this manuscript comes from a principle he taught. He has inspired so many, including me, as to what government can deliver.

One of the finest elected officials I have ever had the opportunity to work with is former Monroe County (Rochester, NY) Executive Maggie Brooks. The first person ever to serve twelve years leading the community, Maggie recently left elected life. She lived out the principles contained in this book throughout her tenure, particularly demonstrating courage in the face of extraordinary challenges. So many would have taken the easier path, yet Maggie made it the norm to do what was hard—often at personal sacrifice. I admire her enormously.

Erika Heilman and the team at Bibliomotion have been terrific. From the beginning they were able to see the vision for the book and embraced its contribution to the conversation regarding performance.

Saving America is a bold conversation. It requires us to acknowledge that the government we have built is no longer serving us but instead serving itself.

But it doesn't have to be that way. We can spend less and get better results. We can dispense with the polls and focus on excellence in performance. We can make government great. And this book provides the tools to begin that transformation.

It is a joy to share it with you.

Mark Aesch
Tampa, Florida

NOTES

Introduction

1. "Best Education in the World: Finland, South Korea Top Country Rankings, U.S. Rated Average," *Huffington Post,* November 27, 2012, http://www.huffingtonpost.com/2012/11/27/best-education-in-the-wor_n_2199795.html.
2. Max Fisher, "Map: How 35 Countries Compare on Child Poverty (The U.S. Is Ranked 34th)," *Washington Post,* April 15, 2013, http://www.washingtonpost.com/blogs/worldviews/wp/2013/04/15/map-how-35-countries-compare-on-child-poverty-the-u-s-is-ranked-34th/.
3. James Andrews, "U.S. Places 21st in Ranking of World Food Systems," *Food Safety News,* January 15, 2014, http://www.foodsafetynews.com/2014/01/u-s-places-21st-in-ranking-of-world-food-systems/#.Vw09JnErK70.
4. Sarah Kliff, "The U.S. Ranks 26th for Life Expectancy, Right Behind Slovenia," *Washington Post,* November 21, 2013, http://www.washingtonpost.com/blogs/wonkblog/wp/2013/11/21/the-u-s-ranks-26th-for-life-expectancy-right-behind-slovenia/.
5. Steve Kroft, "Falling Apart: America's Neglected Infrastructure," CBS News, November 23, 2014, http://www.cbsnews.com/news/falling-apart-america-neglected-infrastructure/.
6. Lydia Saad, "Government Itself Still Cited As Top U.S. Problem," Gallup, January 15, 2014, http://www.gallup.com/poll/166844/government-itself-cited-top-problem.aspx.
7. "150,000 U.S. Bridges Are Rated 'Deficient,'" *Homeland Security Newswire,* July 26, 2010, http://www.homelandsecuritynewswire.com/150000-us-bridges-are-rated-deficient.
8. Erik Brady, "50 Senators Sign Letter Urging Redskins to Change Team Name," *USA Today,* May 22, 2014, http://www.usatoday.com/story/sports

/nfl/redskins/2014/05/22/washington-redskins-senate-nickname-american-indians-daniel-snyder/9439613/.

Chapter 1

1. "Highway Accident Report: Collapse of I-35W Highway Bridge, Minneapolis, Minnesota, August 1, 2007," National Transportation Safety Board, November 14, 2008, http://www.ntsb.gov/investigations/AccidentReports/Reports/HAR0803.pdf.
2. "Garrett Ebling: 'Emotionally, I'm Stuck,'" *Star Tribune*, July 28, 2012, http://www.startribune.com/garrett-ebling-emotionally-i-m-stuck/164144906/.
3. "Garrett Ebling: 'Emotionally, I'm Stuck.'"
4. Philip Rucker, William Branigin, and Amy Goldstein, "Minneapolis Bridge, Like Many in U.S., Was 'Structurally Deficient,'" *Washington Post*, August 3, 2007, http://www.washingtonpost.com/wp-dyn/content/article/2007/08/02/AR2007080200423.html.
5. Rucker, Branigin, and Goldstein, "Minneapolis Bridge."
6. "Deficient Bridges by State and Highway System," U.S. Department of Transportation, December 2007, http://www.fhwa.dot.gov/bridge/defbr07.cfm.
7. "Report Card for America's Infrastructure," American Society of Civil Engineers, 2009, http://www.infrastructurereportcard.org/2009/sites/default/files/RC2009_full_report.pdf.
8. Granted, ASCE is an independent trade association with a "special interest" in ginning up new work, but its work and its words are still important. Just ask Garrett Ebling if bridge improvement is only a special interest. See also, Megan Chuchmach, "Minnesota I-35 Bridge Collapse Anniversary: How Safe Are Drivers Now?" ABC News, August 1, 2012, http://abcnews.go.com/Blotter/bridge-collapse-anniversary-safe-drivers-now/story?id=16907710.
9. "Garrett Ebling: 'Emotionally, I'm Stuck.'"
10. "Garrett Ebling: 'Emotionally, I'm Stuck.'"
11. Steve Kroft, "Falling Apart: America's Neglected Infrastructure," CBS News, November 23, 2014, http://www.cbsnews.com/news/falling-apart-america-neglected-infrastructure/.
12. Michael Corkery, "Bottom Falls Out of Debt-Ridden City," *Wall Street Journal*, January 31, 2013, http://www.wsj.com/articles/SB10001424127887323926104578276044132947694.
13. Lenny Bernstein, "Obama Orders Review of Chemical Plant Safety Steps," *Washington Post*, August 2, 2013, http://www.highbeam.com/doc/1P2-34970251.html.

14. Ramit Plushnick-Masti, "Federal Agency Finds Lax Regulation of Chemicals," AP Online, June 28, 2013, http://lubbockonline.com/texas/2013-06-28/federal-agency-finds-lax-regulation-chemicals#.Vw1NknErK70.
15. Plushnick-Masti, "Federal Agency Finds Lax Regulation."
16. "As Deadline for Decisions Nears, Coalition Launches Video Urging Calls to the White House for Chemical Plant Safety," States News Service, October 22, 2013, http://www.highbeam.com/doc/1G1-346527360.html.
17. Jeff Donn and Justin Prichard, "GAO: Leaks at Aging Nuke Sites Difficult to Detect," AP Online, June 21, 2011, https://www.yahoo.com/news/gao-leaks-aging-nuke-sites-difficult-detect-224706966.html?ref=gs.
18. Donn and Prichard, "GAO."
19. Patrik Jonsson, "West Virginia Chemical Spill: Does It Threaten Clean Water Gains?" *Christian Science Monitor*, January 11, 2014, http://www.csmonitor.com/Environment/2014/0111/West-Virginia-chemical-spill-Does-it-threaten-clean-water-gains.
20. Trip Gabriel, "Thousands Without Water After Spill in West Virginia," *New York Times*, January 10, 2014, http://www.nytimes.com/2014/01/11/us/west-virginia-chemical-spill.html?_r=0.
21. Matt Stroud, "Poisoned: Why West Virginia's Water Crisis Is Everyone's Problem," *Verge*, January 14, 2014, http://www.theverge.com/2014/1/14/5307842/poisoned-why-west-virginias-water-crisis-is-everyones-problem.
22. Gabriel, "Thousands Without Water."
23. Gabriel, "Thousands Without Water."
24. Tim Skillern, " 'I'm Desperate for Clean Water'—and Other Worries from West Virginia," Yahoo News, January 10, 2014, http://news.yahoo.com/water-west-virginia-charleston-chemical-spill-213120682.html.
25. Eric Eyre, "Bad Water Puts Eyes at Risk, Jefferson Delegate Says," *Charleston Gazette*, January 27, 2014, http://www.wvgazette.com/News/watercrisis/201401270117?display=print.
26. Eyre, "Bad Water."
27. Charles Duhigg, "That Tap Water Is Legal but May Be Unhealthy," *New York Times*, December 16, 2009, http://www.nytimes.com/2009/12/17/us/17water.html.
28. Charles Duhigg, "Millions in U.S. Drink Dirty Water, Records Show," *New York Times*, December 7, 2009, http://www.nytimes.com/2009/12/08/business/energy-environment/08water.html.
29. Duhigg, "Millions in U.S. Drink Dirty Water."

30. John Celock and Matt Sledge, "Fire Department Cuts Force Firefighters to Watch and Wait," *Huffington Post,* July 17, 2012, http://www.huffingtonpost.com/2012/07/13/fire-department-cuts-a-thousand-cuts_n_1659671.html.
31. Celock and Sledge, "Fire Department Cuts Force Firefighters to Watch and Wait."
32. John Celock, "FMBA: Decreased Manpower Prevented Ladder Truck Response to Ferraro's," *Patch,* May 10, 2011, http://patch.com/new-jersey/clark/fmba-decreased-manpower-prevented-ladder-truck-respona46fda5889.
33. Celock and Sledge, "Fire Department Cuts Force Firefighters to Watch and Wait."
34. Bill Dedman, "Slower Arrival at Fires in US Is Costing Lives," *Boston Globe,* January 30, 2005, http://archive.boston.com/news/specials/fires/fire_departments_struggle_as_towns_grow/?page=full.
35. Dedman, "Slower Arrival at Fires in US."
36. Dedman, "Slower Arrival at Fires in US."
37. Veronique de Rugy, "How Does the US Debt Position Compare with Other Countries?" Mercatus Center, October 22, 2013, http://mercatus.org/publication/how-does-us-debt-position-compare-other-countries.
38. Matt Cover, "CBO: Federal Revenue to Set Record in 2013," CNS News, February 7, 2013, http://www.cnsnews.com/news/article/cbo-federal-revenue-set-record-2013.
39. Romia Boccia, Alison Fraser, and Emily Goff, "Federal Spending by the Numbers, 2013: Government Spending Trends in Graphics, Tables, and Key Points," The Heritage Foundation, August 20, 2013, http://www.heritage.org/research/reports/2013/08/federal-spending-by-the-numbers-2013.
40. Kasia Klimasinska, "Deficit in U.S. Narrows to Five-Year Low on Record Revenue," *Bloomberg Business News,* October 30, 2013, http://www.bloomberg.com/news/articles/2013-10-30/budget-deficit-in-u-s-narrows-to-5-year-low-on-record-revenue.
41. Greg Giroux, "Voters Throw Bums in While Holding Congress in Disdain," *Bloomberg Business News,* December 13, 2012, http://www.bloomberg.com/news/articles/2012-12-13/voters-throw-bums-in-while-disdaining-congress-bgov-barometer.
42. Giroux, "Voters Throw Bums In."
43. Erik Brady, "50 Senators Sign Letter Urging Redskins to Change Team Name," *USA Today,* May 22, 2014, http://www.usatoday.com/story/sports/nfl/redskins/2014/05/22/washington-redskins-senate-nickname-american-indians-daniel-snyder/9439613/.
44. Chris Zimmer, "Pop Culture Distracts from Political Issues," *Flyer News,* January 22, 2014, http://www.flyernews.com/fn_wp/pop-culture-distracts-from-political-issues/.

45. Tyler O'Neil, "America Distracted: Focused on Miley Cyrus Twerking Instead of Global Crisis in Syria, Possible WWIII," *Christian Post*, August 29, 2013, http://m.christianpost.com/news/american-media-ignore-syria-crisis-possible-wwiii-to-cover-miley-cyrus-vma-controversy-analysis-finds-103306/.
46. Brett Logiurato, "The Moment When MSNBC Cut Off a Former Congresswoman for Breaking News About Justin Bieber," *Business Insider*, January 24, 2014, http://www.businessinsider.com/msnbc-justin-bieber-breaking-news-nsa-andrea-mitchell-2014-1.
47. Oliver Darcy, "Just Watch How Pedestrians React When Jimmy Kimmel Tells Them FDR Died on Monday," *Blaze*, February 18, 2014, http://www.theblaze.com/stories/2014/02/18/just-watch-how-pedestrians-react-when-jimmy-kimmel-tells-them-fdr-died-on-monday/.
48. Erica Ho, "Survey: One in Three Americans Would Fail Citizenship Test," *Time*, May 2, 2012, http://newsfeed.time.com/2012/05/02/survey-one-in-three-americans-would-fail-citizenship-test/.
49. John Ford, "33% of Native-Born Americans Would Fail the Citizenship Test," *Policy Mic*, July 12, 2013, http://www.policymic.com/articles/54255/33-of-native-born-americans-would-fail-the-citizenship-test.
50. "Christie Story Attracts Little Public Interest," Pew Research Center, January 13, 2014, http://www.people-press.org/2014/01/13/christie-story-attracts-little-public-interest/.
51. "Christie Story Attracts Little Public Interest."
52. Philip Bump, "The Majority of Americans Still Don't Care About the NSA Spying on Them," *Wire*, June 10, 2013, http://www.thewire.com/politics/2013/06/nsa-spying-poll-pew/66093/.
53. Bill O'Reilly, *The O'Reilly Factor*, Fox News, February 17, 2014.
54. Rebecca Riffkin, "Climate Change Not a Top Worry in U.S.," Gallup, March 12, 2014, http://www.gallup.com/poll/167843/climate-change-not-top-worry.aspx.
55. Jeffrey Jones, "Americans Say Federal Government Wastes Over Half of Every Dollar," Gallup, September 19, 2011, http://www.gallup.com/poll/149543/americans-say-federal-gov-wastes-half-every-dollar.aspx.
56. David Boyer, "$20 Trillion Man: National Debt Nearly Doubles During Obama Presidency," *Washington Times*, November 1, 2015, http://www.washingtontimes.com/news/2015/nov/1/obama-presidency-to-end-with-20-trillion-national-/.
57. Charles Babington, "Poll: Americans Have Little Faith in Government," Associated Press, January 2, 2014, http://www.apnorc.org/news-media/Pages/News+Media/Poll-Americans-have-little-faith-in-government.aspx.

58. Peggy Noonan, "America and the Aggressive Left," *Wall Street Journal*, Updated February 28, 2014, http://www.wsj.com/articles/SB10001424052702304026804579409551405115662.

Chapter 2

1. "Rare Walt Disney World Aerial Pics," *Disney and More*, February 27, 2013, http://disneyandmore.blogspot.com/2013/02/rare-1971-walt-disney-world-aerial-pics.html.
2. *Wikipedia*, s.v. "Walt Disney World," accessed April 24, 2014, http://en.wikipedia.org/wiki/Walt_Disney_World.
3. Bakari Savage, "50 Years Ago, Walt Disney World Almost Wasn't Built in Florida," News 13 Orlando, November 21, 2013, http://www.mynews13.com /content/news/cfnews13/on- the- town/article.html/content/news/articles/cfn/2013/11/21/walt_disney_orlando.html.
4. Savage, "50 Years Ago, Walt Disney World Almost Wasn't Built in Florida."
5. Savage, "50 Years Ago, Walt Disney World Almost Wasn't Built in Florida."
6. Savage, "50 Years Ago, Walt Disney World Almost Wasn't Built in Florida."
7. Stacy Conradt, "Why Walt Disney Built a Theme Park on Swampland," *Mental Floss*, October 1, 2013, http://mentalfloss.com/article/28174/why-walt-disney-built-theme-park-swampland.
8. Jim Korkis, "WDW Chronicles: Year One—Year of Magical Mouse," *AllEars® Newsletter*, June 21, 2011, http://allears.net/ae/issue613.htm.
9. *Wikipedia*, s.v. "Walt Disney World."
10. Carl W. Stern and Michael S. Deimler, eds., *The Boston Consulting Group on Strategy: Classic Concepts and New Perspectives* (Hoboken, N.J.: John Wiley & Sons, 2006).
11. Walter Isaacson, "The Real Leadership Lessons of Steve Jobs," *Harvard Business Review*, April 2012, https://hbr.org/2012/04/the-real-leadership-lessons-of-steve-jobs/.
12. Isaacson, "The Real Leadership Lessons."
13. Matthew Honan, "Apple Unveils iPhone," *Macworld*, January 9, 2007, http://www.macworld.com/article/1054769/iphone.html.
14. Peter Cohen, "Apple Hits 10 Million iPhone Target Two Months Early," *Macworld*, October 21, 2008, http://www.macworld.com/article/1136284 tenmillion.html.
15. Cohen, "Apple Hits 10 Million iPhone Target."
16. Henry Blodget, "Make No Mistake: The Future of Apple Depends on the iPhone 5," *Business Insider*, July 12, 2012, http://www.businessinsider.com/iphone-5-future-of-apple-2012-7.

17. Heidi Moore, "Live-Blogging the Wall Street CEO Grilling on Capitol Hill," *Wall Street Journal*, February 11, 2009, http://blogs.wsj.com/deals/2009/02/11/live-blogging-the-wall-street-ceos-grilling-on-capitol-hill/.
18. Moore, "Live-Blogging the Wall Street CEO Grilling."
19. Neil Barofsky, "Where the Bailout Went Wrong," *New York Times*, March 29, 2011, http://www.nytimes.com/2011/03/30/opinion/30barofsky.html.
20. Barofsky, "Where the Bailout Went Wrong."
21. *American Morning*, aired February 12, 2009, http://transcripts.cnn.com/TRANSCRIPTS/0902/12/ltm.03.html.
22. "Live-Blogging the Bankers' Showdown on Capitol Hill," Dealbook, *New York Times* online edition, February 11, 2009, http://dealbook.nytimes.com/2009/02/11/live-blogging-the-bankers-showdown-on-capitol-hill/?_php=true&_type=blogs&_r=1.
23. David Boyer, "$20 Trillion Man: National Debt Nearly Doubles During Obama Presidency," *Washington Times*, November 1, 2015, http://www.washingtontimes.com/news/2015/nov/1/obama-presidency-to-end-with-20-trillion-national-/?page=all.
24. Kevin Sack and Megan Thee-Brenan, "Poll Finds Most in U.S. Hold Dim View of Race Relations," *New York Times*, July 23, 2015, http://www.nytimes.com/2015/07/24/us/poll-shows-most-americans-think-race-relations-are-bad.html.
25. Mara Lee, "Median Household Income Up in 2014, but Flat Since Recession Ended," *Hartford Courant*, December 1, 2015, http://www.courant.com/business/hc-median-income-connecticut-20150917-story.html.
26. Ali Meyer, "Record 20% of Households on Food Stamps in 2013," CNS News, January 21, 2014, http://cnsnews.com/news/article/ali-meyer/record-20-households-food-stamps-2013.
27. Glenn Kessler, "The White House's Claim That 7 million Enrolled in Obamacare 'Was Never Our Target Number,'" *Washington Post*, January 3, 2014, http://www.washingtonpost.com/blogs/fact-checker/wp/2014/01/03/the-white-houses-claim-that-7-million-enrolled-in-obamacare-was-never-our-target-number/.
28. Kessler, "White House's Claim."
29. Robert Pear, "U.S. to Extend Sign-Up Period of Insurance," *New York Times*, March 25, 2014, http://www.nytimes.com/2014/03/26/us/politics/obama-administration-extends-health-enrollment-for-some.html.
30. Stephanie Condon, "As Obamacare Reaches Crunch Time, Kathleen Sebelius Faces Congress," CBS News, March 12, 2014, http://www.cbsnews.com/news/as-obamacare-reaches-crunch-time-kathleen-sebelius-faces-congress/.

31. Melanie Hunter, "Sebelius Dismisses 7M Sign-Up Goal for Obamacare," CNS News, February 25, 2014, http://www.cnsnews.com/news/article/melanie-hunter/sebelius-dismisses-7m-sign-goal-obamacare.
32. "Biden: 'We May Not Get to 7 Million' by Obamacare Deadline,'" Reuters, February 19, 2014, http://www.reuters.com/article/2014/02/20/usa-healthcare-biden-idUSL2N0LP02120140220.
33. "Mission," National Park Service, accessed April 24, 2014, http://www.nps.gov/aboutus/index.htm.
34. U.S. Customs and Border Protection, "About CBP," accessed April 24, 2014, http://www.cbp.gov/about.
35. Melinda Plaisier, "Vision/Mission/Values," U.S. Food and Drug Administration: Inspections, Compliance, Enforcement, and Criminal Investigations," accessed April 24, 2014, http://www.fda.gov/ICECI/Inspections/IOM/ucm124442.htm.
36. The Learning Network, "Oct. 4, 1957 | Soviet Union Launches Sputnik Satellite," *New York Times*, October 4, 2011, http://learning.blogs.nytimes.com/2011/10/04/october-4-1957-soviet-union-launches-sputnik-satellite/.
37. Carol Kino, "Boldly, Where No Dog Had Gone Before," *New York Times*, November 4, 2007, http://www.nytimes.com/2007/11/04/arts/design/04kino.html.
38. Mary Roach, "In Space, Nice Guys Finish First," *New York Times*, April 9, 2011, http://www.nytimes.com/2011/04/10/opinion/10Roach.html.
39. John F. Kennedy, "Moon Speech—Rice University," September 12, 1962, http://er.jsc.nasa.gov/seh/ricetalk.htm.
40. John F. Kennedy, speech delivered before a joint session of Congress, May 25, 1961, published on NASA website, May 24, 2004, https://www.nasa.gov/vision/space/features/jfk_speech_text.html#.Vl4LXt-rRAY.

Chapter 3

1. Quote and details from succeeding story from: The Learning Network, "Feb. 22, 1980. U.S.A. Beats Soviet Union in 'Miracle on Ice,'" *New York Times,* February 22, 2012, http://learning.blogs.nytimes.com/2012/02/22/feb-22-1980-u-s-a-beats-soviet-union-in-miracle-on-ice/.
2. "Herb Brooks Quotes," Herb Brooks Foundation, accessed April 24, 2014, http://www.herbbrooksfoundation.com/page/show/740804-herb-brooks-quotes.
3. "Miracle Quotes (2004)," IMDB, accessed April 24, 2014, http://www.imdb.com/title/tt0349825/quotes.

4. Elizabeth Pinkston, "The Past and Future of U.S. Passenger Rail Service," Congressional Budget Office, September 2003, https://www.cbo.gov/sites/default/files/108th-congress-2003-2004/reports/09-26-passengerrail.pdf.
5. Pinkston, "The Past and Future of U.S. Passenger Rail Service," 8.
6. Pinkston, "The Past and Future of U.S. Passenger Rail Service," 5.
7. Pinkston, "The Past and Future of U.S. Passenger Rail Service," 5.
8. Malia Herman, "Amtrak Defends Plan to Get Back on Track," *USA Today*, November 28, 2012, http://www.usatoday.com/story/news/nation/2012/11/28/amtrak-reorganization-house/1733263/.
9. Mike Opelka, "Amtrak Turns 40...Called a 'Massive Failure' by Its Founder," *Blaze*, May 7, 2011, http://www.theblaze.com/stories/2011/05/07/amtrak-turns-40-called-a-massive-failure-by-its-founder/.
10. *Strategic Plan FY2011–FY2015*, Amtrak, 2011, http://www.amtrak.com/ccurl/30/12/Strategic-Plan-2011-2015.pdf.
11. Herman, "Amtrak Defends Plan."
12. Herman, "Amtrak Defends Plan."
13. *Strategic Plan FY2014–FY2018.*
14. *Strategic Plan FY2014–FY2018.*
15. *Strategic Plan FY2014–FY2018.*
16. Alison Vekshin, "The Building Boom That's Sinking Stockton," *Bloomberg BusinessWeek*, April 12, 2012, http://www.businessweek.com/articles/2012-04-12/the-building-boom-thats-sinking-stockton.
17. Vekshin, "The Building Boom."
18. Vekshin, "The Building Boom."
19. Vekshin, "The Building Boom."
20. Vekshin, "The Building Boom."
21. Vekshin, "The Building Boom."
22. Brad Pulmer, "Detroit Isn't Alone. The U.S. Cities That Have Gone Bankrupt, in One Map," *Washington Post*, July 18, 2013, http://www.washingtonpost.com/blogs/wonkblog/wp/2013/07/18/detroit-isnt-alone-the-u-s-cities-that-have-gone-bankrupt-in-one-map/.
23. Tony Morden, *Principles of Management, Second Edition* (Great Britain: Ashgate, 2004), 123.
24. Morden, *Principles of Management*, 125.
25. "Notable & Quotable: Margaret Thatcher on What 'Consensus' Really Means," *The Wall Street Journal*, October 6, 2009, http://online.wsj.com/news/articles/SB10001424052748704471504574445072280951620.

26. Interview with Elizabeth Fretwell, City Manager of Las Vegas, Nevada, April 9, 2014.
27. Interview with Elizabeth Fretwell.
28. Interview with Elizabeth Fretwell.
29. Interview with Elizabeth Fretwell.
30. Interview with Elizabeth Fretwell.
31. Interview with Elizabeth Fretwell.
32. Interview with Elizabeth Fretwell.
33. Interview with Elizabeth Fretwell.
34. Interview with Elizabeth Fretwell.
35. Interview with Elizabeth Fretwell.
36. Interview with Elizabeth Fretwell.
37. Interview with Elizabeth Fretwell.
38. Interview with Elizabeth Fretwell.

Chapter 4

1. Sources for this account include: LocalWiki, s.v. "A's 20 Game Streak," accessed April 24, 2014, https://localwiki.org/oakland/A's_20_Game_Streak; *Wikipedia,* s.v. "List of Major League Baseball Longest Winning Streaks," accessed April 24, 2014, http://en.wikipedia.org/wiki/List_of_Major_League_Baseball_longest_winning_streaks; Wendy Thurm, "Ten Years Later: The A's 20-Game Winning Streak, Scott Hatteberg, and Moneyball," *SB Nation*, August 19, 2012, http://www.sbnation.com/2012/8/19/3250200/ten-year-anniversary-athletics-20-game-winning-streak-hatteberg-moneyball; and http://reds.enquirer.com/2002/09/05/red_as_win_20th_straight.html.
2. "MLB Team Payrolls," *Steve the Ump,* http://www.stevetheump.com/Payrolls.htm.
3. Dan Ackman, "Moneyball: The Art of Winning an Unfair Game," *Forbes*, May 28, 2003, http://www.forbes.com/2003/05/28/cx_da_0528bookreview.html.
4. Michael Lewis, *Moneyball: The Art of Winning an Unfair Game* (New York: W.W. Norton & Company, Inc., 2003), 1.
5. Ackman, "Moneyball."
6. Ackman, "Moneyball."
7. Ackman, "Moneyball."
8. Allen St. John, "Powered by Bill James and Friends, the Red Sox Win (Another) Moneyball World Series," *Forbes*, October 31, 2013, www.forbes.com/sites/allenstjohn/2013/10/31/powered-by-bill-james-and-friends-the-red-sox-win-another-moneyball-world-series/#4466928d41f1.
9. "Disaster Housing: FEMA Needs More Detailed Guidance and Performance

Measures to Help Ensure Effective Assistance After Major Disaster," United States Government Accountability Office, August 2009, http://www.gao.gov/new.items/d09796.pdf.

10. John Bridgeland and Peter Orszag, "Can Government Play Moneyball?" *Atlantic*, June 19, 2013, http://www.theatlantic.com/magazine/archive/2013/07/can-government-play-moneyball/309389/.
11. Bridgeland and Orszag, "Can Government Play Moneyball?"
12. Bridgeland and Orszag, "Can Government Play Moneyball?"
13. Bridgeland and Orszag, "Can Government Play Moneyball?"
14. David Bornstein, "Can Government Play Moneyball?" *New York Times*, April 16, 2014, http://opinionator.blogs.nytimes.com/2014/04/16/can-government-play-moneyball/.
15. "Learn More About Results for America," Results for America: An Initiative of America Achieves, October 9, 2013, http://moneyballforgov.com/learn-more-about-results-for-america/.
16. "Learn More About Results for America."
17. "New RFA Scorecard Looks at How the Federal Government Plays Moneyball," Results for America: An Initiative of America Achieves, October 11, 2013, http://moneyballforgov.com/new-results-for-america-scorecard-looks-at-how-the-federal-government-plays-moneyball/.
18. Jim Collins, *Good to Great: Why Some Companies Make the Leap...And Others Don't* (New York: HarperCollins, 2001), 13.
19. Lou O'Boyle, "Blueprint Chesterfield...Building a Better Community," Case Study, Chesterfield County, Virginia, 2015.
20. *Wikipedia*, s.v. "1988 Notre Dame Fighting Irish football team," accessed April 24, 2014, https://en.wikipedia.org/wiki/1988_Notre_Dame_Fighting_Irish_football_team.
21. John Buntin, *Assertive Policing, Plummeting Crime: The NYPD Takes on Crime in New York City* (Cambridge, MA: John F. Kennedy School of Government Case Program, 1999), 1.
22. Buntin, *Assertive Policing*, 1.
23. Alison Mitchell, "Giuliani Appoints Bostonian to Run New York's Police," *New York Times*, December 3, 1993, http://www.nytimes.com/1993/12/03/nyregion/giuliani-appoints-bostonian-to-run-new-york-s-police.html.
24. Mitchell, "Giuliani Appoints Bostonian."
25. Buntin, *Assertive Policing*, 5.
26. Buntin, *Assertive Policing*, 5.
27. Buntin, *Assertive Policing*, 16.

28. Buntin, *Assertive Policing,* 17.
29. Buntin, *Assertive Policing,* 12.
30. Buntin, *Assertive Policing,* 7.
31. Buntin, *Assertive Policing,* 11.
32. Buntin, *Assertive Policing,* 17.
33. Buntin, *Assertive Policing,* 12.
34. Buntin, *Assertive Policing,* 18.
35. Buntin, *Assertive Policing,* 18.
36. Buntin, *Assertive Policing,* 18.
37. Buntin, *Assertive Policing,* 18.
38. Buntin, *Assertive Policing,* 19.
39. Buntin, *Assertive Policing,* 19.
40. Buntin, *Assertive Policing,* 20.
41. Buntin, *Assertive Policing,* 23.
42. Buntin, *Assertive Policing,* 23.
43. Buntin, *Assertive Policing,* 1.

Chapter 5

1. The following story and its details were provided to the author in an interview with Cathy Clement, January 7, 2014.
2. Carolyn Thompson, "Home-Front Team Gets Kin to Wounded GI's Bedside," Associated Press, August 6, 2004, http://www.utsandiego.com/uniontrib/20040806/news_1n6wounded.html.
3. Suzie Bailey, "How to Develop Strategy in the NHS," *Guardian,* October 23, 2014, http://www.theguardian.com/healthcare-network/2014/oct/23/how-develop-strategy-nhs.
4. Interview with Thad Allen, December 22, 2014.
5. George S. Patton, Paul D. Harkins, and Beatrice Banning Ayer Patton, *War As I Knew It* (Boston: Houghton Mifflin, 1947), 357.
6. Drake Baer, "Netflix's Major HR Innovation: Treating Humans Like People," *Fast Company,* http://www.fastcompany.com/3027124/lessons-learned/netflixs-major-hr-innovation-treating-humans-like-people.
7. Scott Jaschik, "The Creativity Crisis," *Inside Higher Ed,* February 10, 2015, https://www.insidehighered.com/news/2015/02/10/author-discusses-new-book-creativity-crisis-science.
8. Rebecca Roberts, "Parents Rally Around Suspended Preschool Teacher," Fox Now St. Louis, February 19, 2015, http://fox2now.com/2015/02/19/parents-rally-around-suspended-preschool-teacher/.

9. "US Airways Slammed After Flight Attendant Refuses to Hang Up Army Ranger's Uniform Jacket," Fox News, October 11, 2014, http://www.foxnews.com/us/2014/10/11/us-airways-slammed-after-flight-attendant-refuses-hang-army-ranger-jacket/.
10. The following story and its details were provided to the author in an interview with Jim Bennett, December 6, 2014.
11. Michael Lee Stallard, "Scandals Obscure Patriots True Competitive Advantage," Fox Business News, January 30, 2015, http://www.foxbusiness.com/business-leaders/2015/01/30/scandals-obscure-patriots-true-competitive-advantage/.

Chapter 6

1. Stephen E. Ambrose, *The Victors: Eisenhower and His Boys: The Men of World War II* (New York: Simon & Schuster, 1999) via World War II History Info, http://www.worldwar2history.info/D-Day/Pointe-Du-Hoc.html.
2. Brian Williams, "Pointe Du Hoc," Military History Online, 2000, http://www.militaryhistoryonline.com/wwii/dday/pointeduhoc.aspx.
3. Robert Wilde, "Pointe du Hoc: The Sixth D-Day Landing," *European History,* http://europeanhistory.about.com/od/worldwar2/a/Pduhocarticle.htm.
4. Williams, "Pointe Du Hoc."
5. Ronald Reagan, "The Boys of Pointe du Hoc," Real Clear Politics, June 6, 2013, http://www.realclearpolitics.com/articles/2013/06/06/the_boys_of_pointe_du_hoc_96877.html.
6. Wilde, "Pointe du Hoc."
7. Williams, "Pointe du Hoc."
8. Ralph Keyes, "The Quote Verifier: Who Said What, Where, and When," http://www.ralphkeyes.com/quote-verifier/.
9. Charles Duhigg, "How Companies Learn Your Secrets," *New York Times,* February 16, 2012, http://www.nytimes.com/2012/02/19/magazine/shopping-habits.html?adxnnl=1&pagewanted=all&adxnnlx=1421680144-RoFixMtLVD53GVoph7CKnw.
10. Alison Vekshin, "The Building Boom That's Sinking Stockton," *Bloomberg BusinessWeek,* April 12, 2012, http://www.businessweek.com/articles/2012-04-12/the-building-boom-thats-sinking-stockton.
11. Don Thompson, "Lawyer Warns of 60 Percent Pension Cuts in Stockton Bankruptcy Case," *San Jose Mercury News,* October 1, 2014, http://www.mercurynews.com/california/ci_26643087/lawyer-warns-60-percent-pension-cuts-stockton-bankruptcy?source=infinite.

12. Alison Vekshin, James Nash, and Rodney Yap, "Police Chief's $204,000 Pension Shows How Cities Crashed," *Bloomberg Business,* July 31, 2012, http://www.bloomberg.com/news/articles/2012-08-01/police-chief-s-204-000-pension-shows-how-cities-crashed.
13. Regan Morris, "Californian City of Stockton Files for Bankruptcy," BBC US & Canada News, June 27, 2012, http://www.bbc.com/news/world-us-canada-18605326.
14. Elaine Kamarck, "Lessons for the Future of Government Reform," Brookings, June 18, 2013, http://www.brookings.edu/research/testimony/2013/06/18-reinventing-government-future-reform-kamarck.
15. David Bornstein, "Can Government Play Moneyball?" *New York Times,* April 16, 2014, http://opinionator.blogs.nytimes.com/2014/04/16/can-government-play-moneyball/.
16. Chad Vander Veen, "Gov. Martin O'Malley Uses StateStat to Transform Maryland," *GovTech,* August 4, 2009, http://www.govtech.com/featured/102492329.html.
17. David Leonhardt, "Study Finds Gains from Teacher Evaluations," *New York Times,* October 17, 2013, http://economix.blogs.nytimes.com/2013/10/17/a-new-look-at-teacher-evaluations-and-learning/?_r=0.
18. Jessica Bakeman, "NYSUT President Loses Ground As 'Divisive' Election Nears," *Politico New York,* January 30, 2014, http://www.capitalnewyork.com/article/albany/2014/01/8539552/nysut-president-loses-ground-divisive-election-nears.
19. Kate Taylor, "Cuomo's Education Agenda Sets Battle Lines with Teachers' Unions," *New York Times,* January 20, 2015, http://www.nytimes.com/2015/01/21/nyregion/cuomos-education-agenda-sets-battle-lines-with-teachers-unions.html.
20. "Caucus History: Past Years' Results," *Des Moines Register,* 2015, http://caucuses.desmoinesregister.com/caucus-history-past-years-results/.
21. Theodore White, *America in Search of Itself: The Making of the President 1956–1980* (New York: Warner Books, 1988), 245–53.
22. M. J. Stephey, "Top 10 Memorable Debate Moments," *Time,* http://content.time.com/time/specials/packages/article/0,28804,1844704_1844706_1844582,00.html.
23. John F. Kennedy, speech delivered before a joint session of Congress, May 25, 1961, published on NASA website, May 24, 2004, https://www.nasa.gov/vision/space/features/jfk_speech_text.html#.Vl4LXt-rRAY.

Chapter 7

1. "Detailed Description of the bin Laden Assassination Raid," *Apartment 26,* August 2, 2011, http://apt46.net/2011/08/02/detailed-description-of-the-bin-laden-assassination-raid/.
2. Rob O'Neill, interviewed by Peter Doocy, *The Man Who Killed Osama Bin Laden,* Fox News, air date November 11 and 12, 2014.
3. "The Man Who Killed Osama Bin Laden," filmed November 11, 2015, uploaded November 14, 2014, YouTube video, 36:29, https://www.youtube.com/watch?v=W6YpWSfZ150.
4. For the United States Census Bureau's population of Nassau County, see http://www.census.gov/quickfacts/table/PST045215/36059,00; for Nassau County's population relative to other states, please see, http://www.infoplease.com/us/states/population-by-rank.html.
5. David Usborne, "The Moment It All Went Wrong for Kodak," *Independent,* January 19, 2012, http://www.independent.co.uk/news/business/analysis-and-features/the-moment-it-allwent-wrong-for-kodak-6292212.html.
6. Interview with Max Stier, November 18, 2014.
7. For a profile of James D. Green, please see, http://servicetoamericamedals.org/honorees/view_profile.php?profile=374.
8. For a profile of Susan Hanson, please see, http://servicetoamericamedals.org/honorees/view_profile.php?profile=377.
9. "Constructive Dissent Awards," American Foreign Service Association, accessed April 24, 2014, http://www.afsa.org/dissent.
10. Guy Taylor, "State Department Has a Dearth of Diplomats to Award for Dissent," *Washington Times,* June 26, 2013, http://www.washingtontimes.com/news/2013/jun/26/state-department-has-a-dearth-of-diplomats-to-awar/?page=all.
11. Jessica Talarico, "How D-Day Was Delayed by a Weather Forecast," Imperial War Museums, accessed April 24, 2014, http://www.iwm.org.uk/history/how-d-day-was-delayed-by-a-weather-forecast.
12. Walter Bedell Smith, *Eisenhower's Six Great Decisions: Europe, 1944–1945* (London: Longmans, Green Publishing, 1956).
13. Brett and Kate McKay, "Leadership Lessons from Dwight D. Eisenhower #3: How to Make an Important Decision," *The Art of Manliness,* June 24, 2012, http://www.artofmanliness.com/2012/06/24/leadership-lessons-from-dwight-d-eisenhower-3-how-to-make-an-important-decision/.

14. Leon Watson, "'Any Fault Is Mine Alone': How General Eisenhower Planned to Take Full Blame If D-Day had FAILED (And It Could Teach Today's Politicians a Thing or Two!)," *Daily Mail,* June 5, 2014, http://www.dailymail.co.uk/news/article-2649562/Any-fault-How-General-Eisenhower-planned-blame-D-Day-FAILED-teach-todays-politicians-thing-two.html#ixzz3NKFy8GB0.

Chapter 8

1. Ken Adelman, *Reagan at Reykjavik: Forty-Eight Hours That Ended the Cold War* (New York: HarperCollins, 2014), 64.
2. "Reagan and Gorbachev: Geneva Summit 1985," uploaded December 5, 2013, YouTube video, 59:04, https://www.youtube.com/watch?v=jA4XxUEb_EE.
3. Interview with Ken Adelman, February 16, 2015.
4. Adelman, *Reagan at Reykjavik,* 233.
5. Peter Robinson, "'Tear Down This Wall': How Top Advisers Opposed Reagan's Challenge to Gorbachev—But Lost," *Prologue Magazine,* National Archives, Summer 2007, http://www.archives.gov/publications/prologue/2007/summer/berlin.html.
6. Lucy Madison, "Remembering Reagan's 'Tear Down This Wall' Speech 25 Years Later," CBS News, June 12, 2012, http://www.cbsnews.com/news/remembering-reagans-tear-down-this-wall-speech-25-years-later/.
7. Adelman, *Reagan at Reykjavik,* 274.
8. "25 Years Since Reagan's Berlin 'Tear Down Wall' Speech," Fox News, September 19, 2012, http://www.foxnews.com/opinion/2012/09/19/25-years-since-reagan-berlin-tear-down-wall-speech.html.
9. Adelman, *Reagan at Reykjavik,* 295.
10. Jim McElhatton, "GSA Scandal Widens; Dozens of Conferences Now Under Investigation," *Washington Times,* August 1, 2012, http://www.washingtontimes.com/news/2012/aug/1/gsa-scandal-widens-dozens-conferences-investigated/?page=all.
11. Steve Kroft, "Falling Apart: America's Neglected Infrastructure," CBS News, November 23, 2014, http://www.cbsnews.com/news/falling-apart-america-neglected-infrastructure/.
12. Eric Eyre, "Bad Water Puts Eyes at Risk, Jefferson Delegate Says," *Charleston Gazette,* January 27, 2014, http://www.wvgazette.com/News/watercrisis/201401270117?display=print.
13. Andrew C. Revkin, "Wanted: A New Salt Mine; One-Industry Town Presses for State Aid," *New York Times,* December, 10, 1995, http://www.nytimes.com/

1995/12/10/nyregion/wanted-a-new-salt-mine-one-industry-town-presses-for-state-aid.html.

14. Revkin, "Wanted: A New Salt Mine."
15. William M. Kappel, Todd S. Miller, and Richard M. Yager, "Effects of the 1994 Retsof Salt Mine Collapse in the Genesee Valley, New York," *Department of the Interior US Geological Survey,* October, 1998, http://ny.water.usgs.gov/pubs/fs/fs01798/FS017-98.pdf.

Epilogue

1. Interview with Max Stier, November 18, 2014.

INDEX

ABOUT THE AUTHOR

Mark Aesch passionately believes that public sector agencies can operate as efficiently and as focused on meeting customer needs as private sector businesses. Mark is the chief executive officer of TransPro, a management consultancy that guides public organizations to new levels of performance excellence with TransPro's 7 Steps to Success strategic planning, performance scorecard systems, leadership coaching, and customer satisfaction programs.

Mark introduced the concept of managing a public sector agency with a private sector mind set in his best-selling business book *Driving Excellence.* His work to drive change in public sector management has been reported on in the *New York Times,* the *Wall Street Journal,* the *Washington Post,* on *Fox National News, CBS Morning Show, CNBC,* Bloomberg Radio and TV, National Public Radio, and many other media outlets.

Mark also serves as a senior advisor at Boston Consulting Group specializing in public sector management and transportation issues, and as a Senior Fellow for the Alliance for Innovation, an international network of progressive governments and partners committed to transforming local governments. He also provides executive leadership coaching and mentoring.

Mark lives in Tampa, Florida, and is represented by Washington Speakers Bureau and Leading Authorities. Mark can be reached at mark@TransProConsulting.com and www.savingamerica2016.com.